THE
FAMILY
CREATIVE
WORK
SHOP

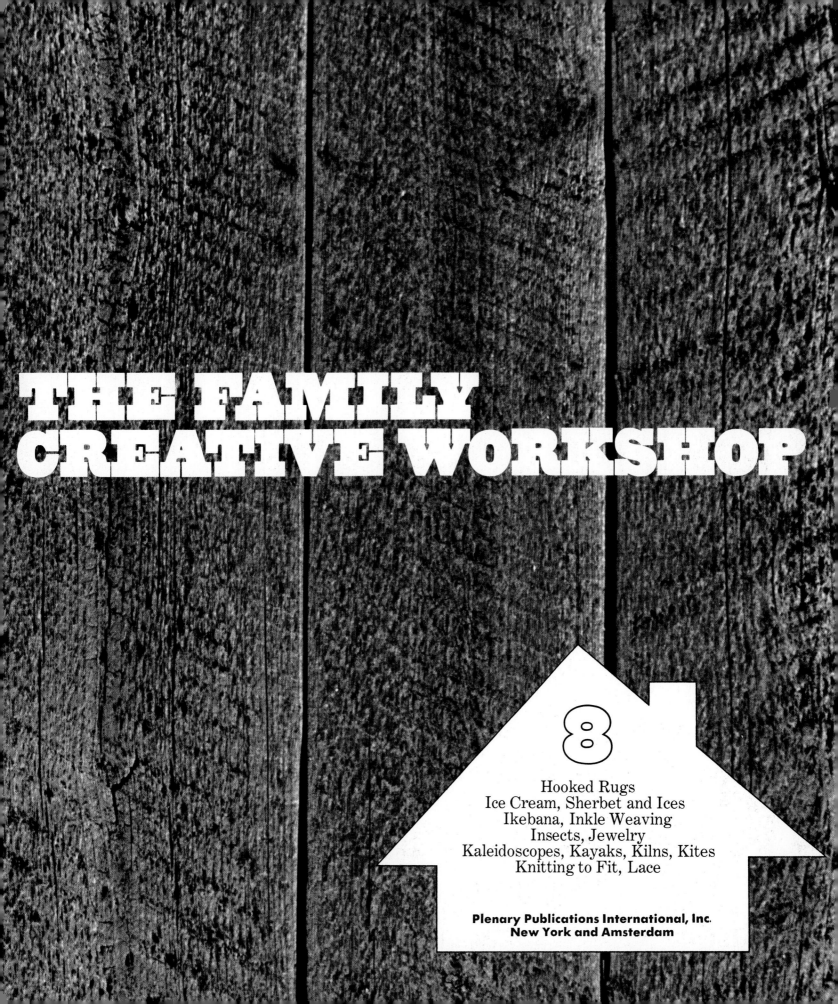

# THE FAMILY CREATIVE WORKSHOP

**Plenary Publications International, Inc.**
**New York and Amsterdam**

Published by Plenary Publications
International Incorporated
300 East 40 Street, New York, N.Y.
10016, for the
Blue Mountain Crafts Council.

Library of Congress Catalog Card
Number: 73-89331.
Complete set International Standard
Book Number: 0-88459-021-6.
Volume 8 International Standard
Book Number: 0-88459-007-0.

Manufactured in the United States
of America. Printed and
bound by the W. A. Krueger
Company, Brookfield, Wisconsin.

Printing preparation
by Lanman Lithoplate Company.

**Publishers:**
Plenary Publications
International, Incorporated
300 East 40 Street
New York, New York 10016

Allen Davenport Bragdon
EDITOR-IN-CHIEF AND
PUBLISHER OF THE FAMILY
CREATIVE WORKSHOP

Nancy Jackson
ADMINISTRATIVE ASSISTANT

Jerry Curcio
PRODUCTION MANAGER

**Editorial preparation:**
Tree Communications, Inc.
250 Park Avenue South
New York, New York 10003

Rodney Friedman
EDITORIAL DIRECTOR

Ronald Gross
DESIGN DIRECTOR

Paul Levin
DIRECTOR OF PHOTOGRAPHY

Donal Dinwiddie
CONSULTING EDITOR

Jill Munves
TEXT EDITOR

Sonja Douglas
ART DIRECTOR

Rochelle Lapidus
ASSOCIATE DESIGNER

Betty Friedman
ADMINISTRATIVE MANAGER

Barnet Friedman
COPYREADER

Lucille O'Brien
EDITORIAL PRODUCTION

**Editors for this volume:**
Andrea DiNoto
KILNS

Donal Dinwiddie
KAYAKS

Michael Donner
INSECTS

Linda Hetzer
HOOKED RUGS
INKLE WEAVING

Nancy Bruning Levine
JEWELRY

Jill Munves
KITES

Marilyn Nierenberg
IKEBANA

Marilyn Ratner
ICE CREAM, SHERBETS AND
ICES

Mary Grace Skurka
KALEIDOSCOPES
KNITTING TO FIT
LACE

**Contributing illustrators:**
Marina Givotovsky
Nancy Bruning Levine
Lynn Matus
Sally Shimizu

**Contributing
photographers:**
Nancy Baldwin
Marsha Janota
Paul Levin
Frank Lusk

**Acknowledgement:**
CONTRIBUTING CONSULTANT
FOR KITES: Will Yolen,
editor and president of the
International Kite
Fliers Association.

**Photo and illustration credits:**
HOOKED RUGS: Shaker
Hooked Rug, page 903, courtesy of Index of American
Design, National Gallery of
Art, Washington, D.C.
IKEBANA: Rikka and Shoka
designs by Senei Ikenobo,
courtesy of Ikenobo Ikebana
Society of San Francisco,
Calif. KALEIDOSCOPES:
Photographs taken through
the Karelitz Kaleidoscope
are the property of Judith
Karelitz. *Hue View* is a
trademark of Judith Karelitz
registered with the U.S. Pa-
tent Office. Designs and
photographs are not to be
reproduced for commercial
use without the written
permission of the artist.
KILNS: Temperature Equi-
valent Chart, page 979, courtesy of the Edward Orton,
Jr. Ceramic Foundation.
LACE: *Woman Making Lace*,
page 1012, by Nicolas Maes,
courtesy of The Metropolitan
Museum of Art, The Michael
Friedsam Collection, 1931.
INSECTS: Lithographs and
Etchings, pages 940, 944 and
945, courtesy of New York
Public Library Picture Collection. ICE CREAMS, SHER-
BET AND ICES: Freezers,
page 912, manufactured by
Proctor Silex, Inc., and
Salton, Inc.

The Project-Evaluation
Symbols appearing in the
title heading at the
beginning of each project
have these meanings:

**Range of approximate cost:**
¢ Low: under $5 or free
and found natural materials

$ Medium: about $10

$$ High: above $15

**Estimated time to completion
for an unskilled adult:**
⊠ Hours

◑ Days

Weeks

**Suggested level of experience:**
Child alone

Supervised child or
family project

Unskilled adult

Specialized prior training

**Tools and equipment:**
Small hand tools

Large hand
and household tools

Specialized
or powered equipment

**On the cover:**
Pendant of turquoise wrapped in a cage of
silver wire, spotted turkey and pheasant
feathers, coil of silver wire, pin of polished
Jasper Canyon agate, and half-round pliers,
on a bed of beach pebbles. See Jewelry
entry, beginning on page 948.

**Contents and craftspeople for Volume 8:**

*Lisa Deiches, a graduate of Antioch College, is a young craftswoman deeply involved in the textile crafts. She has been accepted at the Textile Institute in Boras, Sweden, to do graduate research on textile techniques, and, in her own work, has woven rugs and tapestries, spinning her own yarn and dyeing it with natural dyes. Lisa has woven a large number of tapestries for a corporation and has exhibited her work in both Ohio and New York.*

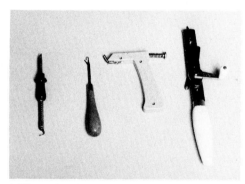

1: The various hooks used in making rugs by hand are (left to right) a punch needle, a latch hook, a latch gun, and a speed hook.

# HOOKED RUGS
## Latching onto an Heirloom

Hooking rugs by hand is an ancient technique of rug-making that has come to us through two very different cultures. Each culture made rugs with a soft, thickly woven surface called the pile. Craftspeople in the Scandinavian countries developed a thick pile rug called *rya*, which means "rug" in Swedish. Perhaps the cold arctic winters inspired the creation of these rugs. The original rya rugs were made on looms with the pile woven in during the weaving process.

Today, rya rugs can be made by knotting the pile by hand onto a woven fabric backing. People in the Middle East and the Orient developed a similar method of making rugs—one that involved tying the pile onto a backing, using what became known as an Oriental knot. From these two rug-making methods have come the various techniques that are used today in rugs hooked by hand.

Hooked rugs are made by forcing loops of yarn or cloth strips through a backing fabric to create a pile surface, which can be either looped or cut. The materials used are generally very coarse and usually economical. Good use was made of this technique in early America: Coarse handmade cloth was available for backing, and cloth strips cut from worn but still valuable clothing or bedding served as the tight pile loops. Designs portrayed notable events or scenes, simple geometric patterns, or adaptations of flora and fauna motifs such as the Shaker representation of a horse (opposite). These sturdy rugs are still economical. Making them requires no large equipment. With only a few special tools, some backing fabric, and suitable fabric or yarn, you are ready to start.

### Materials

Although rugs can be hooked by machine today, making them by hand is still a popular craft. Most hooking methods require a frame, backing fabric, yarn or cloth strips in various colors, and one of the many types of hooks. To make a frame, use four strips of wood that, with joints butted together rather than lapped, will give you a rectangle 2 inches longer and wider than the rug to be hooked. Nail these wood pieces together and use 90-degree angle irons on each interior corner to keep the rectangle true and rigid. One-by-twos or two-by-twos are suitable, but even two-by-fours may be used for large rugs. Canvas-painting stretchers, available in many sizes at art supply stores, can be reinforced as above to make a suitable frame. The backing fabric should be a coarse material with a fairly open weave. Burlap usually works well, but for finer work—intricate wall hangings or carefully matched designs—a higher quality fabric such as monk's cloth is the best choice. This can be purchased in widths up to 72 inches, and like the burlap, it can be pieced together to make very large or unusual shapes. This backing is stretched taut and tacked or stapled to the frame. The type of hook used will depend on the design and personal preference. Photograph 1 shows the instruments used for the two basic methods of rug-hooking. The punch needle is used on the back of the fabric backing to force a continuous piece of yarn in and out, causing loops to form on the right side. The speed hook is used in similar fashion and produces the same results as the punch needle, but at a greater speed as the in-and-out motion is accomplished by turning a handle, much as one would operate an egg beater. The latch hook is used to knot short pieces of yarn or cloth strips to a canvas backing, working from the front, while the latch gun simplifies the knot-tying process into one step, and is, therefore, faster than the hook. Each of the following projects makes use of a different hook so the advantages and disadvantages of each can be learned.

Rug yarns of wool, cotton, synthetics, and various blends are suitable for these projects. They are sold at craft shops, variety stores, and by mail order houses, and are designed to wear well underfoot and make long lasting products. Cloth strips cut from partly worn articles or new yardage should be very narrow—about ¼ inch wide—so they work smoothly in the various hooks. Yarn strips can be bought pre-cut, or prepared by hand—small cutting machines are available to facilitate

[Text continues on page 904]

Made by a member of the Shaker religious community in Pleasant Hill, Kentucky, in the nineteenth century, this museum rug has pile made from rags of homespun wool hooked into a heavy canvas backing. The outer border is a braid made from the same rags of homespun wool. The Shakers were noted for the simple beauty and economy of all their arts.

The rug design, using one geometric motif in several sizes, was created by moving paper shapes around until a dramatic pattern was achieved.

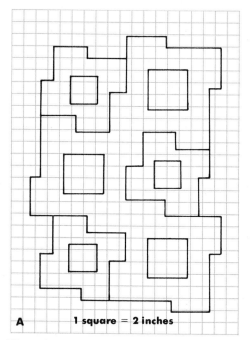

**A**          1 square = 2 inches

Figure A: Follow this pattern if you would like to duplicate the geometric rug. See page 57, Volume One, for instructions for enlarging it.

this. With yarn or cloth strips, count on using about ½ pound per square foot of rug area. Be careful not to mix yarns that will wear unevenly or require different care. Wool must be dry-cleaned and should not be combined with washable cotton.

### Design Possibilities

Sculptured effects may be achieved by varying the pile heights in one rug or combining two or more methods of hooking. Using additional needlework methods, such as embroidery with hooking, opens up an exciting range of possible texture and pattern ideas. Emphasis on the important design elements is possible through color, as well as by varying the pile height. The general rule that cool colors—blue, green and purple—recede and warm colors—red, yellow and orange—appear to come forward is useful in planning rug designs. Remember, too, that light tints may seem to float off the floor and dark shades sink into it, if concentrated heavily in one area. Light and dark colors also tend to show soil more readily than do medium tones.

Hooked rugs should be shaken and vacuumed often to stay fresh and clean. If the materials used are washable, then the rug can be washed safely with a mild detergent. Wool rugs require drycleaning, but will remain fresh for a long time if vacuumed regularly. This is true for hooked pillows and wall hangings as well.

**Weaving, Braiding, Knotting**
# Geometric-pattern rug

The geometric rug shown in the photograph at left was made with a speed hook, probably the best method for working large contemporary designs. This kind of hook can fill in large areas very quickly—this rug was completed in one week. There are several makes of speed hooks; they vary in cost and complexity. The Scandinavian-type hook used here is efficient and inexpensive. Speed hooks are advertised in craft magazines or may be purchased in craft supply shops. The advantage of a speed hook is its speed, of course. It uses a continuous length of yarn. Leftover yarn is appropriate only if the design has small areas of color. For this 32-by-46-inch rug, I used about 6 pounds of yarn, 3½ of red and 2½ of purple.

The geometric pattern of this rug is created with one motif repeated several times in two sizes. I made the plan by cutting out paper shapes and shifting them around until I had a pleasing effect. When pasted to a backing paper, the shapes became the sketch for the rug. Unusual shapes, well suited to hooking, will often suggest themselves with this planning method.

To transfer this design to a backing fabric, enlarge the pattern (Figure A). Cut backing fabric at least 6 inches longer and wider than the design area. The rug shown here, 32 by 46 inches when finished, needs a backing fabric 38 by 52 inches. If the fabric you use is not wide enough, seam two or more pieces together. Let the seams face the underside of the rug. Use colored chalk to plot the general pattern lines, allowing for the 3-inch-wide border. This border will be used for tacking the fabric to the frame, and, later, for hemming the finished rug. When the placement seems right, begin exact measurements of the design parts according to your pattern grid. Draw the final pattern lines in a bold color, using an indelible marking pen (photograph 2). (Water-soluble colors may run when the rug is blocked or cleaned, so be sure you use indelible ink.) For a more comprehensive guide, fill in small or complex areas with color (photograph 3).

The frame should be as large as the rugmaker finds comfortable to use, but the entire pattern does not need to fit within the frame at one time. One area can be stretched on the frame, and, when that hooking is completed, the backing can be shifted to stretch an unhooked area in the frame opening. If you use a small frame, decide which part of the pattern you want to work and place it drawing side up on the frame so that none of that section is over the wood. Staple or tack the cloth to the wood, attaching it at the middle of each frame piece, and stretching the backing slightly. Check the placement again to see that none of the design is resting on wood. Continue stretching the fabric, stapling at 2-inch intervals, working from center of wood toward the corners. Stretch the cloth taut so it sounds like a drum when tapped. This tension allows the hook to pass in and out of the cloth smoothly.

2: Follow a small sketch above, as you draw the pattern directly on the back of the backing fabric with an indelible marking pen.

3: Completely color in any intricate area of the pattern, making color identification easier and forestalling errors as you hook.

4: To start hooking, first outline the shape to be filled in, then fill it in, working back and forth in rows or in a random pattern.

To begin working the rug, thread the hook according to package directions. Working from the back or drawing side, hook the outline of the shape (photograph 4), keeping the yarn just inside the lines of that area. Then fill the entire shape with loops of yarn arranged in rows or random patterns. The speed hook is adjustable so you can use different pile heights for each project or even within a project for a sculptured effect. Some experimenting is necessary to decide which height or combination of heights you prefer. I made high loops in the red areas and smaller ones in the purple areas to get contrasting textures as well as colors. As you work with any hooking device, check to see that the yarn is feeding into it freely; otherwise, some loops will be too short.

When one area is complete, pull the hook out of the cloth until the point appears, and guide 3 inches of yarn out of the hook. Cut the yarn next to the hook. Continue working, either completing another area of the same color, or threading the hook with the next color. I find it is easier (and time-saving) to continue working areas of the same color. As you develop an area, check the density of the stitches. If they are so close together that they seem to bend the backing away from you, allow more space between rows. If the pile is too dense, the rug will not lie flat; too few loops, on the other hand, will give a bald effect with the backing fabric showing through.

5: Before hemming, trim the backing fabric border to 1 inch, and cut out the corners so the hem will not be bulky when it is turned under.

After one section of the rug is complete, you may need to shift the cloth on the frame to stretch an unfinished area. Continue in this way until the entire design is worked. During the hooking process, the backing fabric is often pulled off grain, and the finished rug may need blocking. This will adjust the final shape of the rug slightly and help it relax in its final position, but it will not correct too dense a pile or other defects of workmanship.

To block, chalk the outline of the rug on a large board or workroom floor. Place the rug face up over the outline and tack it in place, using rustproof tacks or staples just outside the last row of loops. Place two or three layers of damp towels over the entire rug, cover it with a piece of plastic and let it stand overnight. Remove the plastic the next day, and the towels the third day. Allow the rug to dry thoroughly in this position and then remove it from the board.

Spray or paint-on latex backing used to keep scatter rugs from slipping can also be used to hold the loops in place. Apply it liberally to the underside of the hooked rug, and it will glue the loops firmly to the backing fabric.

6: Fold back the 1-inch hem allowance, pin it in place, and stitch it to the back of the rug with heavy-duty thread.

To finish the rug, hem it, using the 3-inch border trimmed down to 1 inch as the hem allowance (photograph 5). Fold this hem allowance under, stitching it down with heavy-duty thread (photograph 6). An alternate method is to use an iron-on tape. In this case, cut the hem allowance down to ¾ inch. Fold it to the rug backing, and hold it in place with the iron-on tape. Follow the package directions for the tape exactly, and protect your iron by using a pressing cloth. Work small areas of the edge, and, if necessary, cut the tape into small sections where the rug silhouette changes direction.

The wise and solemn owl becomes a bird of fantasy when worked in pink, yellow and orange.

Figure B: The pattern for the owl can be worked in a smaller version for a pillow by reducing the background grid; see page 57, Volume One.

**B          1 square = 2 inches**

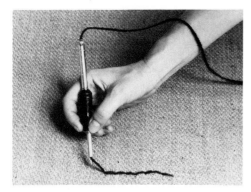

7: To form loops with the punch hook, just push the threaded needle through the back of the fabric and pull it out again.

## Weaving, Braiding, Knotting
# Intricate owl rug

A punch hook, while not as fast as a speed hook, is a much more flexible tool. It can be used with many more yarn weights, it makes more varied pile heights, and it is inexpensive. In many ways these advantages make up for the loss of speed. Punch hooks are available in needlework shops and department stores. The punch hook process is basically the same as the speed hook process. The planning, the design transfer, the use of the frame, and the hooking itself are the same as for the geometric rug (page 904). But the punch hook is suited to making a different kind of design. Because it is excellent for outlining and filling intricate areas and provides the greatest degree of control, it is used for detailed designs such as the owl pictured (left). The feathery outline and the fine detailing of the claws and eyes are easily managed with the punch hook. These hooks are inexpensive and you may want to have several, each threaded with a different color and ready to be picked up when needed. This is particularly useful if you are filling in small areas such as animal spots and foliage.

### Preparation and Hooking
To make this rug, you will need a 35-by-39-inch piece of backing fabric and rug yarn in the following amounts: 26 ounces of green, 14½ ounces of brown, 13 ounces of yellow, and 6½ ounces each of orange and pink. The design used for such a rug can be adapted from children's books, fabric or wallpaper patterns. With a grid placed over the original design, larger grids can be laid out on the backing cloth and the pattern transferred square by square (see page 57, Volume One). To copy the owl shown here, use the grid in Figure B. Center the motif on the fabric. Leaving a 3-inch border around the outside of the pattern for a hem allowance, stretch the backing on the frame.

Thread the hook, following package directions and using dark brown yarn, since you will outline the central animal shape first (photograph 7). Make sure the yarn is flowing freely so that loops are being formed on the right side. Using pink, yellow, and orange, or any other colors desired, fill in the body areas. One way to adapt this design to your own decor is to fill in the body areas using three colors that coordinate with a child's room. Do the border after the owl's body, using dark brown yarn, and complete the hooking by working the green background area. Secure the loops with latex following the directions on page 905.

### Design Effects With Pile
The final effect of the hooked rug will change with the next step. Decide on the effect you want: uncut loops, cut loops—they will impart a velvety appearance—or a blend of the two textures. Even within one color area, there will be a marked visual difference between cut ends and loops. There is a variation in texture and a dramatic difference in color. Loops catch the light and highlight the rug, giving it an overall lighter color, while cut ends do not catch the light and make the rug seem much darker. This variety in texture gives you a good way to achieve added interest. Cut the loops after the latex backing is applied. Slip one blade of a sharp scissor through a group of loops, and slice upward while pressing the blades closed. This motion helps to fluff the ends and keep the loops uniform. When a section is completely cut, the ends may be slightly uneven. If you do not want this effect, use the scissors like a hedge trimmer to sheer the pile, checking the level frequently by fluffing the pile. Be careful not to trim the pile too closely as the backing fabric may show through.

You may want to experiment with different pile heights for the separate design elements. Working the owl in longer loops and the background in shorter loops, for example, makes the owl stand out from the background. Or perhaps you might work the orange feathers in longer pile and the pink background in shorter pile to give the wings added texture. Adjust the hook and try a small section of each texture before continuing to hook the rug. To finish the rug, hem it, following the directions on page 905.

Love comes to the fore when spelled out in vibrant primary colors.

**Weaving, Braiding, Knotting**
# Design for love

Another type of hook used for making pile rugs is the latch hook. This is a simple tool to operate, and can be mastered with only a little practice. The differences between hooking with a latch hook and the methods previously described are: (1) it is not necessary to stretch the backing onto a frame; (2) the work is done from the front of the rug; and (3) the hook requires the use of pre-cut yarns. The latch hook makes longer pile and therefore opens up a whole new range of design possibilities.

Without a frame, you are free to fill in any area of the backing at any point in the work, and can complete one color throughout the rug before going on to the next. Working from the front of the rug also means that you may tack the canvas to a wall and step back to consider the general effect of the design, making changes as you go along, much as a painter works at his easel. Pre-cut yarns make much longer pile than the punch-hooking techniques, and these yarns are used for the luxurious ryas—the Scandinavian shag-type rugs. These rugs emphasize color more than specific designs, and one excellent way to achieve this effect in sketching a design is to use watercolors on wet paper, applying liberal washes so the paints can run into each other. The combination of pure and blended areas of color will suggest ways to mix yarns in the rug.

The fabric backing for latch-hooked rugs must have a very coarse, open mesh, similar to that used for needlepoint, so rug canvas is used. This has double horizontal and vertical threads for extra strength and the mesh ranges from a coarse 3½ or 4 squares per inch to 18 or more squares per inch in needlepoint canvas. Generally, the coarsest mesh is best for rug work, but in adapting designs to a finer scale for pillows or wall pieces, investigate smaller meshes.

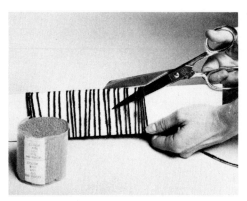

8: For latch-hooking this rug, purchase yarn in pre-cut 2⅝-inch lengths, or cut leftover yarn to this dimension as shown above.

9: To begin working with a latch hook, insert the hook under and through one pair of the double threads of the rug canvas.

10: Fold the yarn under the hook. Attaching the yarn to the latch hook at this stage allows you to make sure the ends will be even.

11: Moving the hand that is holding the yarn slightly away from the hook, catch the yarn into the latch in a smooth motion.

12: Pull the latch hook back through the mesh and out to tighten the knot. Latch knots can not be pulled loose by tugging on the yarn ends.

The design for latch hooking is transferred to the backing in the usual fashion (page 904), except that a wider marking pen is used since the meshes are open and tend to break the drawing lines. Solid areas of color are harder to fill in.

To make the love-pattern rug, you will need a piece of rug canvas 27 by 39 inches (allowing a 1½-inch border around the 24-by-36 inch design), and the following yarn: 16 ounces of yellow, 13 ounces of blue, 11 ounces of red, and 9 ounces of white.

Yarn for latch hooking can be purchased pre-cut to prcisely 2⅝ inches, and packaged in small rolls of one color. This is very convenient, but you may want to economize and cut your own yarn lengths—an excellent way to use scrap yarn from other projects. Decide what length yarn you will use and cut a piece of cardboard to one-half that width (photograph 8). Make the cardboard fairly long so you can wrap a continuous length of yarn around it. Hold the yarn in place as shown and cut it at one edge. To keep the cut pieces neat, gather them into a pompom and bind lightly with a rubber band. (Craftsperson's hint: Another way to do this, and for many people an easier way, is to cut the cardboard as wide as the yarn pieces will be long. Wrap the yarn as before, but secure it with a rubber band running the length of the cardboard and cut the yarn on both edges. In this case, the rubber band used to hold the yarn around the cardboard is used to bind the cut lengths.) The lengths need not be precisely even if the desired effect of the rug is one of bold color. The uneven pile resulting from uneven ends creates a casual appearance.

Using the latch hook requires four motions. The first inserts the hook under the double canvas thread (photograph 9). The second attaches the yarn. (This may be done before or after the hook is inserted into the canvas. Photograph 10 shows the yarn being attached after the hook was inserted. Experiment to discover which method is easier for you.) The third step is to hook the yarn into the latch (photograph 11). This should be done as smoothly as possible. Finally, the latch hook is pulled through the backing and out of the canvas to close the knot (photograph 12). The latch knots can not be loosened by tugging on the yarn ends; this will only tighten the knot. To remove a knot, if necessary, use a needle to loosen it at the center first. (There is a latch gun that speeds this type of hooking process. To use it, follow the package directions.)

For the love-pattern rug, transfer the pattern using the grid in Figure C. Since the design has some complex areas, color in any areas that might be confusing in the hooking process. The pile should be about 1 inch high. If the pile is too long, it will tend to distort the pattern. To get this length, the precut 2⅝-inch yarns are ideal; the knot uses approximately ½ inch of yarn so the pile will be about 1 inch high. The pile must also be kept even to prevent distortion of the design; if you cut your own yarn lengths, make sure they are as even as possible. The design can be worked from top to bottom or done by color area. Experiment to find the most comfortable method for you. When finished, trim any uneven yarn ends.

To finish the rug, you need rug binding (available at department stores); heavy-duty thread; and a sewing needle. First, trim the excess canvas to leave 1 inch along the sides and, by cutting diagonally, ½ inch at the corners (Figure D). Fold the canvas to the rug back and stitch it down (Figure E). Starting at one corner of the rug, stitch the binding all around the outside rug edge (Figure F). Stitch the inside edge of the rug binding to the backing (Figure G) mitering the corners as shown (Figure H).

For related crafts and projects, see "Braided Rugs" and "Rya Rugs."

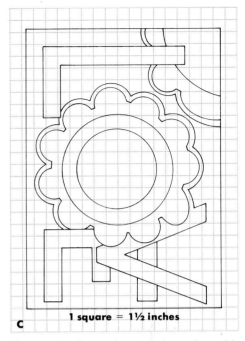

1 square = 1½ inches

Figure C: For instructions on how to enlarge this rug design, see page 57, Volume One.

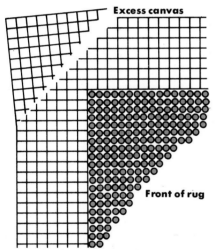

Excess canvas

Front of rug

**D**
Figure D: To start a hem, trim excess canvas to 1 inch along sides; cut corners diagonally.

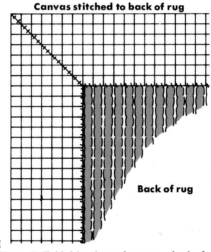

Canvas stitched to back of rug

Back of rug

**E**
Figure E: Fold this trimmed excess to back of rug and stitch it down.

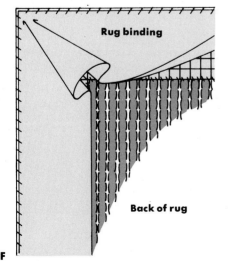

Rug binding

Back of rug

**F**
Figure F: Stitch rug binding around the outside edge of the back of the rug.

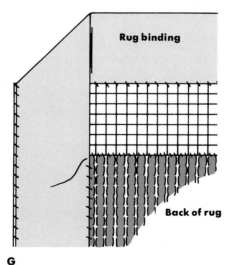

Rug binding

Back of rug

**G**
Figure G: Stitch inside edge of rug binding to rug back covering the excess canvas as shown.

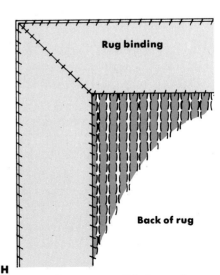

Rug binding

Back of rug

**H**
Figure H: Miter corners of binding as shown, having folded the excess binding to the inside.

# ICE CREAM, SHERBERT AND ICES
## Hooked on Homemade

*Lari Siler, a writer—often of food articles, learned to make homemade ice cream while writing a make-your-own ice cream article for* Epicure *magazine—she concocted 63 flavors as part of the research. In this, Lari had the help of her six children—some of them eager crankers and all eager tasters.*

Homemade ice cream, once an old-fashioned treat rarely encountered, has made a strong comeback with the return to natural foods and to meals made from scratch. The reasons behind its rebirth are not hard to find: It seems to taste better than store-bought ice cream—perhaps due to the rich, fresh ingredients used and perhaps due to the energy invested in it; it invites experimentation so flavors can be made to suit your own taste; and, finally, the making itself can turn into an exercise in pure, unadulterated fun. You may not achieve perfect results the first time you make ice cream, because each person has his own idea of what this is — but chances are you will be very satisfied with your effort.

Making—and, of course, eating—homemade ice cream is a project to intrigue and involve the whole family, from nostalgia-seeking grandparents to toddlers. The latter are often surprised to find out what ice cream is made of. Just for fun, ask your children if they can name its ingredients. Even if they can't, they will be willing helpers—and tasters—at all stages of the making process.

Armed with a knowledge of freezing techniques and some basic recipes, you will find that there is little mystery in making first-rate ice cream. The only piece of equipment you will need is an ice cream freezer, and even this is not absolutely essential; all of the recipes here can be made in a pan placed in the freezer compartment of your refrigerator. The texture of ice cream made this way is generally not as fluffy as the churned kind, and with this method the mixture must be taken out and whipped once or twice during the freezing. This serves to aerate the mix, making it lighter, and is essential; air is as important as any other ingredient.

Because the United States is the world's largest consumer of ice cream and has the widest—and weirdest—variety of flavors, people are often surprised to discover that the roots of this and other frozen desserts go back to Europe—and beyond. Marco Polo encountered water ices and sherbets in the Far East in the late thirteenth century, and when he returned to Italy, he brought with him a recipe for a frozen dessert that included milk. The popularity of ices and sherbets grew in Italy, reaching its peak during the sixteenth century.

We do not know who first churned a pint of homemade ice cream, but presidents and kings were among the first consumers. A queen, Catherine de Medici, introduced this dessert into France at her Paris wedding to Henry II in 1533. Across the Atlantic, George Washington was a later devotee; there is record of his having bought a "cream machine for making ice." Another fan, Thomas Jefferson, recorded a recipe for French ice cream while at the court of Louis XVI, and carried it home with him. The flavor was vanilla; the making involved 18 separate steps.

If the elite were the first to enjoy ice cream, the taste soon filtered down to the rest of the population, and ice cream parlors flourished. With the invention in the mid-1800s of a hand-cranked freezer for home use, the dessert was on its way to becoming the all-time U.S. favorite.

The mechanical processes that were perfected for the mass production of ice cream gave it a characteristic hard, light, uniform texture; the addition of commercial stabilizers added to its shelf-life. But homemade ice cream, denser and somewhat less uniform than commercial ice cream, is held in high regard by many families. True, it will not last as long as the store-bought variety, but in our house, at least, this poses no problem; homemade ice cream is rarely in the refrigerator long enough for its stability to matter. More temperate consumers, however, will be glad to know that it will keep for several weeks.

The taste's the thing, say members of the Siler family and friends as they practice the easy art of eating ice cream. Recipes for ice cream and other frozen desserts begin on page 914.

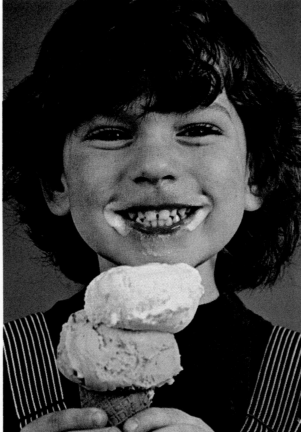
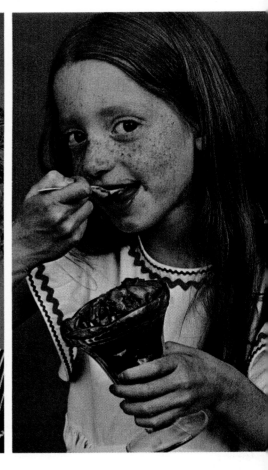

Ice cream makers representative of those available for churn-freezing include (left to right) a 4-quart hand-crank tub freezer, a 6-quart electric tub freezer and a 1-quart electric churn-freezer. The latter operates in the freezer compartment of a refrigerator. Ice cream can also be frozen in refrigerator ice trays.

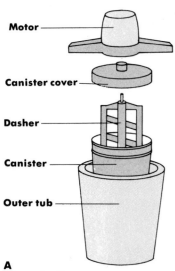

**Motor**

**Canister cover**

**Dasher**

**Canister**

**Outer tub**

**A**

Figure A: The major parts of a churn-freezer are the outer tub or bucket, the canister, the dasher, and the hand-crank or motor.

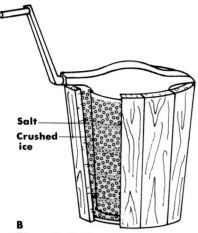

**Salt**

**Crushed ice**

**B**

Figure B: To churn-freeze, pack ice and salt in alternating layers to the top of the canister, beginning with a 2-inch layer of crushed ice topped with a thin layer of salt. Add ice and salt, as necessary, to maintain this level; brine will drain.

## Ice Cream Basics and Methods

Cream, milk, sugar, and occasionally eggs are the starting ingredients for ice cream, no matter what the flavor. Originally, a bowl of mixed ingredients was set in a pan filled with salt and ice and shaken or stirred until the mixture froze. This tiring process, known as the "pot freezer" method, became obsolete with the invention of hand-cranked freezers. To churn the sweetened cream mixture, you turned a handle attached to a wooden paddle that rotated in a metal container. The container held the ingredients and rested in a wooden bucket filled with crushed ice and coarse salt. Improvements in ice cream freezers since the invention of the first crank-and-paddle model have been slight. A wooden tub still usually holds the ice and salt because it provides good insulation; the inner container is still made of metal because that is the best conductor of cold. Most of today's electric freezers differ from their precursors only in that a motor—instead of the cook—moves the crank. Some models have outer tubs made of heavy plastic instead of wood, and there are a few that do the churning job inside a refrigerator freezer, eliminating the need for crushed ice and salt. One of these freezers is shown above, left, along with an electric freezer and a traditional hand-cranked model.

The function of a churn-freezer is to churn the ingredients into a smooth mix while freezing it. Churning also aerates the mix, increasing its volume by about one-third. After the ice cream has been churned, it is still soft, and it must be hardened, or ripened, either in the freezer compartment of a refrigerator or in the churning tub itself. So the process is a two-stage one—the churn-freezing, then the hardening. The critical stage is the first, where fast freezing must occur in order for the finished product to be smooth. By following the directions on the next page you should be able to make delicious ice cream using any type of home freezer.

## Essentials of Freezing

Making ice cream is one of those delightful bits of kitchen alchemy in which everything seems to happen at once. A liquid mixture is poured into the churn-freezer, and, as you crank it, you cause the ingredients to mix, aerate and begin freezing all in one step. With so much going on, it seems that something could go wrong—and sometimes it does. Ice cream, to be at its best, must be smooth and light, so you must be careful neither to over-churn nor under-churn the mixture. The correct churn-freezing time is determined by the temperature of the mixture at the start (it must first be chilled in the refrigerator) and the salt-to-ice ratio. This ratio influences the texture of the finished product. The salt melts the ice, and the faster the ice melts, the faster the mixture freezes. Too much salt will freeze a mixture too fast, resulting in coarsely-textured ice cream. Too little salt causes slow freezing, in which case the product is likely to be butter instead of ice cream. Ice cream recipes call for ice-to-salt ratios that may vary from a ratio of 10 parts ice to 1 part salt down to a ratio of 4 parts ice to 1 part salt. In my own churning, I have found that with my recipes ice cream freezes best when a ratio of 7 parts ice to 1 part salt is used. The recipes that follow, each making a 2-quart batch, should use this ratio.

## Preparing Ice and Salt

Follow the instructions for your particular freezer for amounts of ice and salt needed. Crushed or cracked ice rather than ice cubes is always called for, because the finer the ice the smoother the ice cream will be. If you start with ice cubes, crush them by putting them in a plastic bag, wrapping the bag with a towel, and hitting the cubes with a hammer or mallet. Freezing may be unsatisfactory with coarsely crushed ice. Coarse rock salt, sometimes called sidewalk salt, should be used unless your freezer manual substitutes table salt (in which case you should follow the salt-ice proportions suggested by the manual.) Rock salt is available at most hardware stores.

A final variable is the sweetness of the mixture. Sugar slows the freezing process, so if a very sweet mix is used, such as the fruit ice on page 917, more rock salt is needed; in general, use 5 parts ice to 1 part salt for freezing ices and sherbets. This is the proportion suggested for recipes given here. If you find that the product is grainy you may have to use more ice for churn-freezing. Remember that frozen desserts hardened in the churning tub out of the food freezer will take more ice and salt, usually twice the amount needed for churn-freezing.

Three cooks are better than one when it comes to homemade ice cream. Lari Siler (right) layers ice while Brooke (left) adds salt and Matthew turns the crank to churn the mixture.

### How to Make Ice Cream

Prepare the ice cream mixture and chill in the refrigerator for at least an hour. Make sure all parts of the churn-freezer are clean.

Crush the ice and measure the salt. The amount of ice to be used depends on the freezer's capacity. A one-gallon freezer requires about 14 pounds. You should use this much even if you make only 2 quarts. This amount of ice is needed just for churning. If you plan to harden the churned mixture in the churn-freezer as well, you will need about 25 pounds of ice in all, to allow for repacking the tub for hardening. The ratio of 7 parts ice to 1 part salt means you will need about 2 pounds of rock salt (about 2 cups) for the initial 14 pounds of ice. If you are using table salt, use about ¾ cup with this much ice. Position the canister in the freezer tub and insert the dasher. Keep the drainage hole clear and place a cup under it as the brine will drain during churn-freezing.

Pour the chilled mixture into the canister but fill only ⅔ full to allow for expansion during churning. You can pour in slightly more of the mixture for ices and sherbets. Replace the cover and position the motor or hand-crank mechanism. If you have a motor, plug it in and allow it to run for about one minute before you begin adding ice and salt.

While the dasher is turning, pour about 2 inches of crushed ice in the bottom of the tub, then sprinkle about ¼ cup of rock salt on top of the ice. Continue to alternate such layers of ice and salt until they reach the top of the canister. As the brine drains, add ice and salt to keep this level.

When the motor slows or stops or the cranking becomes difficult, the mixture is sufficiently churned. This usually takes about 25 minutes. If you are using an electric freezer, unplug the motor the minute it stalls.

The ice cream will be the consistency of mush or whipped cream at this point and it is ready to be hardened—though not before tasting, of course. Clear away the ice and salt from around the can cover, remove the motor or crank, and carefully remove the can cover and the dasher.

Push the mixture down into the canister with a large spoon, replace the cover (but not the dasher), and prepare to harden. The ice cream can be hardened in one of two ways: by placing the canister in the freezer compartment of your refrigerator, or by putting it back in the freezer tub and repacking the tub with salt and ice. If you decide to use your refrigerator-freezer, you may want to divide the partially frozen mix into several small plastic containers for easy handling. After a few hours, the ice cream will be ready to eat.

If you opt for using the freezer tub, drain off the leftover ice and salt, then place the canister back in the churn-freezer tub and repack it with additional crushed ice and rock salt. Finally, wrap the tub in several layers of newspaper or a large towel for additional insulation and let it stand in a cool place for two or three hours.

Brooke takes her turn at cranking but finds it exhausting as the mixture, which must be churned for about half an hour, begins to thicken.

# Start with vanilla

Each spring, the trade magazine for the dairy industry surveys frozen desserts to see which flavors are the most popular, and every year vanilla comes in first, followed by chocolate and strawberry. Even if vanilla is not one of your favorites, it is the first flavor to make since all of the others are but variations on it. The question, then, becomes *which* vanilla to try first, for there are quite a few. Some vanillas have a custard base—these are generally called French vanilla, and they always contain eggs. Another type, known as Philadelphia vanilla, is pure white rather than yellow in color. Some recipes are no-cook while others require top-of-the-stove cooking. And finally, the different types will vary from each other in terms of calories and fat content.

The following basic vanilla ice cream recipes can be modified to make other flavors by the addition of fruit, nuts, chocolate, coffee and other flavorings. Each recipe yields two quarts of ice cream, but may be halved or doubled. The mixtures can be frozen in the ice trays of your refrigerator if you do not have a churn-freezer, but if you do this, be sure to cover the filled ice trays with aluminum foil or plastic wrap and to whip the mixture with an egg beater or a wire whisk once or twice during the freezing time. All the recipes are best made following the churn-freezing instructions on pages 912 and 913.

## Old-Fashioned French Vanilla
This custard-based ice cream is the creamiest of the vanillas.

**6 egg yolks**
**2 cups milk**
**1 cup sugar**
**¼ teaspoon salt**
**2 tablespoons pure vanilla extract or 1 vanilla bean, split lengthwise**
**2 cups heavy cream**

In the top of a double boiler, beat the egg yolks and milk until well blended. Stir in sugar, salt, and vanilla bean. (If vanilla extract is used, add after cooking.) Cook, stirring constantly, over hot, but not boiling, water until the mixture is thick enough to coat a wooden spoon.

Remove from heat and let cool, and then cover and refrigerate. When the mixture is well chilled, stir in the cream and the vanilla extract. (If a vanilla bean was used, remove it and scrape the insides into the mixture.) Pour the chilled cream into the freezer canister and churn-freeze according to the previous instructions.

## No-cook Country Vanilla
This superbly easy-to-do ice cream is one version of French vanilla requiring no cooking. To save on clean-up, all ingredients may be mixed directly in the freezer canister.

**2 eggs**
**1⅛ cups sugar**
**2½ cups milk**
**2 cups heavy cream**
**2½ teaspoons pure vanilla extract**
**dash of salt**

Beat eggs lightly and add sugar gradually while beating, until mixture thickens. Add the remaining ingredients and mix well.

## Philadelphia Vanilla
Philadelphians believe that the only vanilla ice cream worthy of the name is a pure white ice cream, laden with specks of vanilla bean.

**5 cups light cream**
**1¼ cups sugar**
**1½ vanilla beans, split lengthwise**

Mix 2 cups of cream, all of the sugar and the vanilla beans in the top of a double boiler and stir over boiling water for 10 minutes. Remove vanilla beans and scrape pulp into the cream mixture. Cool. Add remaining 3 cups of cream. Chill, then churn-freeze.

## No-cook Philadelphia Vanilla
This is a no-cook version of Philadelphia vanilla. Ingredients can be mixed directly in the freezer canister.

**5 cups light cream**
**1 cup sugar**
**2 tablespoons pure vanilla extract**

Mix all ingredients directly in the freezing canister and churn-freeze.

## Vanilla Ice Milk
Ice milk contains less butterfat than ice cream and therefore is not as rich.

**3 eggs**
**1 cup sugar**
**4 cups milk**
**1½ tablespoons pure vanilla extract**

Beat eggs until creamy. Add sugar and stir until dissolved. Add the remaining ingredients, and chill, then churn-freeze. Note: Skim milk can be used instead of whole milk. Artificial sweeteners may also be substituted, but adjust the measurement, as these are usually sweeter than sugar.

## Condensed Milk Vanilla
Canned condensed milk is concentrated, and pre-sweetened therefore no additional sugar is required in the next two recipes. This recipe makes about 2½ quarts.

**2 14-ounce cans sweetened condensed milk**
**4 cups light cream**
**2 cups cold water**
**2 tablespoons pure vanilla extract**

Combine all the ingredients and stir until well blended. Chill and churn-freeze.

## Ice Tray Condensed Milk Vanilla
This makes about two ice trays full, or 1 quart of ice cream.

**2/3 cup sweetened condensed milk (about half a 14-ounce can)**
**½ cup water**
**1½ teaspoons pure vanilla extract**
**1 cup heavy cream**

Combine the milk, water and vanilla, and refrigerate. Whip the cream to a soft, custard-like consistency and fold it into the chilled mixture. Pour into ice cube trays with the partitions removed, cover with aluminum foil, and freeze for one hour. Pour the still-soft mixture into a chilled bowl and beat until fluffy. Return to the ice cube trays, cover with aluminum foil, and continue freezing until firm.

1: A wire whisk is an effective utensil for beating eggs as well as for adding sugar to beaten eggs when making No-cook Vanilla.

2: Once the vanilla mix has been chilled it is poured into the freezer canister for churn-freezing. The can should be filled to no more than ⅔ capacity to allow for expansion.

3: After ½ hour of churning, the ice cream mixture is partially frozen and is the consistency of whipped cream. Some invariably sticks to the dasher, which is now removed and licked.

4: For hardening, ice cream is poured into small plastic containers. Nearby are walnuts and marshmallows which can be added now, before the ice cream is fully frozen.

## Kitchen Favorites and Celebrations
# Concocting flavors

Any of the vanilla recipes on the previous page can be used as a base for the ice cream flavor of your choice—but a little caution is necessary here. Adding chocolate, strawberries, bananas, or coffee, for example, is a simple procedure but it must be done at the right time—which can be either before churn-freezing or after—and the ingredients must be added in the right proportion.

The flavoring suggestions on the next page are all geared to a 2-quart recipe. Remember to use the best quality ingredients available—the freshest milk, cream and eggs, pure vanilla extract, and fully-ripened fruit, fresh if possible.

Crushed fruits and candy should be added to the ice cream mixture after churning, but before it is hardened. Nut ice cream is made by adding 1 to 2 cups of nuts to the ice cream mixture after churning, if you want a chunky texture, such as for butter pecan ice cream.

5: Inventing flavors such as chocolate chip marshmallow is easy when homemade vanilla ice cream is the base. Ingredients are simply worked into the churn-frozen mixture before hardening it.

### Chocolate Ice Cream

Melt 2 squares of unsweetened baking chocolate in the top of a double boiler and add to the French vanilla ice cream base while it is cooking. Chill and freeze in the usual manner.

### Quick Chocolate

Add 1 cup of chocolate syrup to any vanilla ice cream mixture just before churn-freezing. Lessen the amount of sugar in the vanilla recipe by ½ cup or more, depending on the sweetness of the syrup.

### Coffee Ice Cream

Add 3 to 4 tablespoons of instant or freeze-dried coffee to French vanilla ice cream while it is cooking.

### or

Substitute 1 cup of very strong, freshly brewed coffee for 1 cup of milk in any of the no-cook vanilla ice cream recipes.

### or

Put 5 to 6 tablespoons of ground coffee in a cheesecloth sack, tie it tightly with a piece of string, and place it in the saucepan while French vanilla ice cream is cooking. Remove the sack and chill and freeze mixture as in the original recipe.

### Butter Pecan Ice Cream

Brown 1 cup of finely chopped pecans in 2 tablespoons of butter. Cool. Add nuts to churned and still-soft vanilla ice cream. Harden in the usual fashion.

### Banana Ice Cream

Mash 3 ripe bananas and sprinkle with ½ tablespoon of fresh lemon juice. Add to cooled vanilla ice cream before churn-freezing.

### Strawberry Ice Cream

Add 2 cups of crushed, fresh strawberries, which have been sprinkled with sugar, to churned vanilla ice cream mixture while it is still soft. Harden according to original recipe.

Note: Peach, pineapple and other fruit ice creams are made the same way. For pineapple, add an extra ⅛-teaspoon of vanilla extract to the basic mixture. When adding mashed fresh fruit or crushed berries, sprinkle them with sugar so they will not freeze; a sprinkling of lemon juice can be used to heighten the flavor.

### Peppermint Candy Ice Cream

Add ½ cup of crushed peppermint candy to French vanilla ice cream while it is cooking. After the ice cream has been cooled and churned, add another ½ cup of crushed peppermints for additional texture and taste.

### My Favorite Crunchy Ice Cream

Add 2 cups of corn flake crumbs to vanilla ice cream while it is still soft. Harden as directed.

### More Flavor Fun

Any of these recipes can be altered to suit your taste preference, but remember that ingredients that should be whole in the final (eating) stage—chocolate chips, for example—should be added after the churn-freezing process while the ice cream is still soft. Crushed candy or peanut brittle must be broken into very fine bits. Raisins should be ground fine and you may want to soak them in rum. Butterscotch sauce or fudge sauce can be swirled through vanilla or chocolate ice cream after it has been churned, but if the syrup is very sweetened, the amount of sugar in the recipe should be reduced.

Ingredients for ices and sherbets include milk, sugar, lemons, bananas, oranges and strawberries. In back is a bottle of grape juice. Fruit ices and sherbets are frozen the same way as ice cream, but the ratio of salt-to-ice should be 1-to-5.

**Kitchen Favorites and Celebrations**
# Sherbet made simple

Sherbets, like ice cream, come in infinite variety. They are made with milk, not cream, and while the freezing process is the same as for ice cream, the correct salt-to-ice ratio is 1 to 5. These recipes can be varied by adding different fruits.

### Lemon Sherbet

½ cup fresh lemon juice
1 tablespoon finely grated lemon rind
1½ cups sugar
5 cups milk
dash of salt

Combine milk, salt, and sugar and stir until the sugar is dissolved. Add lemon juice and rind, stirring as you do so. Churn-freeze according to earlier directions.

### Orange Sherbet

2 cups fresh orange juice
4 cups milk
1-1/3 cups sugar
3-6 tablespoons lemon juice
2 tablespoons grated orange rind
⅛ teaspoon salt

Mix milk, sugar and salt together, and stir until the sugar dissolves. Add orange juice, orange rind and lemon juice very slowly to the milk mixture, stirring constantly. Churn-freeze in the usual manner.

### Low-fat Orange Sherbet

2 6-ounce cans of frozen orange juice, undiluted
1½ cups skimmed milk
1 teaspoon pure vanilla extract

Combine all the ingredients in a blender until the mixture is thick and creamy. Churn-freeze.

### Strawberry or other Fruit Sherbets

2 cups berries
2 cups sugar
2 tablespoons lemon juice
1½ quarts milk

Crush berries in a blender or by mashing them through a strainer. Mix with sugar and lemon juice. Add milk and churn-freeze according to previous directions.

**Kitchen Favorites and Celebrations**
# Ices ¢ ⊠ 🚶 🔔

Ices are much like sherbets but contain no milk, and are generally made from sweetened fruit juice diluted with water. The following lemon ice recipes have different proportions of lemon and sugar-water and you will probably want to experiment, as I did, to see which one you like best.

To make other fruit ices, such as orange, grape, raspberry, cherry, or pineapple, follow the proportions used in the lemon ice recipe you like best, simply substituting the orange, grape, or other fruit juice for the lemon juice, adding 2 tablespoons of lemon juice to enhance the fruit flavor. To make pops, pour the churned mixture into paper cups and place in the refrigerator freezer. After an hour, insert wooden or plastic sticks into the center of each up. Continue freezing until hard.

### Lemon Ice No. 1

2 cups sugar
4 cups water
2 cups lemon juice (4 to 5 fresh lemons)
grated rind of 2 lemons

Boil sugar and water for 5 minutes. Chill. When cool, add lemon juice and rind. Chill in the refrigerator and freeze.

### Lemon Ice No. 2

3 cups sugar
4½ cups water
1½ cups lemon juice

Boil sugar and water for 5 minutes. Cool. Add lemon juice. Chill and churn-freeze.

### Lemon Ice No. 3

1½ cups sugar
1 cup water
3¼ cups lemon juice
4 cups water
grated rind of 1 lemon

Boil sugar and 1 cup of water for 5 minutes. When cool, add lemon juice, rind, and 3 more cups of water. Chill and churn-freeze.

Ices, which originated in the Orient, were the forerunners of sherbets. Cooling raspberry and grape ices are made with water and fruit juice.

### For Further Reference
Related entries in this series include "Birthday Celebrations" and "Confections and Comfits." Useful books, most of which give recipes, are:

Arbuckle, W. S., *Ice Cream*. AVI Publishing Company, Inc., 1966.

Anderson, Carolyn, *The Complete Book of Homemade Ice Cream*. Saturday Review Press, 1972.

Dickson, Paul, *The Great American Ice Cream Book*. Atheneum, 1972.

*Horizon Cookbook*. American Heritage Press, McGraw Hill, Inc., 1971.

Ice Cream review: *The History of Ice Cream*, published by the International Association of Ice Cream Manufacturers, Washington, D.C.

生花

These are the calligraphic characters for ikebana. The word derives from a phrase that means "to arrange flowers."

This 4-foot-high arrangement set in an earthenware bowl uses the mixture of plant materials permitted in classical *shoka* designs. A blade of pandanus grass is used for the primary branch, and wisteria vines form the second and third branches. Pink mums and foliage, used to support the three essential branches of the ikebana triangle, balance the composition.

# IKEBANA
## Japanese Floral Art

*Senei Ikenobo is the 45th headmaster of the Ikenobo school of ikebana, the Japanese art of flower arranging, in Kyoto. More than 1,000 years ago the Rokkakudo temple at this school became the birthplace of ikebana, and the art is still being taught there. Mr. Ikenobo designed the arrangements below and opposite to illustrate two variations of classical Ikenobo styles of flower arranging.*

Ikebana, the Japanese art of flower arranging, was being practiced in Buddhist temples more than 1,000 years ago. The temple priests created *tantebana*—standing floral designs whose materials were arranged to symbolize a balanced, harmonious universe. By the sixteenth century, the *tantebana* had developed into two distinct types of floral arrangements: the rigidly formal *rikka* (meaning "standing flowers") shown opposite, and the somewhat less formal *nageire* (meaning "thrown-in flowers") that emphasized the natural shape of the plants used; the photograph on page 925 shows a *nageire* arrangement you can make.

Elaborate rules governed the choice and relationships of floral materials and containers that could be used in these early *rikka* and *nageire* arrangements. For this reason, a less restrictive form of ikebana called *shoka* (meaning "living flowers") was introduced in the late seventeenth century and became popular with Japanese noblemen and warriors who had taken up flower arranging as an avocation. *Shoka*, demonstrated in the arrangement at left, permitted wider experimentation with plant materials and containers. But it retained the relationship of three main branches—representing universal harmony—that had by then become characteristic of all ikebana work. Of these three main branches, heaven was represented by a primary branch called *shin* (meaning "sincerity" or "truth"), man by a second branch called *soe* (meaning "add to"), and earth or nature by a third branch called *tai* (meaning "substance"). Additional branches (the "*ashirai*") played a supporting role in the arrangement, somewhat like counterpoint in music. The most important characteristic of *shoka* was that the three central branches were arranged without symmetrical balance, as shown at left.

As *shoka* superseded *rikka* in popularity, the emphasis shifted from formal religious symbolism to decorative flower arrangement, even though the basic principle of harmony was retained. The trend toward still freer forms of expression has continued to this day. Early in this century, the Ohara school contributed to *moribana* (meaning "heaped-up flowers"), an arrangement of fresh plant materials designed to represent a natural setting. Using a long, low bowl with a pin holder to anchor stems, you can make a *moribana* like the one on page 922. In recent years the Sogetsu school has developed a truly avant-garde, freestyle approach that permits combining fresh plants with those that had been dried, bleached and even painted. Containers can be traditional or totally unconventional. The freedom from restraining rules is so complete that inanimate materials—plastic, metal, glass—can be introduced at the discretion of the arranger. The stick construction containing lilies, roses and foliage on page 926 is an example of this approach. The unbalanced triangle shape is not required in a modern Sogetsu design.

The projects that follow illustrate the principles of the three schools of ikebana most widely practiced today; the original Ikenobo (still teaching the classical forms of *rikka, nageire* and *shoka*), the naturalistic Ohara, and the freestyle Sogetsu.

For more than two hundred years, large flower arrangements such as the 6-foot-tall *rikka* in the porcelain vase opposite were popular with the Buddhist priesthood and ruling classes of Japan. Here, as permitted by the classical rules, a bleached grass shoot is centered alongside a stalk of flowering strelitzia which is the main branch right of center. Another branch material—pine—is used for the two shorter branches. Wisteria vines, lilac mums and broad leaves complete the composition.

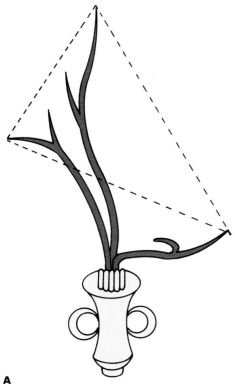

**A**

Figure A: In traditional forms of ikebana, the three main branch tips are placed according to imaginary lines (shown dotted here) to form an irregular triangle.

## Some Design Fundamentals

The ikebana arranger always works with an odd number of branches or flower groups, placing them to form one or more irregular triangles that give the art a dynamic balance (Figure A). Beginners who want to try the traditional forms can use the following guidelines.

For a *rikka* arrangement, the height of the tallest branch above the top of the container should be three to five times the height of the container. The visible height of a *shoka*'s tallest branch should be one-and-one-half to three times the height of its container. Traditionally, for either arrangement, the lengths of the second and third branches should be about two-thirds and one-third the height of the tallest, respectively, as suggested in Figure A. In more modern forms, this relationship can be changed, as it is in the *rikka* arrangement on page 919. Traditionally, additional groups of supporting plants or flowers are shorter and do not extend beyond the tips of the three main branches, but even this fundamental rule is not always observed today.

In an ideal arrangement, any supporting elements could be removed without affecting the harmony of line and the balance of the three main branches. A good test is to photograph an arrangement with black-and-white film; the harmonious balance of lines, shapes and textures (or the lack of it) shows more clearly without the distraction of color.

Ikebana materials are broadly divided into two categories—the pliable, woody tree plants and the more delicate flowers or grasses. Within these two categories are groups classified as vines, leafy plants, berry plants, hanging plants and aquatic plants. A list of plants appropriate for the upright *moribana* (page 922), the cascading *nageire* (page 925), and the freestyle modern arrangement (page 926), accompanies the instructions for each of the projects.

1: A tall, slender section of privet, a handsome evergreen with lustrous leaves, is chosen for the center line of the natural-looking *moribana* arrangement on page 922.

2: Here the privet has been pruned to enhance the structural line of the main branch. The base of the branch was freshly cut to make sure it would continue to take up more water.

3: This pine branch is being bent to conform to the shape of the cascading *nageire* on page 925. To bend any branch, rest thumbs on the top of the curve and place fingers underneath for support. Bring elbows into your chest for leverage and flex the branch gently, gradually working along the curve until the shape is set.

Some traditional rules governing ikebana, while not sacred, can be applied to advantage by the modern arranger. Try not to mix flowers from different seasons, or plants from different regions (mountains and seashore, for example), in the same arrangement. Select branches whose stem lines conform as closely as possible to the lines you want to establish (photograph 1). Do not hesitate to remove twigs and foliage to enhance the natural structural line of a branch (photograph 2). Never cut two branches or flowers to identical heights. Do not hesitate to bend branches if that will create more interesting curves (photograph 3). The secondary branch in the cascading *nageire* on page 925 was flexed to accent its graceful flowing line.

The plant materials and their container should always be related in scale, texture and color. Flowers can be used singly or in clusters to help lead your eye through the design, but use them with discrimination; colors should be subordinate to the structural composition. Flowers should seem to be growing from the container and, with rare exceptions, at least half of the vase rim should be free of blooms or foliage. Colorful stones (see *moribana*, page 922), shells or glass bits can add seasonal effects: green stones for spring, white for summer, red for fall and black for winter.

### Preserving the Plants

There are several things that you can do to branches and flowers before and after you arrange them to help them stay fresh longer. You may be able to get even the most fragile flowers in your arrangements to last a week if you are diligent.

To prolong the life of flowers, cut them early in the morning or in the evening, when they are full of water. Remove any foliage you can spare—leaves continue to take up and give off water after the stem is cut. Immediately plunge the cut ends in a pail of warm water, about 100 degrees Fahrenheit. Before arranging the flowers, make fresh cuts near stem ends to be sure the tubes in the stems are unclogged and not mashed shut (photograph 4). Many arrangers make these cuts on a slant but scientific tests have not been able to demonstrate that this extends a flower's life, since there are only so many stem tubes to take up water.

It is a good idea to sear the stem tips of some plants, like poinsettias, dahlias and poppies, that exude a milky substance that coagulates and clogs the tubes. First, wrap the blossom and most of the stem with a damp cloth or newspapers. Expose only the tip of the stem to the flame momentarily (photograph 5). Some foliage will stay soft indefinitely without water if branches stand for about two weeks in a mixture of one part glycerin and two parts water.

 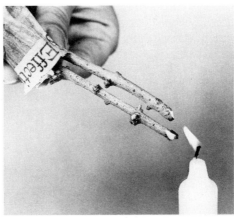 

4: To help preserve flowers, submerge stem tips in warm water and make fresh cuts with scissors-type pruning shears. Submersion lets stems begin absorbing more water as soon as the cut is made.

5: To preserve plants that exude a milky substance, char about ½ inch of the stem tip. Wrap most of the branch with damp newspaper, then hold stem tips over a flame for a few moments.

6: Revive wilted flowers by covering petals with damp newspaper, then soaking stem tips in boiling water. Let them soak until the water cools. Unwrap and mist leaves with cool water.

Many notions about extending the life of cut flowers are of little or no value. An aspirin or a copper penny in the water does no harm, but no good either. Sugar is a source of plant energy, but used with cut flowers it is actually harmful, since it stimulates the growth of bacteria. Commercial preservatives are useful, but the best trick of all is scrupulous cleanliness.

To help preserve any arrangement, space flowers so that fresh air circulates around them and change the water daily with a syringe. If an arrangement is beginning to wilt, you sometimes can revive the flowers by wrapping the petals in damp newspaper, then placing the stem ends in an inch or two of boiling water and letting them stand there until the water cools (photograph 6). Remove paper and dunk the stems in a pail of cool water. Then unwrap the flowers, spread them out and spray them with cool water.

The life of woody branches can be lengthened by splitting an inch or two of the thick stem end with garden shears, or by stripping bark from this area, or by crushing the end with a hammer.

*Audrey Jocelyn studied ikebana in Japan, where she attained a professorship. Later she founded the New York City Chapter of Ikebana International. Today she teaches classes in the art at her shop,* The Flower Arrangers, *in New York City. Throughout the years she has won many awards for her floral designs.*

## Greenery and Growing Things
# Upright moribana design

Unlike classical Ikenobo arrangements that stress precision of line and strict proportions, the *moribana* designs of the modern Ohara School seek to represent a natural scene or landscape. The container used is lower and wider than that for *rikka* or *shoka*. But *moribana* designs are still based on the irregular triangle essential to all ikebana (Figure A, page 920).

To make the upright *moribana* shown below, I used a flat-bottomed porcelain bowl 14 inches in diameter, a round lead pin holder 4 inches in diameter, 3 ounces of floral clay, pruning shears, and half a dozen white pebbles. At left is a list of flowers and branches suitable for *moribana*. I chose a low, blue porcelain bowl to symbolize water, privet hedge branches, 7 yellow chrysanthemums (they symbolize courage and are the national flower of Japan), and 9 yellow Peruvian lilies. The Peruvian lilies blend well with the mums while providing a pleasant contrast with the mum petals and privet leaves.

Select a container that will complement the size, shape, texture and color of your arrangement. Expensive containers are not necessary—an old soup plate or a wide ashtray would do, for example, or even an aluminum pan sprayed with waterproof paint. The round wooden pedestal base that I used is optional, but if you have a saber saw or jigsaw, it is an easy job to cut a wood circle of an appropriate size and stain or paint it.

The pin holder can be placed on the left side of the bowl for a right-handed arrangement, or on the right side for a left-handed arrangement. The terms right- or left-handed arrangement refer to the direction the lowest of the three main

## Plant material suitable for the upright moribana

**Branches:** All pines, Scotch broom, cedar, cypress, pussy willow, arborvitae, privet, rhododendron, magnolia, camellia, dogwood, azalea, horse chestnut, lilac, nandina, elm and driftwood are suitable, as are flowering fruit trees such as apple, quince, cherry, plum and peach.

**Calendar of flowers:** Any appropriate flowers can be used for festive arrangements but in general, only flowers that are in season are used in the more traditional Japanese arrangements. Floral representatives of each month are: January, pine; February, plum; March, peach and pear; April, cherry; May, azalea and wisteria; June, iris; July, morning glory; August, lotus; September, grasses; October, chrysanthemums; November, maples; December, camellia. (When I designed the **moribana** at right I used seasonal Peruvian lilies and chrysanthemums.)

Since the lowest branch points left, this is termed a left-handed *moribana* arrangement. Privet of varying lengths is used for all three main branches, and their tips form an irregular triangle. At the base, a triangular cluster of yellow mums and Peruvian lilies balances the design.

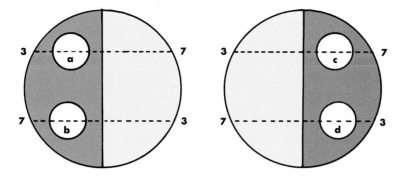

**B**

Figure B: To fix the location of the pin holder in the container, turn the container so that its vertical center line would face you. Then separate it into imaginary quadrants (by any one of the dotted lines above) that divide the vertical center line into either a 3-to-7 or a 7-to-3 ratio. For a right-handed arrangement (where the lowest branch will extend to the right), locate pin holder at either *a* or *b*. If the lowest branch will extend to the left, making it a left-handed arrangement, locate pin holder at either *c* or *d*. The arrangement opposite uses the *c* location.

7: To fix the pin holder firmly in the container, apply a bit of floral clay at four spots around the bottom of the pin holder. Position pin holder according to a right-hand or left-hand placement (see Figure B) and press holder so clay grips the bowl bottom.

branches or flowers points. Thus, the *moribana* opposite is a left-handed arrangement. Always place the pin holder toward the back or the front of the container and toward one side (Figure B) so that it will be off-center. To fix the pin holder to the bottom of the bowl, put four pieces of floral clay on the edges of one holder (photograph 7) and press the holder firmly in place.

Select a main branch (or flower, if only flowers are to be used in your design) that is one to two times the width of the container plus its height. This will represent the main trunk of the arrangement. If you wish, this branch can be shaped into a slight curve by bending it in the center (photograph 3). Remove all twigs and leaves from the bottom 4 inches of the stem. When you cut off a branch large enough to leave a scar, camouflage it with cigarette ashes or paint it the color of the branch. Clip the tip of the stem and impale the branch in the middle toward the back of the pin holder. The *moribana* design represents nature so don't remove all imperfect leaves.

The second branch or flower should be about two-thirds the height of the first. Leaves, blossoms or tips of twigs should face upward in a sun-and-dew-catching position. Impale this branch toward the front and right-hand side of the pin holder, so that it is under the first branch and leans outward at about a 45-degree angle. This branch should extend beyond the edge of the container. Traditionally, the third branch would be about one-third the length of the first, but the actual length is not as important as the balance achieved; the arrangement pictured needed a somewhat longer third branch. Insert this last branch toward the front left of the pin holder, angled left 15 to 18 degrees from the horizontal (Figure C and color photograph opposite).

**C**

Figure C: Placement of the three main branches in the *moribana* arrangement opposite achieves the irregular triangle of traditional design.

Groupings of from 3 to 15 flowers (always an odd number) can be added to the arrangement for color and counterbalancing. If possible, select each flower to represent a different stage of development and cut each stem to a different length. To mount the thin-stemmed mums in the pin holder, first insert each mum stem in a short piece of a larger hollow, woody stem (photograph 8). Place the flowers where weight is needed to counterbalance the tall, angled main branch. Flowers in front of this branch (closest to the sun) should be full blown; buds, imperfect leaves or smaller plants should be placed toward the back as if they were in the shade. This is traditional with *moribana*. Place leaves of branches and small flowers inconspicuously at the base of the stems and in the pin holder to balance the composition and to conceal the holder.

Check the arrangement to make sure that there are an odd number of branches and flowers. Eliminate any unnecessary or confusing branches that obscure the principal lines. Make sure the tips of the three main branches and the flower cluster form irregular triangles. Add a trail of pebbles to the container for a touch of scenic realism. And, since a Japanese landscape without water is unthinkable, fill the container with enough fresh, warm water to cover the pin holder. The arrangement will last a week if you change the water daily with a syringe. Place the bowl on a mat or a wooden disc, as shown opposite, to enhance the design and protect table top.

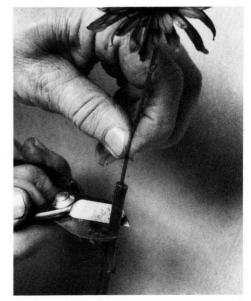

8: To attach a slender-stemmed mum to a pin holder, cut the stem to the desired length, then insert the end of this stem into a segment of a larger stem that is hollow or soft at the core. The larger stem can be impaled.

## Plant material suitable for a nageire

**Trees and shrubs:** Pines, witch hazel, cork, beech, podocarpus, Scotch broom, boxwood and bamboo are suitable. (See **moribana** plant list, page 922, for more materials.)

**Flowers:** Any strong-stemmed flower can be used, including roses, carnations, asters, strelitzia, and many others.

**Flowering fruit trees:** Branches of quince, cherry, weeping cherry, plum, pear, apple, crab apple, apricot, or almond can be used.

9: Join horizontally cut upper branch with a vertically cut support stick as illustrated. The slits will lock the pieces together so the upper branch maintains the desired angle.

# Cascading nageire design

Classical *nageire* arrangements of the Ikenobo school emphasize the natural shapes of the plant material rather than following formal rules governing proportions and the relationships of the main branches. A cascading *nageire* arrangement like the one opposite should be composed in a tall vase made of a traditional material such as bamboo, bronze, porcelain, pottery or stone. Flowers may be used at the container mouth (as are the roses serving as the lowest branch here) but the mouth should not be jammed with blooms or foliage.

I pruned a branch of white pine to serve as a middle branch. This is the most important branch in a cascading *nageire* and, in this case, I made it the longest branch, the one whose graceful line flows out of the container and to the left. Try to select a long, irregular branch with an interesting shape, one that slopes upward briefly before flowing outward and downward. Or pick a slender branch that can be easily bent into a beautiful curve. You can use any pliable branch or vine that grows naturally in an irregular or drooping form; select from the list on page 922 or at left. The visible part of the cascading branch should be equal in length to the height of the vase plus its width. The visible part of the nearly vertical branch should measure one to two times the height of the container, so that its height helps stabilize the composition. How much you add to these visible lengths will depend on how each branch fits into the container. If the branch is light, little additional

10: The slit-stick support method (photograph 9) can be used in conjunction with a crossbar wedged in the container. The crossbar here (arrow) is a pine stick cut to serve as a wedge between support stick and side of vase.

length may be needed. Simply cut the stem end diagonally so that it can be braced against the inside of the vase at the desired angle. If the branch is heavy, and too short to reach the bottom of the container, cut a separate piece of branch that will fit squarely against the bottom of the container and serve as an upright support. To attach an upper branch to this support branch, cut a slit in the end of each branch with garden shears and wedge them together (photograph 9). Then put the support branch into the container and brace the upper branch against the wall of the container at whatever angle is desired. If additional bracing is needed to fix the branch position, cut a short section of pine and use it as a cross-brace, as in photograph 10.

Red roses were used for the lowest branch position. Cut the roses so their visible portions measure one third to one half the height of the vertical branch, adding extra length for support within the vase. Their height is influenced by the size and curvature of both the branches, but visually the roses should appear to be about one third the height of the vertical branch. Rose leaves in varying lengths can be placed along the rim of the vase to balance the composition.

This cascading *nageire* is an arrangement of white pine and red roses. Japanese arrangers often contrast a bold pine branch with a fragile flower like a rose.

## Greenery and Growing Things
# Avant-garde ikebana

**Plant materials suitable for a freestyle design**

Any plant material, fresh or preserved, can be used in a freestyle arrangement. Plants can be preserved to maintain their natural colors, or dried and spray-painted, dyed or shellacked. Florists can supply you with unusual plants to use, but some suitable ones that are cultivated in home gardens are hydrangea, canna lily, tulip, caladium, coleus, begonia, pachysandra, forsythia, aspidistra, cabbage, dracaena, hosta and zinnia, or climbing vines such as ivy, clematis and honeysuckle.

While most schools of ikebana follow the traditional rigorous rules, there is one avant-garde school—the Sogetsu—in which almost anything goes as long as the artist doing the arranging is satisfied with the results. It is this school that I attended in Japan, and I have followed its recent evolution with great interest. I have seen ovals, circles, fans, crescents and even abstract shapes successfully substituted for the classic triangular form. Every kind of plant material imaginable has been used in one Sogetsu arrangement or another: fresh, dried, bleached, painted and even—perish the thought—artificial. Nor are other inanimate materials excluded. Such found objects as old TV and radio tubes and scraps of telephone wire have been integrated into some of these arrangements; colorful plastic tubing into others. Almost anything seems to find its way into this free-form. I personally am anxious to try an arrangement using discarded umbrellas.

To hold these disparate elements, you can use a conventional container if you like. But just about everything else your imagination suggests can be substituted —even a container that does not contain, such as the garden-stake-and-foam holder in the color photograph below.

If Sogetsu ikebana is distinguished from traditional ikebana primarily by its free style, it also stands alone in its sculptural quality. Every other form of ikebana calls

Rubrum lilies in this tall stick construction suggest ikebana's basic triangular shape in a freestyle arrangement. Yellow roses and a lily bud at lower right balance the composition. Sprigs of leather-leaf fern and ivy fill out the design and conceal a vial holder within the sticks and a cup holder resting on top of the post-and-crossbar support.

for a definite front which faces the viewer; a freestyle Sogetsu arrangement is intended to be viewed from all angles, much as sculpture is.

Because of the sculptural quality of Sogetsu ikebana, the container here is merely a frame for the arrangement. It is an integral part of it; indeed, frequently the most important part. Let your imagination run free in creating unusual containers. Not only plastic foam and sticks, but cans (sprayed on the inside with waterproof paint), seashells or tiles embedded in plaster, and vinyl, leather or wood scraps glued onto glass jars can be made into arresting, inexpensive containers. The colors, textures, shapes and sizes of such invented containers will help you decide the color and placement of the plant materials you will use.

### Stick Sculpture

To make the foam-and-stick composition, cut a 1-by-12-by-16-inch block of plastic foam with a saw or sharp knife. This will be the base. For the two containers you will need 63 pointed ⅛-by-18-inch garden stakes, an 8-inch length of cord, an 8-foot roll of 1-inch-wide black masking tape, black floral spray paint, one dozen No. 23 floral wires, four ounces of green florist's foam, a 1½-by-5-inch plastic vial (a frozen juice can would do) a 2¼-by-2¼-inch black cup holder (or any similar plastic container, such as the bottom of a sewing-kit box, covered with black tape), and 1-by-1-inch pin holder to put in the cup. Floral spray paint and masking tape come in enough colors to suit almost any design. I have used silver and gold colors when I wanted a metallic effect. For the arrangement at left I felt black would best set off the bright rubrum lilies, roses, leaf ferns and ivy.

I prefer to spray-paint the sticks and plastic foam first, but you can do this just as easily after the containers have been fully assembled. Conceal the rough edges of the plastic foam with masking tape. Align the flat top ends of three garden stakes, placed side by side, with the rim of the vial. Wire the sticks to the vial, then bind with black masking tape (photograph 11). Fill the vial with green florist's foam. This soft substance will act as a holder to support the ferns and lilies. Gather 52 sticks flat ends up and tie them loosely in the middle with a cord. To separate the sticks, use your fist to open up the top half of the bunch (photograph 12). Adjust the sticks until you are satisfied with the angles they form top and bottom. Then embed the pointed ends of these sticks in the plastic foam toward the left side of the base and cut the cord. Add the sticks holding the vial, pressing them into the plastic foam so that the top faces out at the left side.

Use the remaining eight sticks to make two H-shaped post-and-crossbar supports. Cut six of them into thirds so you will have 16 six-inch segments. Divide sticks into groups of four with flat ends up. Wire-wrap each bunch of four sticks 2 inches down from the top to form four posts. Cut two sticks to make four 5-inch crossbars. Pair them with points facing in the same direction. Wire-wrap each crossbar pair 1¼ inches from each end. Leave enough space between posts and crossbars to fit the cup with the pin holder snugly. Fasten crossbars to posts with wire at the wire joints (photograph 13), forming two "H" shapes. Align both pairs of posts with the crossbars on the outside and insert into foam. Posts and crossbars positioned toward the front on the right side will balance the tall sticks on the left. Fit the cup holder in place on the crossbars.

Rubrum lilies, yellow roses, leather-leaf ferns and ivy are used in these arrangements. Cut the flower stems to different lengths and insert them into the holders. Arrange the three lilies to create the irregular triangle so important in ikebana design. Let the blossoms face upward as if they were receiving sunlight. Arrange ferns around the flowers, and fill in with smaller pieces of foliage. Three yellow roses at the lower right harmonize with the yellow-centered lilies. Since the arrangement is to be viewed from all angles (unlike the earlier arrangements that have a definite front and back), buds and full blown flowers can be interspersed. Arranged in a triangle, the roses are set off from the curved line formed by the lily bud that cradles the design. As you place ivy around the flowers, put smaller pieces of foliage between them and make sure some of it conceals the pin holder. When the arrangement is complete fill the containers with enough water to saturate the florist's foam in the vial and to cover the pin holder in the cup.

For related entries, see "Bonsai," "Dried Flowers," "Greenhouses," "Herbs," "Lighted Indoor Gardens," "Terrariums," and "Window Gardens."

11: Line up the flat ends of three 18-inch garden stakes, painted black, with rim of the vial and fasten them together with wire. Then bind the sticks to the vial with masking tape.

12: Position a bunch of sticks tied in the middle with string on the left side of the plastic foam base, then insert your fist into the top half of the bunch to separate the sticks as shown.

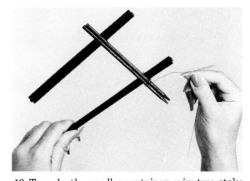

13: To make the smaller container, wire two-stake crossbars to each pair of four-stake posts. The cup pin holder will rest on the crossbars when the posts are pushed into the plastic foam.

# INKLE WEAVING
## Belts, Bands and Straps

*Gudrun Mirin is a self-taught weaver. After taking only one course in weaving, she was so taken with the craft that she learned inkle weaving on her own. Her work, both weaving and pottery, has been exhibited and sold in galleries and at craft fairs. President of the Queens Craft League and a member of the board of the New York Handweavers' Guild, Gudrun was born in Austria. She lives in Ithaca, New York.*

1: In inkle weaving, heddles made of string are attached to the heddle bar (center), tension is adjusted by a movable tension bar (bottom right), and length is adjusted by a movable peg (arrow).

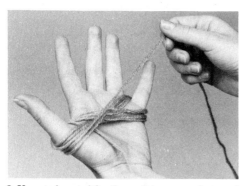

2: Yarn to be used for the weft is wrapped around the thumb and little finger to form a figure-eight shape called a butterfly. This facilitates passing the weft through the warp threads.

One of the simplest kinds of loom weaving is the one that creates the inkle—a narrow strip of woven material that can be used as a belt, a strap, a handle or a headband. To form a wider piece of fabric, several inkles can be sewn together. Inkle is a Scottish word that means band, tape or strip. The inkle loom used in the U.S. can indeed be traced back to Scotland, but the history of inkle weaving goes back much farther.

Narrow belt-like braids were introduced into southern Gaul by Egyptian weavers during the Roman Empire. These braids were the forerunners of the woven band and, in their simplest form, could be made without a loom. Subsequently, narrow loom-woven strips were developed in various parts of the world—in Madagascar and other parts of Africa, in South America, and in Latin America. In fact, the belts woven in Guatemala today closely resemble inkle belts.

Inkle weaving is also well recorded in English literature. Shakespeare, Chaucer and Swift all mentioned inkles woven of linen and alluded to the fact that inkle weavers had less status than did weavers of wider cloth. The British inkle looms of those times were adapted from the Scottish, the type of loom originally used to make intricate braids. English and Scottish weavers both worked with sturdy, inexpensive fibers—linen, cotton and wool—and the inkles they made served as the poor man's trimming in place of costly lace and silk.

History has it that a woman named Mary Atwater, author of *Byways in Handweaving* (published in 1968 by Macmillan Publishing Co., Inc.), introduced the inkle loom to the U.S. in the 1930s, and then, with great ingenuity, went on to improve the basic technique. Dissatisfied with the plain-weave instructions sent with the loom, she devised intricate patterns using several colors of thread.

Today, inkles are becoming popular again, though no longer as a poor man's trim. The striking color and texture combinations that can be achieved through inkle weaving have brought inkles to the attention of craftspeople who have never woven before. Learning to weave on an inkle loom makes possible the creation of a satisfying product and serves as a good introduction to yarns, looms and the more complicated forms of weaving.

Inkle looms are available through mail-order loom suppliers, including E. E. Gilmore, 1032 Broadway, Stockton, Cal. 95205; Lily Mills Company, Shelby, N.C. 28150; and School Products Co., Inc., 312 East 23rd St., New York, N.Y. 10010.

### Threading the Loom

All weaving is the process of interlocking lengthwise and crosswise threads. In the weaving done on an inkle loom (photograph 1), the pattern of the woven piece depends entirely on how the lengthwise threads are arranged on the loom, since the crosswise threads will show only at the edges. These lengthwise threads, known as the warp, are strung on the loom so they are parallel to each other. The variously colored threads are tied to each other to form one continuous strand around and around the loom, so the tension is equal throughout. The process of putting these threads on the loom is known as warping the loom.

The crosswise threads, which constitute the weft of the fabric, are added as the weaving progresses. To make it easier to pass the weft thread from one side of the loom to the other, it can be wrapped around two of the weaver's fingers to form a figure eight, called a butterfly (photograph 2), or wrapped on a shuttle.

In inkle weaving, there are two sets of lengthwise threads on different planes on the loom, and the weft thread is passed between them, producing what is termed a warp-faced band because the visible pattern is formed solely by warp threads. The weft serves the important function of holding the lengthwise strands together.

Inkle belts are not only functional but can be twisted and sewn together to create unusual wall hangings such as this one the artist has titled "A Twist of Inkles."

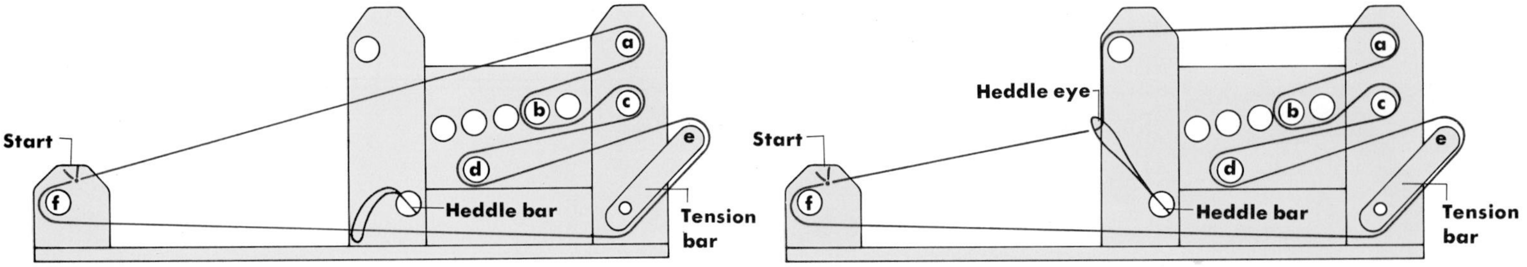


A

Figure A: To warp the loom, thread the yarn alternately through the open space between heddle loops (left) and through the heddles themselves (right). The path from a to f for both warps is the same.

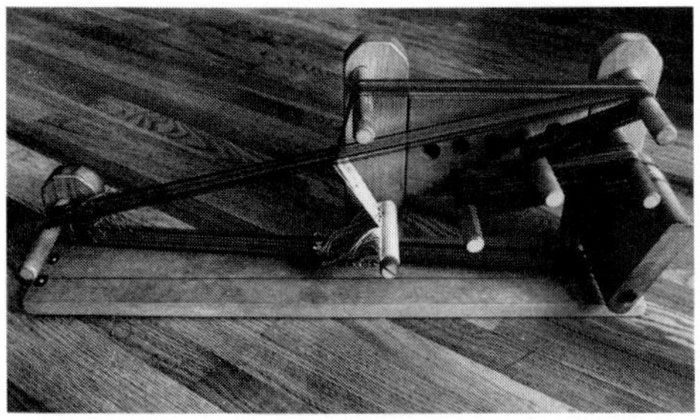

3: The loom is warped (threaded with warp yarn) to make the hat band and tote bag handle pictured on page 932.

Due to the way the loom is threaded (Figure A), the two sets of warp threads—known as the heddle warp and the open warp—can exchange planes as a unit, although only the open warp moves. When the loom is being warped, every other thread is passed through a loop of string called a heddle, one loop for each thread. These become the heddle warp; the alternating threads—the open warp—do not go through string loops. The space between the two sets of warp threads is called a shed.

To fill the loop with warp threads, tie the first thread temporarily to the front bar of the loom. Figure A, left, shows the path taken by an open warp thread. When the first thread gets back to where it started, it can continue around again, or it can be cut and the end tied to a thread of a different color, depending on the pattern planned. The second warp thread goes through a heddle eye; Figure A, right, shows the path taken by such a heddle warp thread. The warp threads continue to alternate between the two paths as they are placed on the loom until the desired width is reached; when all are in place, the last end is tied temporarily to the front bar. When it becomes necessary to move the warp threads around the loom (after about 5 inches of belt are woven), both first and last warp threads are untied from the loom peg and tied to their adjacent warp threads.

One of the central pegs is adjustable, depending on which of a row of holes is used; its position determines the length of the belt that can be made. The loom pictured can produce a belt 6 to 8 feet long. The number of threads placed on the loom depends on the thickness of the thread used and the planned width of the finished belt. Photograph 3 shows warping completed for the hat band and tote bag handle pictured on page 932.

## Weaving

When all of the warp threads are in place on the loom, weaving can begin. In this process the weft thread is passed through the open space between the upper and lower sets of warp threads. The threads of the open warp are then shifted with pressure of a finger so the positions are reversed; if the open warp was on top, it is

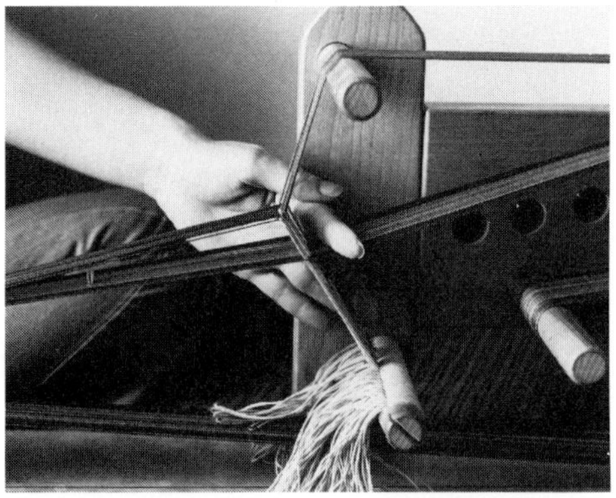

4: To make the first shed—a space between the two sets of warp threads—push down on the open warps so the heddle warps are on top and the open warps on the bottom.

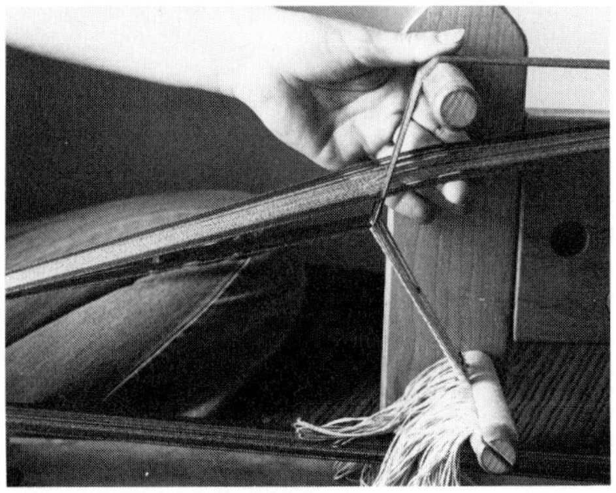

5: To make the second shed, push up on the open warp threads. The shed is now reversed, with open warp threads on top and the heddle warp threads on the bottom.

6: To weave, put the weft through a shed. This is known as making a shot. Then change the shed for the next shot of the weft, thus weaving the weft thread through the warp threads.

7: To make the weave firm, push each shot of the weft thread down with a ruler or other flat stick, as shown. This procedure is known as beating down.

## Glossary

**Beating:** Tamping down each crosswise (weft) thread after it is inserted and shed changed, to make the fabric firmly woven.

**Butterfly:** Thread arranged in a figure-eight shape in order that it might easily be passed back and forth through the loom.

**Draft:** A weaving pattern drawn on graph paper to show the order of various colors of lengthwise (warp) threads.

**Heddles:** A series of loops made of string and attached to the loom, through which half of the lengthwise threads pass.

**Heddle eye:** The string loop through which a lengthwise thread passes.

**Heddle rod:** The projecting bar on the loom that holds the string loops.

**Pick-up stick:** A flat, thin stick used to lift certain lengthwise threads when special pattern effects are sought.

**Selvage:** The side edges of a strip of woven cloth.

**Shed:** The open space between the two sets of lengthwise (warp) threads; as these sets successively exchange top-and-bottom positions, the crosswise (weft) threads pass through the sheds that are created.

**Shot:** The passage of one crosswise thread through a shed.

**Shuttle:** A flat wooden paddle for holding the weft (the filling thread) so it can be easily passed through the shed.

**Take-up:** The shortening of the lengthwise threads that results as they go over and under the crosswise threads.

**Tension bar:** An adjustable rod that can be loosened so thread is not stretched.

**Warp:** The lengthwise threads that are strung directly on the loom, through which the crosswise (weft) threads are woven.

**Warp-faced:** A weaving, as in these projects, in which the lengthwise threads show on the surface; the crosswise threads are visible only along the edges.

**Weaving:** The interlacing of lengthwise and crosswise threads to form fabric.

**Weft:** The crosswise threads that are woven through the lengthwise threads on the loom.

moved to the bottom. Photographs 4 and 5 show the two sheds that can be formed successively by raising and lowering the open warp.

Weaving on the inkle loom is the process of passing the weft thread through a shed (called making a shot, photograph 6), changing the shed, tamping down the weft to make it firm (photograph 7), then passing the weft thread back through the new shed. A small ruler (as shown), a tongue depressor, or a beater made specifically for this purpose can be used to press the weft into place, a process called "beating down." The weaving process then continues—make a shot, change the shed, beat down, make a shot, change the shed, beat down . . .

## Designing Inkles

One of the reasons why inkle weaving is growing in popularity is that the design of the inkle is established as soon as the loom is threaded. Weaving is a continuous process of filling the threaded loom with weft. For a solid-color inkle, the loom is filled with one color. If a pattern is desired, the loom must be carefully threaded, and a graph-paper pattern, called a draft, is the easiest way to note the number of colors and their order. This is done as shown in Figure B, page 932.

To make lengthwise stripes, the colors are placed alternately on the loom. If a stripe one thread wide is desired, two threads of the same color must be used side by side—one through a heddle loop and the other through the open space. This is done because only the threads on the top are visible at any one shot of the weft. The change of shed for the next shot of the weft brings the bottom warp threads to the top, so for a continuous lengthwise stripe, both one open warp thread and its adjacent heddle warp thread must be in the same color. For wider stripes, any multiple of two will work.

To make crosswise stripes, on the other hand, contrasting colors are used for the open warp and the heddle warp. When the open warp threads form the top of the shed, only that color will be visible. On the next shed, when the heddle threads are on top, that color will form a contrasting stripe, thus producing a pattern of crosswise stripes in alternating colors. Figure D (page 933) shows a pattern for crosswise stripes; the watch band made from this pattern is on page 933.

The only place where the weft thread shows is at the edges. The weft is shot through the sheds from either side; if you start the weft on the right and pass through to the left (photograph 6), the next shot will be from left to right. The small loops of weft that show from one shot to another form a woven edge called selvage. In order to make this selvage edge an integral part of the weaving, use the same color thread for the weft as the outermost warp threads. As you gain experience in weaving and can make selvages that are even and of an equal tension, you might use leftover yarn in a coordinated color for the weft.

The thickness of the weft thread determines the speed of the weaving: The thicker the weft thread, the faster the weaving goes. Too thick a weft, however, will result in a loose, uneven belt. When working with a thin yarn such as No. 5 pearl cotton, I use a double strand for the weft to accentuate the design in the warp.

An inkle belt used as a hat band and bag handle is an attractive way to coordinate a hat and bag.

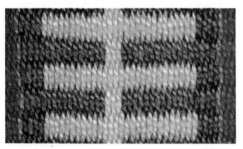

This detail shows the design created when the loom is warped following the pattern in Figure B.

8: To remove the finished belt, cut across the warp threads, leaving several inches for fringe.

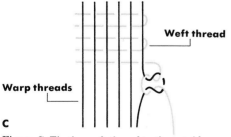

Weft thread

Warp threads

C

Figure C: Tie the weft thread to the outside warp thread to secure the weaving at both the beginning and the end of the weaving.

## Weaving, Braiding, Knotting
# Hat band and bag handle

The hat band and matching bag handle at left were made with No. 5 pearl cotton thread in 5 colors. You will need a total of 4 ounces of thread and a sewing needle.

Measure the crown of the hat and decide the length of the handle you want, allowing 1 foot extra for tying the inkle on the hat, making the fringe, and sewing on the handle. I needed a belt about 6 feet long, so I warped the loom with the adjustable peg in the position shown (photograph 3, page 930). To make the band 1¾ inches wide, warp the loom following the pattern, called a draft, in Figure B. These graph patterns are a convenient and concise way of showing how to warp a loom. Reading from left to right, the first thread is maroon and it is threaded through the open warp. The path of an open warp was shown in Figure A, page 930. The next thread is also maroon and it is a heddle warp, also in Figure A. The

middle repeat from right to left →

| Heddle | M | M | M | M | P | | B | B | B | B | L | L | L | L | L | L | L | L | L | L | G |
| Open | M | M | M | M | P | B | | B | B | B | G | G | G | G | G | G | G | G | G | G | G |

B    Key: M = maroon   P = purple   B = blue   G = gold   L = light blue

Figure B: Warping the loom according to this pattern will produce the design pictured (left).

threads are warped alternately through the open space and through a heddle. This creates the two sets of warp threads between which the weft passes in the process of weaving. To continue warping, follow the draft. Each lettered block indicates one thread: The letter tells what color and the placement of the letter tells whether it is warped open (bottom line) or through a heddle (top line). After 8 maroon threads are warped, a purple thread is attached. To do this, cut the maroon thread, leaving enough to tie to the purple thread, just in front of the front bar (photograph 3). Tie the purple to the maroon; all new colors are tied on this way to form a continuous warp. The knots can be cut off together when the weaving is completed.

To make the draft—the graph-paper pattern—more concise, any belt that is symmetrical from left to right can be shown with only half a draft. The first half is written out and the second half is a repeat of the first, but worked in reverse. When you get to the last gold thread at the far right of Figure B, for example, you will be at the center of the belt. To warp the second half, follow the colors backwards (from right to left), but ignore the placement, simply alternating open and heddle warps. The last thread warped according to the pattern was a gold through the open space. To warp the second half, repeat the gold but since the last thread was through the open space, this gold must be threaded through the heddle. The next thread (second from right) is also gold and goes through the open space. A glance at your loom will tell you whether the next thread is open or heddle, and the pattern indicates which color is used. The pattern ends with 3 gold threads; when you repeat it backwards, you add 3 gold for a total of 6. Then alternate the gold and light blue, followed by 8 blue, 2 purple, and 8 maroon. The draft shows 43 threads; the completed warp will have 86. To make the stripes appear thicker, I used 2 strands of maroon (the color of the outer warp threads) for the weft.

To weave, raise the warp to form a shed (photograph 4), insert the weft (photograph 6), change the shed, and beat down (photograph 7). Continue weaving this way until the shed is so small that it is difficult to pass the weft through. Loosen the tension bar and rotate the woven area under the first peg; then tighten the tension bar and continue weaving. Repeat this procedure each time the shed becomes too small. To remove the finished belt, hold the warp threads and cut across as shown in photograph 8. The weaving will unravel if the weft threads are not secured, so tie a knot at the edge of the weaving (Figure C), both at the beginning and end of weft. Trim the fringe to approximately 2 inches.

For the hat band, tie the belt around the crown of the hat, knot it, and cut off the excess. Unravel 2 inches of weave of the cut end to match the fringe on the other end, and knot the weft. Use the remaining belt for the bag handle, folding one end around one ring of the tote bag and hemming it under. Adjust the length of the strap until it is comfortable for you, then secure the other end.

A narrow inkle band and a small buckle make a durable and attractive watch band.

A vase for dried flowers is made from a length of inkle belt and a juice can.

**Weaving, Braiding, Knotting**
# Watchband and vase

The watchband and vase cover pictured above were made from No. 5 pearl cotton thread. The navy and raspberry stripes are bordered in light blue; and a double strand of the same color is used for the weft. You will need 1 ounce each of navy and raspberry, less than 1 ounce of light blue, a small buckle (available at jewelry or department stores), a sewing needle, a 6-ounce juice can and white household glue. Since the inkle belt is very narrow, the complete pattern for warping the loom is shown in Figure D. I needed less than 1 foot of inkle for the watchband and, thinking it would be a shame to waste the extra warp threads, I wove a 6-foot length and used the excess belt to make a vase cover.

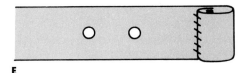

Figure E: To finish the watch band, fold the end under so the warp threads are covered, as shown, and stitch down.

| Heddle | B | N | N | N | N | N | N | N | N | N | N | N | N | N | N | N | N | B |
|--------|---|---|---|---|---|---|---|---|---|---|---|---|---|---|---|---|---|---|
| Open | B | N | N | R | R | R | R | R | R | R | R | R | R | R | N | N | | |

**D**      Key: **B** = light blue    **N** = navy    **R** = raspberry

Figure D: This pattern is used to warp the loom for a narrow band with crosswise stripes.

To warp the loom, follow the pattern, reading from left to right. Each lettered block indicates one thread. There are 36 threads indicated which, placed on the loom, make a ⅝-inch-wide band. To determine the width inkle you need, measure the strap opening on your watch. Push the warp threads close together (but not overlapping) to determine the width the inkle will be after weaving, and warp as many threads as you need for the strap opening on the watch.

Weave the belt following the directions on page 930. Remove the belt from the loom, and knot the weft. Measure your wrist, allowing 3 inches extra for hemming. Divide this measurement in half (for the two parts of the strap), and cut two pieces of inkle to this half measurement. Slipping one end through the opening on the watch, hem the belt on the reverse side. Repeat for the other strap, then slip one loose end through the buckle, and hem it under, securing it to the buckle. At this point, try the watch on to determine the placement of the holes for the buckle. Measure for two holes so the watchband is adjustable. Fold the end of the band as shown in Figure E, and hem. To make the holes, simply move the weaving aside until you can push the needle through from one side to the other. Using a needle threaded with one of the colors of the belt, outline a hole with small stitches (Figure F). Repeat for the second hole.

To make the small vase with the leftover inkle belt, I used a 6-ounce juice can. Measure the circumference of the can and, allowing ¾ inch for overlap, cut six pieces of inkle to this length. Use white household glue to attach the inkle belt lengths to the can, folding the cut ends under. Continue gluing all six rows, overlapping the ends at the same place, and let dry for 2 hours. To keep the ends secure, stitch the folded ends under, keeping this seam in the back of the can.

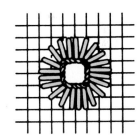

Figure F: The belt holes are made by separating the threads to form a hole, which is bound with a buttonhole stitch (see Crewelwork Sampler, page 544, Volume Five).

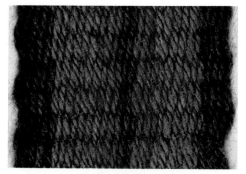

A detail shows the design that results from warping the loom following Figure H, top.

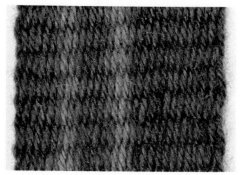

This is the belt woven following the second from the top pattern in Figure H.

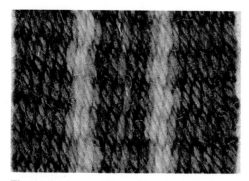

The third pattern in Figure H produces the design shown here.

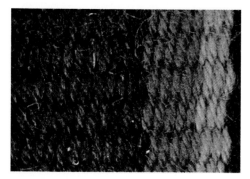

Warping for this inkle belt is shown in the bottom pattern in Figure H.

## Weaving, Braiding, Knotting
# A twist of inkles

The wall hanging (page 929) is made from four inkle belts, which are twisted together as shown in Figure G. The pattern calls for stripes of different widths made in several shades of brown and gold. I used 3-ply wool yarn and hand-dyed it, using commercial acid dyes. The stripes are made by warping an even number of threads, as shown in Figure H. You can change the width of the stripes simply by warping any even number. You will need a total of 20 ounces of yarn and a ¼-inch dowel 14 inches long to make the hanging.

Warp the loom, following the patterns in Figure H or varying the design if you so desire. Use one strand of the outside warp color for the weft, and make each belt 8 feet long, following the directions on page 930. Knot the weft to prevent unravelling, and leave the fringe slightly uneven for a casual effect.

To make the wall hanging, cut each belt in half and stitch the cut end of each piece over the dowel so that it is completely covered. (I arranged the belt halves symmetrically, starting in the center and working out toward each end, and overlapped the third and outermost belt pieces slightly.) To arrange the belts, start with the outermost belts, stitching their inner edges together about 1 foot down from the dowel (Figure G, far left). Turn the belt pieces over so the back faces out and stitch them together just above the fringe. To sew inkle belts together, use the same color thread as the outer warp color and pick up the piece of weft that shows along the edge. This way the stitches are hidden in the weaving. Now join the belts that lie next to the center belts, bringing the inside edges together about 7 inches down from the dowel and stitching as before (Figure G, center left). Let the ends hang loose until the next two belts are joined. The third belt (Figure G, center right) is next. Bring the pieces to the center under the stitching on the second belt, turn the belt so the back faces front, and stitch the pieces to both the second and fourth belts. Lastly, bring the innermost belt pieces to the outside and stitch to the second belt (Figure G, far right). Trim the fringe if you want an even edge; I prefer the casual look of uneven fringe.

Figure G: The wall hanging shown on page 929 is put together by arranging each of the four belts as shown below. Work from left to right, positioning and stitching the belts as indicated.

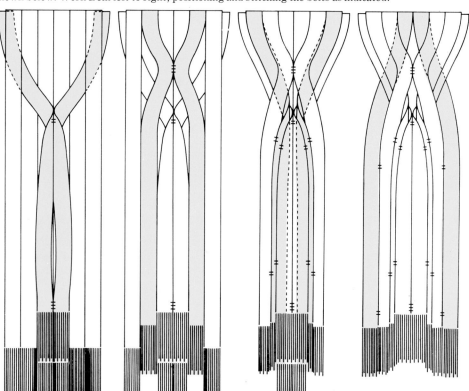

G

| | | | | | | | | | | | | | | | | | | | | | | | | | | | | | | | | | |
|---|---|---|---|---|---|---|---|---|---|---|---|---|---|---|---|---|---|---|---|---|---|---|---|---|---|---|---|---|---|---|---|---|---|---|
| **1** Heddle | C | C | C | C | P | P | P | P | P | P | R | R | R | C | ← middle repeat from right to left | | | | | | | | | | | | | | | | | | | |
| Open | C | C | C | C | P | P | P | P | P | P | P | R | R | R | C | | | | | | | | | | | | | | | | | | | |

end →

| | | | | | | | | | | | | | | | | | | | | | | | | | | | | | | | | | |
|---|---|---|---|---|---|---|---|---|---|---|---|---|---|---|---|---|---|---|---|---|---|---|---|---|---|---|---|---|---|---|---|---|---|---|
| **2** Heddle | C | C | C | C | C | R | G | G | R | C | C | C | C | R | G | G | R | C | C | C | C | C | C | C | C | C | C | C | C | C | C | C | C | |
| Open | C | C | C | C | C | R | G | G | R | C | C | C | C | R | G | G | R | C | C | C | C | C | C | C | C | C | C | C | C | C | C | C | C | C |

| | | | | | | | | | | | | |
|---|---|---|---|---|---|---|---|---|---|---|---|---|
| **3** Heddle | B | B | B | B | B | G | Y | Y | G | B | B | ← middle repeat from right to left |
| Open | B | B | B | B | B | G | Y | Y | G | B | B | R |

| | | | | | | | | | | | | | | | | | | | | | | |
|---|---|---|---|---|---|---|---|---|---|---|---|---|---|---|---|---|---|---|---|---|---|---|
| **4** Heddle | D | D | D | D | D | D | D | D | D | D | D | D | D | C | C | C | C | C | G | G | G | D ← end |
| Open | D | D | D | D | D | D | D | D | D | D | D | D | D | C | C | C | C | C | G | G | G | D |

**Key:** Y = yellow  G = gold  C = cinnamon  R = rust  P = pumpkin  B = brown  D = dark brown

**H**

Figure H: Follow these patterns to warp the loom for the four belts used in the wall hanging.

## Weaving, Braiding, Knotting
# A pick-up belt  ¢ ▯ ☖ ⚒

Inkle belt design possibilities are greatly increased with the use of a pick-up technique. This is easily learned but is slower than plain weave. To make the belt shown below, warp the loom following the pattern in Figure I. You will need 4 ounces of 4-ply wool (2 ounces of each color). Pick-up patterns are plotted on graph paper (as shown in Figure J). Each square represents one pair of warp threads. The pattern is read from the bottom up and represents one complete motif. In this pattern, 8 rows form the stylized flower which is repeated along the belt.

| | | | | | | | | | | | | | | | |
|---|---|---|---|---|---|---|---|---|---|---|---|---|---|---|---|
| Heddle | G | G | R | R | R | R | R | R | R | R | R | R | R | R | ← middle repeat from right to left |
| Open | G | G | R | R | R | R | R | G | G | G | G | G | G | G | R |

**I**  Key: G = gold  R = red

Figure I: Warp the loom according to this pattern to make the flower-motif belt below.

In plain weave, you open each shed and weave completely across the row; there is no manipulation of threads. If weaved this way, the belt would be alternating red and gold horizontal stripes separated by a center vertical red stripe. In the pick-up technique, you pick up certain warp threads with your fingers, a knitting needle, or a smooth stick called a pick-up stick to form a pattern. The pattern alternates a row of plain weave with a pick-up row. Weave one row as usual, change the shed, beat down, then pick up the indicated warp threads and hold all of these threads on top. Put weft through this newly-created shed, change shed, and beat down. Repeat these steps, picking up the warp threads as indicated in Figure J.

Since one warp thread is part of the top warp several weaves in a row—it is on top, then it is picked up, then it is on top in the usual weave—the pattern also takes on a new dimension of texture, as the lifted warp threads create a raised effect.

A flower motif is created by following the pick-up pattern in Figure J.

a b c d e f g  h i j k l m n

**J**

Figure J: The pick-up pattern for the flower motif is a repeat of these 8 rows.
Row 1: weave as usual.
Row 2: pick up threads d-e-f-i-j-k.
Row 3: weave as usual.
Row 4: pick up threads a-b-c-l-m-n.
Row 5: weave as usual.
Row 6: pick up d-e-f-i-j-k.
Row 7: weave as usual.
Row 8: pick up g-h.

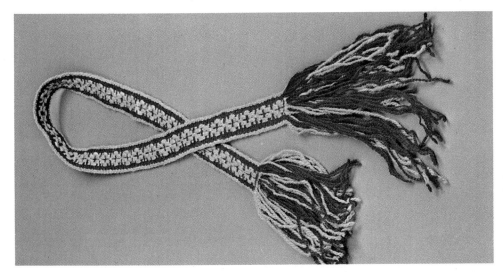

A pick-up pattern is repeated along the entire length of the belt to form a chain of flowers.

# INSECTS
## Observing and Collecting

Many secrets of a mysterious world of nature — that of the insects — can be unraveled with careful and patient observation. The exotic is all around us. Mayflies of certain types, for example, spend several years growing and developing in the water; then one spring day they take flight, deposit their eggs, and die. Some live only two hours out of the water. Queen ants and termites, on the other hand, live up to 18 years. There is one beetle, called the bombardier, that defends itself by shooting streams of hot water and chemicals at its predators. The female of the praying mantis may eat the male alive.

There are ants that cultivate their own food crop in the form of a fungus that grows only in their underground colonies. The 17-year cicada appears punctually for a six-week visit every 17 years. The ichneumon wasp has a three-to-four-inch egg depositor, several times longer than its own body, with which it bores deep into a tree and there inserts its egg into the grub of another insect. There are insects called fairy flies that grow only 1/100 of an inch long and live in the eggs of other insects; each one probably has as many muscles as a man.

Aphids live only three or four weeks and have 10 to 20 overlapping generations a year. Because different generations feed on different plants, aphids differ markedly among themselves in form, color, size and even method of reproduction. Some aphids spend their entire lives, like domesticated animals, in the service of ants. The ants care for aphid eggs during the winter and feed the young when they hatch in the spring. In the summer, the ants put the aphids out to pasture on the roots of corn. The aphids are valued by the ants because they produce a sweet liquid, which the ants obtain by milking the aphids as if they were cows.

Every one of these creatures, far from being an isolated phenomenon, is part of a mysterious world. If you happen to have a cabbage patch in your garden and were to examine it closely, you might find, as one researcher did, that there are more than 200 insect species living harmoniously in it. Each has a life pattern of its own that insures it a place in that little universe. Even an indifferent and rationalistic observer, facing such intricacy of adaptation, profuse artistry, inscrutable richness of invention, will, despite himself, occasionally be awed.

### The Vast Unknown

There are an estimated three to four million varieties of insects in the world. Of these, some one million have been described and classified by scientists — one quarter of them beetles. These totals do not include spiders, ticks, mites, centipedes and millipedes, which are separate classes of life, not insects. (What most obviously distinguishes an insect is its legs — every insect has six.) There are more known species of insects than there are of all other animals and plants combined, and thousands of new ones are discovered and named each year. Ironically, thinking up appropriate names poses some of the scientists' biggest problems.

If the thought of exploring the unknown tempts you to undertake observing insects or collecting them, you might be encouraged to know that scientifically, there are many more unknowns than knowns. Concerning the mystery of where houseflies go in the winter, for example, even the most precise research can offer but a few speculations. With the study of insects, the painstaking accumulation of bits of information in the hope of obtaining a new answer sometimes leads only to the recognition that real understanding cannot be found in a pile of facts. Rather, it calls for an especially inquisitive way of looking at things that lets you see them whole, the biggest obstacle to which is the presumption of "knowing."

*Peter Chabora, associate professor of biology at Queens College, New York, received his doctorate in entomology from Cornell University and was a research associate at Oxford University, England. Among his many published works are studies in parasite-host interactions, hereditary variation and dynamics of insect populations.*

*August Schmitt of Northport, New York, has been collecting and raising insects as a hobby since 1931. In pursuit of specimens, he has travelled to South America, Africa, Asia and the South Pacific. A retired machinist, he runs the Northport Butterfly Farm and has donated his collection, photographed here in part, to Cornell University.*

A rare instance of gynandromorphism (the incorporation of both male and female characteristics in a single individual) is seen in this *Ornithoptera priamus poseidon* found in New Guinea. The male colors — predominantly green — are mixed with the predominantly brown of a female in this freak of nature. Enlarged views of gynandromorph from above and below can be compared to the small photographs of the ordinary male and female at left and right. •

## Insects vs. Man

The insect world is not alien to that of man, as we realize when we wear silk or eat honey, or even when we enjoy watching a passing butterfly. We appreciate insects less when we become their victims, as when we are stung by a mosquito or annoyed by a buzzing housefly. In some underdeveloped countries, insects are man's greatest natural competitor and regularly destroy up to 40 per cent of the food crops. On occasion, an insect can even become man's predator: Malaria, transmitted by insects, kills more people than any other parasitic disease, and some people are so allergic that they can be killed by a sting of a bee. (Earwigs, however, do not in fact invade people's ears, as they once were believed to do.)

## The Other Side of the Coin

But all in all, only a tiny percentage of the earth's insects can be considered harmful to man. Without them, many plants would simply not exist; insects are their only means of being pollinated. Other insects hasten the process of decay that is an essential part of the natural life cycle. In fact, to look at any aspect of the natural world as if it were in a vacuum—or to say that one thing is good and another bad—is to miss the essential interrelatedness of things. If some things could be different, then everything would be different. The modern-day abuse of insecticides is perhaps based on this misapprehension. But many gardeners, preferring to exercise a more harmonious stewardship over nature, introduce the eggs of the fierce-looking praying mantis and the colorful ladybird beetle (the ladybug) into their gardens, since both will consume great quantities of harmful insects. If an occasional bright orange ladybug, freckled with black spots, finds its way into the house, it will do yeoman work cleaning aphids from houseplants.

If this suggests that by collecting insects, you might upset the balance of nature, you need have little fear. Insects, more than any other creature, depend on sheer numbers for survival. If a certain species of fly that reproduces frequently, laying 550 eggs at a time, were not decimated by outside forces, it would blanket the earth in only a few years.

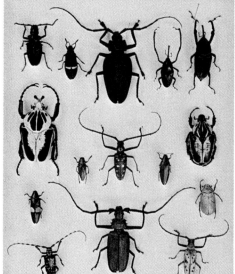

Beetles the world over include, left to right: (top) *Cyrtognathus indicus*, India; *Magaloxantha nigricornis*, Sumatra; *Ctenoscelis coeus*, Brazil; *Cyrtotrachelus buqueti*, Malaysia; *Macrochirus praetor*, Java; (second row) *Goliathus regius* (male), Nigeria; *Paracupta helopioides*, Solomon Islands; *Batocera albofasciata*, Malaysia; *Chrysochroa vittata*, India; *Goliathus regius* (female); (third row) *Chrysochroa buqueti*, India; *Tricholeptis lactea*, Thailand; (bottom) *Melanauster malasiacus*, India; *Gallipogon armillatus*, Peru; *Batocera flavescens*, Malaysia.

New World butterflies include, left to right: (top) *Morpho adonis* (male), Peru; *Callithea sapphira* (male and female), Brazil; *Morpho thamyris* (male), Brazil; (second row) left and right, *Agrias amydon* (males), Peru; center, *Morpho helena* (male), Peru; (third row) *Thecla coronata* (male and female), Ecuador; (bottom) left and right, *Catopsilia avellaneda* (male and female), Cuba; center, *Morpho hecuba obidonis* (male), Brazil. Most of these specimen are rarely found in collections because they live deep within the Amazon jungles.

Many of these moths, native to the U.S. and other parts of the New World, are easy to find. The collector found the smaller ones in his home state of New York. The larger ones are: at top, *Thysania agrippina*, Peru; below it, *Othreis serpentifera*, Brazil; flanking it, *Erebus odora*, (male and female), Florida, South America and Hawaii; at bottom, *Thysania zinobia* (male and female), Texas to South America. "The moths are the heralds, or better yet, the guardians of eternity. They carry a dark gold dust on their wings, the dust of knowledge."—don Juan

## Watching or Capturing

The observation of insects does not necessarily require that you collect them—an insect collection is not an end in itself but a means of studying life. Nevertheless, most people who become intrigued by the insect world do make collections. You might use insects you have collected to create a diorama, a three-dimensional miniature stage set that illustrates a scene from life. Or you might want to mount a collection in a box, as specialists often do. Some people mount insects in shadow boxes or glass showcases; these are often hung on the walls of English pubs and make interesting decorations for an informal room.

More unusual are the ways insects are sometimes put to use in Brazil. A certain species of butterfly is so common there that its iridescent wings are asembled into collages. And the Jivaro Indians, headhunters of the Amazon, use the iridescent wings of a green beetle to make stunning headdresses. Beetles, the largest and best known order of insects, are of such size and beauty that they intrigue all collectors. One beetle, the scarab, was even held sacred by the ancient Egyptians.

But whether you actually collect insects or only observe them in their native habitats, you will be wise to restrict yourself at the beginning to a very limited area, perhaps to your own backyard or to a nearby field or patch of woodland. See how much you can learn about the insect life there. You might even want to limit yourself to the study of a single variety of insect, following it through all the stages of its life and its daily and seasonal activities.

### Finding Insects

There are dozens of places where an insect hunt might prove especially rewarding. Look for them under stones, in unmowed fields, on tree stumps and decaying logs, among wet or dry leaves, near street lamps and porch lights, on garden plants and inside their flowers, near house windows, in pantries and closets, on mosses and lichens, in mud puddles and around compost piles.

In fact, there is hardly a place in the world where you will not find insects. A typical acre of moist land in the temperate zone shelters millions of them, though a casual observer walking through might notice only an occasional beetle, butterfly or bumblebee.

Once you have spotted your quarry, you might find it more intriguing to watch it than to trap it and take it home. Some extraordinary things have been learned by

The common honey bee (*Apis mellifera*), left, is proverbially busy on a marigold flower. It has been estimated that to gather an ounce of honey, a bee has to fly the equivalent of the distance from New York to San Francisco. At right, a butterfly known locally as a skipper (*Polites vibex*) poses languidly during its midday rest period.

## Sources for Entomological Supplies

Emil Arlt, Specialnadelfabrik, Box 36, Salzburg 1, Pfeifergasse 18, Austria. (For pins.)
Bio Metal Associates, 316 Washington Street, El Segundo, California 90245.
BioQuip East, 1115 Rolling Road, Baltimore, Maryland 21228.
BioQuip West, Box 61, Santa Monica, California 90406.
N. Bourbee & Cie, 3 Place Saint-Andre-des-Arts, Paris 6, France.
Carolina Biological Supply Co., Burlington, North Carolina 27216.
L. Christie, 137 Gleneldon Road, Streatham, London, S.W. 16, England.
General Biological Supply House Inc., 8200 South Hoyne Avenue, Chicago, Illinois 60620.
T. Gerrard & Co., Biological Laboratories, 46a-48 Pentonville Road, London, N. 1, England.
Survival Security Corporation, Division of Entomological Research Institute, 4000 6th Avenue, Lake City, Minnesota 55041.
Wards Natural Science Establishment, Inc., Box 1712, Rochester, New York 14603.
Wards of California, Box 1749, Monterey, California 93942.
Watkins & Doncaster, 110 Parkview Road, Welling, Kent, England.
Robert G. Wind, 827 Congress Avenue, Pacific Grove, California 93950.

**Cicada plebia**

watching insects that would look quite ordinary in a collection. There is, for example, a moth that a certain bat hunts at night by using ultrasonic cries like sonar waves. The bat can zero in on the moth by interpreting the echoes that return to it. But the moth, which has very sensitive ears, can hear the cry of an approaching bat and go into an evasive flight pattern. It might even drop suddenly to the ground. There is a tiny mite that nests in the ear of this moth, destroying the hearing in that ear. But the mite never invades *both* ears, since a totally deaf moth would be easy prey for the bat and both moth and mite would perish. That leaves one question unanswered: How does the mite know?

Another mite lives deep inside a certain flower in Central America. This flower blooms throughout the year, but the individual flowers die and when they do, the resident mites also perish. Some mites, though, survive by moving from one flower to another in the nostrils of hummingbirds that visit the flowers for their nectar.

### Questions for Insects

Such discoveries suggest the excitement that awaits the discerning observer of insect life. Doing your best to remain unobserved yourself, watch how an insect goes about the business of living. How does it move? How do its senses work? What is it doing? How and what does it eat? What eats it? How does it protect itself? How is it related to others of its species? To other forms of life? To the elements? To you? Not only will you find answers to your questions—you may think of questions to ask that have never occurred to anyone else before.

The tomato sphinx moth (*Protoparce sexta*) has an extended proboscis (sucking tongue) that plays an important role in the pollination of flowers. Scientists wondered how a certain orchid in Madagascar with a 10-inch-deep flower cup ever managed to be pollinated, until they discovered a cousin of the species shown here, with a tongue 12 inches long. At right is the ravenous larva of the same insect, which has just finished devouring one leaf and is headed for another, at the Northport Butterfly Farm.

Tarantula spider (*Eurypelma hentzii*), at top, found in Brazil but with varieties ranging as far as Southwestern U.S., is not only harmful to humans; the female tarantula often eats the male. The female of the pepsis killer wasp, bottom left, is a mortal enemy of all tarantulas, killing them and taking their bodies home to its nest. There she lays her eggs in the spider's body, which her young, on emerging from the eggs, devour. The male, bottom right, does not attack spiders though it has a powerful bite.

**Environmental Projects**
# Trapping insects

There are several effective and inexpensive ways of catching insects for a collection. You can catch many by hand or with a household container and deftly maneuvered lid. Of course, exercise caution in this and any other method, because a few insects can hurt you. Although the vast majority of insects are harmless, bees and wasps do sting. Blister beetles contain a chemical that causes blisters on human skin; squash bugs emit a stench when disturbed, like skunks.

Another simple trap—expedient and effortless—consists of burying a coffee can or similar container up to its rim in the earth and leaving it overnight. Crawling nocturnal insects, rarely seen by light of day, will fall into the container and remain there, unable to climb back out.

## A Butterfly Net

There are just so many types of insects you can catch with primitive methods. A slightly more sophisticated trap is the classical butterfly net. (You won't catch a tremendous number of insects with it either, and you will use a lot of energy running after them; but you are likely at least to have a good time in the course of the hunt.) There are many types of nets, some quite sturdy for beating the grass, some delicate with a very fine mesh for small insects. You can make a simple butterfly net from inexpensive, easy-to-get materials.

Bend a length of 14-gauge wire into a roughly circular shape 15 inches in diameter (48 inches in circumference), and, keeping the circle open, extend the two ends of the wire about 6 inches out from the circle, making them parallel with each other (Figure A). Cut a shape known as an isosceles trapezoid (Figure B) from a piece of fine, netlike material 48 inches by 36 inches. Use an open-weave fabric such as mosquito netting, old organdy curtains, nylon net or gauze. (A close-weave material defeats itself in the hunt by blowing insects away with the pressure of trapped air.) Cut half-inch slits one half inch below the 48-inch edge, and run this end of the material around the circumference of the wire circle so the sloping sides of the material meet at the break in the circle as the ends of the wire pass through the slits. Fasten the top of the netting to the hoop by sewing a narrow hem to enclose the wire. At the same time close the slits around the wire ends. Sew the sloping sides together from the hem all the way to the 8-inch edge and darn or patch the circular hole that remains in the bottom of the net. Use a 1-foot length of 1-inch dowel (a cut-down cast-off broomstick would do) for the handle. Attach the wire ends to this by whittling two 6-inch grooves in the surface of the dowel, cutting them opposite one another and deep enough to receive the wire ends (Figure C). Embed the wire firmly into the grooves by wrapping electrician's tape or 18-gauge wire around the dowel over the full length of the grooves. You can change the dimensions to suit the materials you have at hand, but the net should be at least twice as long as the diameter of the hoop, so you can close the trap by draping the net over the frame with a flick of the wrist.

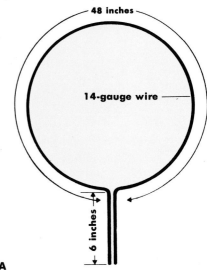

**A**
Figure A: For the frame of a butterfly net, bend a 5-foot length of 14-gauge wire into a circle and extend the two ends 6 inches out from the circle at right angles to it.

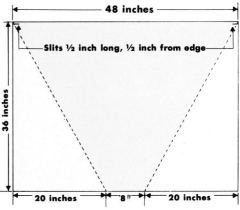

**B**
Figure B: Make the net by cutting a trapezoid shape from a 36-by-48-inch piece of open-weave cloth, with bases of 48 and 8 inches.

Entomologist Schmitt stalks his prey with a net much like the one described on this page. Some collectors find a short handle — 6 inches long in this case — easy to wield.

## A Black-Light Trap

The black-light trap is a most effective means of catching a wide variety of flying insects with a small investment of time and money. Get a 15-watt black fluorescent light bulb and fixture from a lighting store. This is the type of bulb used for atmospheric effects in discotheques. Connect the fixture to your household wiring with an extension cord and mount the light in your yard in front of a white sheet washed in a detergent containing fluorescent dyes (Figure D). If this sounds

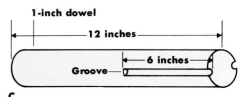

**C**
Figure C: For the net handle, cut a 1-foot length from an old broomstick or other 1-inch dowel and incise two 6-inch grooves opposite one another as shown. Make the grooves deep enough to receive the wire ends.

esoteric, just use any laundry product that claims to get your clothes brighter or whiter. Such detergents impregnate the sheet with fluorescent particles so that the sheet lit by the black bulb will glow in the dark. This will attract insects and as they light on the sheet, you will be able to remove them and place them in a container. Rolling up the bottom of the sheet will catch additional insects.

The best way to pick up a live insect is with a specially made flexible forceps available from biological and entomological supply houses. This is used like an ordinary tweezer, but its tongs are extremely flexible so they can hold the insect without damaging it (Figure E).

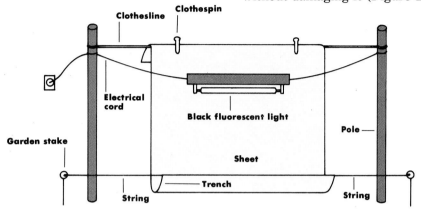

**D**

Figure D: A black-light trap consists of a black fluorescent light mounted in front of a sheet washed in fluorescent dyes. Hang the sheet and the light with clothesline and clothespins. Make a trench to catch insects in the bottom of the sheet by suspending the lower corners, as shown.

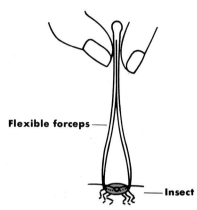

**E**

Figure E: Use flexible forceps to hold insects without damaging them. The tongs spread apart so as not to damage anything held between them.

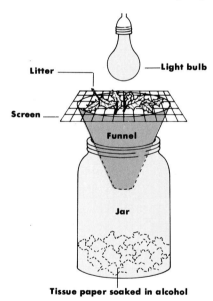

**F**

Figure F: In the Berlese funnel trap, a light bulb is used to dry out litter (decomposing matter) inhabited by insects. Fleeing, they fall through a screen and down a funnel into a jar, where tissue paper treated with alcohol preserves them.

## A Berlese Funnel

You can make a Berlese funnel (Figure F) to trap the types of insects that inhabit the litter (the uppermost, slightly decayed layer of organic matter) that covers the forest floor. Line the bottom of a jar with tissue paper soaked in alcohol. Place a funnel in the mouth of the jar and cover it with a coarse screen or sieve. Put a handful of litter on top of the sieve; then put a light bulb directly on top of the litter. As the bulb begins to dry the litter, the insects will flee, falling through the screen, down the funnel into the jar, and will be preserved by the alcohol. The process takes three or four days.

Many other ways of catching insects have been developed by ingenious entomologists, and you may want to invent or adapt your own methods, depending on what and where you hunt. Each of the methods I have described above has a fixed and limited application, because each type of insect presents a different trapping problem. Creatures who live on or in the water, for example, present special challenges. A good manual with complete instructions for this area is *Guide to the Study of Fresh Water Biology*, by J. G. Needham and P. R. Needham.

**Environmental Projects**

# The insect collection

From a child's playful impulse to capture fireflies in a jar to the serious business of raising silkworms, insect collections fascinate young and old alike. Ant farms (see Volume 1) rival aquariums in popularity, and some collectors breed certain insect species as a means of obtaining specimens in good condition. Breeding insects is a difficult and complex activity, however, because the conditions required for the complete life cycle—mating, egg-laying, hatching, successive nymphal or larval molts, pupation and the emergence of a new adult—are exacting and diverse. An attractive compromise is a free-living collection, such as some gardeners make of ladybird beetles (ladybugs) or praying mantises. They will help you keep insect pests to a minimum and add color and interest to your yard.

If you wish to make a mounted collection of insects, the techniques to use are described in the sections that follow.

## A Killing Jar

The easiest way to kill insects without otherwise damaging them is to drop them (directly from your traps when possible) into a jar lined with tissue paper or cotton that has been treated with ethyl acetate, a safe chemical available from biological supply houses. (Cover the tissue paper or cotton with a sheet of paper so your specimens do not get stuck in it.) For your own safety, avoid completely other common insect poisons such as cyanide and carbon tetrachloride (these can poison humans) and lighter fluid (dangerously flammable when used this way). Choose a jar with a mouth that is wide enough to allow you to reach in later and retrieve the insects with a forceps. And have a cover handy to prevent flying insects from escaping before the poison takes effect.

## Examining Insects

At this point, you will probably want to look more closely at the insects you have caught. For most species, a good magnifying glass or jeweler's loupe is all you need to view this miniature wonder. Looked at in such a Gulliverian way, these creatures can take on a new identity. A praying mantis becomes a fearsome lion or dragon; cicadas and wasps, Boschlike monstrosities.

The things to look for and the questions to ask in these conditions are somewhat different than they were back in the natural setting. How is the insect anatomically adapted for doing what it has to do? Notice the positions, relative sizes, shapes and structures of such parts as antennae, eyes, mouth, wings, legs, and predatory and defensive mechanisms. Try not to lose sight of the life of the insect as it once was, and use your new vantage point to expand the picture that nature presented.

## Preserving Insects

In most cases, it is not necessary to do anything at all to preserve specimens. Except for water insects, spiders and a few other soft-bodied creatures, the hard exoskeleton by which the insect is recognized will last indefinitely. Preserve other types of insects in vials or jars containing a 70 percent alcohol solution (30 percent water). Cap the vials tightly with rubber, rather than cork stoppers.

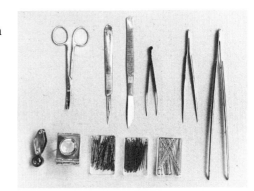

Tools used in collecting and studying insects. Clockwise from upper left: delicate scissor for dissections; lightweight scalpel with long, fine blade; large dissecting scalpel; featherweight forceps for live insects and fragile parts (see Figure E); straight-tip forceps for mounting; long forceps with curved tips for handling folded specimens; insect pins in sizes ranging from No. 000 to No. 7; stand magnifier for general use; 20x magnifier for minute detail.

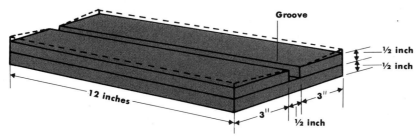

**G**

Figure G: A simple spreading board, for drying and fixing the wings of moths and butterflies, consists of three pieces of soft wood glued together, as shown. Dotted lines indicate a sloping variation of the board used to raise wings into a more naturalistic posture.

## Spreading Insects

For a collection of large-winged insects, such as moths and butterflies, specimens are pinned to a special spreading board (Figure G) for one to three weeks while they dry. This causes uniform wing spread and makes a better display. The board is available from entomological supply houses. It is made of soft wood for easy pinning, and consists of two faces, either parallel to each other or sloping toward a central slot at about a 5 degree angle. You can make a similar board by gluing three pieces of balsa wood or soft composition board together (Figure G).

Here and in later stages of mounting, use pins obtained from biological or entomological supply houses (rather than the household variety), because these are more suitable for mounting specimens, and are made of materials—usually fine, stiff stainless steel or japanned (varnished) wire—that afford the best display and preservation possible. The pins are manufactured in a number of standard heights and in a range of diameters indicated by the gauge numbers 000 (the thinnest) up to 8 (the thickest). In Europe gauges run even higher. Technically, each thickness is suited for mounting a particular size insect, but initially you can make do with a small supply of gauges No. 1, 2 and 3.

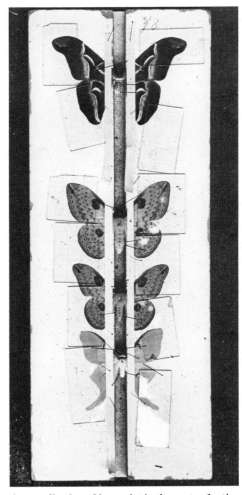

A spreading board has a slot in the center for the bodies of large-winged insects, and two flat or gently sloping surfaces where their wings are held with pins, paper strips and weights until dry.

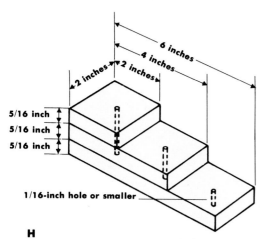

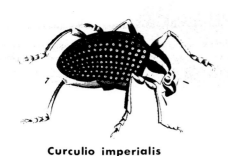

**H**

Figure H: A pinning block, for mounting insects and labels on pins at uniform heights, consists of three pieces of wood glued in a stairway arrangement with a hole drilled through the center of each step.

*Curculio imperialis*

Place the body of the insect in the slot of the spreading board so the wings rest on the parallel (or sloping) faces, and pin it through the center of the thorax (between the front wings). Cover the wings with small pieces of glass to weight them down and flatten them (stiff paper pinned to the board could be substituted). Allow the insect to dry out in this position, and its wings will be permanently fixed at the angle you have chosen.

### Pinning Insects

Whether you decide to house your collection in a box, a glass showcase or some other container, or to display it as a diorama, you will need to know how best to mount your specimens after they are dried. Piercing them with pins, which are then stuck into a soft wood or foam backing, is the commonest method, because it does least damage to the insects, allows them to be picked up and examined later on, and provides a handy way of attaching descriptive labels.

For display, a simple device called a pinning block will be helpful in mounting both insects and labels at uniform heights on the pins. To make a pinning block, cut three rectangles—6-by-2 inches, 4-by-2 inches and 2-by-2 inches—from a scrap of 5/16-inch-thick wood. Fasten the three rectangles together in the stairway pattern shown in Figure H (solid lines) with white resin glue, and weight or clamp the assembly for the drying time recommended for the glue you use—usually 30 minutes. When dry, drill holes 1/16 inch or smaller all the way through the assembled blocks at the center of each platform (Figure H). Pinning blocks can also be bought ready-made from entomological supply houses.

### Using the Step Block

To use the pins and the step block, place the specimen over the hole on the top step. (If the insect is so small that it might fall or be pushed by the pin into the hole, put a thin piece of paper over the hole and place the insect on top of it. Later, when the insect stands at the proper height on the pin, remove the paper.) The anatomical part that you pass the pin through depends on what type of insect it is. Pin butterflies, moths, dragonflies and damselflies through the center of the thorax between the front wings; and true bugs (distinguished by their divided fore wing and piercing beak) in the triangular shield between the base of the wings. In all cases, the pin is inserted through the back (top) side so that the point comes out through the front. Make sure the insect stands at right angles to the pin from side to side and from head to tail, then insert the pin and push the point through to the bottom of the hole. If all your specimens are mounted this way, they will form a neat and attractive collection. Use the two lower steps on the pinning block in the same way to attach descriptive labels to the pin underneath the insect at uniform heights. If this is to be a lasting display, avoid touching the specimens as they are too delicate to last long if handled.

For clarity and durability, cut labels from a stiff grade of paper with good rag content, such as index cards, about ½ inch by 1 inch in size. This will force you to write small, but if you make the labels much larger, they will compete with the insects for attention. Print in black ink, and for a start, use the labels to indicate where and when you caught the specimen, and the family it belongs to (see page 946 for simple identification keys). Later you may want to get into more elaborate identification, down to the genus and even the species. Such a study can be tedious in the beginning, as it usually involves painstaking research. The complexity and difficulty of identification is multiplied by the fact that a given species often exists in different castes, as with bees, different seasonal forms, as with aphids, and different life stages: egg, nymph, larva, pupa, adult; and within these stages there are many gradual changes (molts), not to mention aberrations. Some useful guidebooks are *How to Know the Insects*, by H. E. Jaques; *Collecting, Preserving and Studying Insects*, by Harold Oldroyd; *Insects*, by Herbert S. Zim and Clarence Cottam; *Field Book of Insects*, by Frank E. Lutz; *A Field Guide to the Insects of North America North of Mexico* and *An Introduction to the Study of Insects*, by D. J. Borrer and D. M. DeLong, and *The Insect Guide: Orders and Major Families of North American Insects*, by R. B. Swain, but many others are available, some for specific regions or insect groups.

## Getting it Together

The commonest type of insect collection, and one well-suited for starting, consists simply of a wooden box, preferably air tight, into which the pins, bearing insects and labels, are inserted in an orderly arrangement. The interior of the box should be of sheet cork or balsa, or a comparable soft wood, that will act as a good pincushion. Plastic foam works well, too. These boxes are available from entomological supply houses. (Note: In any type of insect collection, include a few ordinary mothballs or flakes—they can be glued inconspicuously to the corners of the container. There are live insects—carpet beetles—that can ruin a collection.)

The glass showcase collection, which involves an investment best made after you've gathered a sizeable variety of insects, is mounted the same way as the box collection, but labels could be larger and additional information could appear on the backing just below each specimen. This is the time to display your research in the form of detailed identification and any interesting facts you may have discovered in the field or in the library. If your supplementary information seems likely to overwhelm the collection itself, key your specimens by writing letters next to them, and present your research in another area of the display with cross-references to the letter key. Multipurpose glass and plexiglass cases are available from hobby shops and collectors' supply stores, and these can be adapted for mounting with a balsa wood or foam insert.

A totally different kind of glass showcase collection is the diorama, or true-to-life tableau. Take your pointers from the elaborate displays that are on view in many natural history museums, and limit yourself to a real situation, or a composite of real situations, as you have actually been able to observe them. Use natural materials for your background when possible: soil, sand, twigs, stones, acorns and plants such as reeds, cattails and strawflowers, that will not wilt. Most important, exercise your own ingenuity in devising the display and your own powers of observation in selecting its subject matter.

If dioramas do not appeal to you, but you are interested in the ecological relationships among insects, and between them and other living things, try making a schematic diagram of a habitat. For this, little handcrafting is necessary, and the display can be effectively mounted on a wall, whether you use real specimens, draw pictures of them, or combine the two methods. Use arrows and explanations to show how each creature exists in relationship with the others.

## Identification

Scientists have divided all of the animals in the world into 16 major groups called phyla. One phylum, Arthropods, includes all of the animals with segmented bodies and, as its Greek name indicates, jointed appendages. The Arthropods include shrimp, lobsters, crabs, centipedes, millipedes, spiders, ticks, mites, scorpions and insects. The thing that most obviously distinguishes the class insects from the ten other classes of Arthropods is that they alone have six legs. Some of the important orders of insects, and the common names of some family members are: *Orthoptera* —cockroaches, grasshoppers, locusts, praying mantises, crickets; *Isoptera* — termites; *Ephemeroptera*—mayflies; *Odonata*—dragonflies; *Hemiptera*—bugs; *Homoptera*—cicadas, aphids; *Coleoptera*—beetles; *Lepidoptera*—butterflies, moths; *Diptera*—mosquitoes, gnats, flies; *Siphonaptera*—fleas; and *Hymenoptera* —bees, wasps, ants, ichneumon flies. Within the orders, further subdivisions include family, genus, species and subspecies. The rationales for identification are complex and include such minutiae as the configuration of the veins on wings, the structure of the eyes, and the number and shape of the joints in the legs. The official-sounding Greek and Latin terminology, which translates into phrases like "two wings" and "house fly," was invented to facilitate international communication, but in the layman's ears it may ring with a deceptive authority. For, the fact that we have categorized and named a thing does not necessarily mean that we understand it.

Despite the incredible variety among the millions of different kinds of insects, all are alike in having bodies that are divided into three parts: head, thorax and abdomen. Insects generally have two compound eyes (eyes within eyes), two or three simple eyes, and a pair of antennae. Some have mouths adapted for chewing (but they chew, as if comically, from side to side), others for sucking, others for

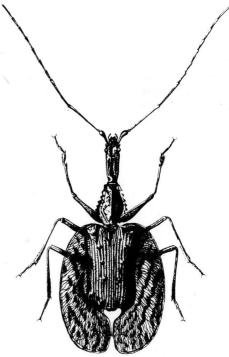

**Marmolyce phyllodes**

945

lapping, and still others for a combination of these. Breathing is through rows of holes in the abdomen. There are, of course, many other characteristics which are used to distinguish them and to set them off from other creatures.

The following illustrated list of the major families of insects will help you with the initial identification of many specimens. When one resembles that pictured, it will likely belong to the same order. Such distinguishing characteristics as metamorphosis (changes of form during the life cycle—as when a caterpillar is given a new existence as a butterfly, for example), mouth parts, number and kinds of wings, and types of legs divide the insects into 26 orders (some authorities give other figures); 11 of the more important ones are represented here by typical members.

I
Figure I: Below are representatives of 11 important orders of insects. Common names of the more familiar members are given in the text on page 945.

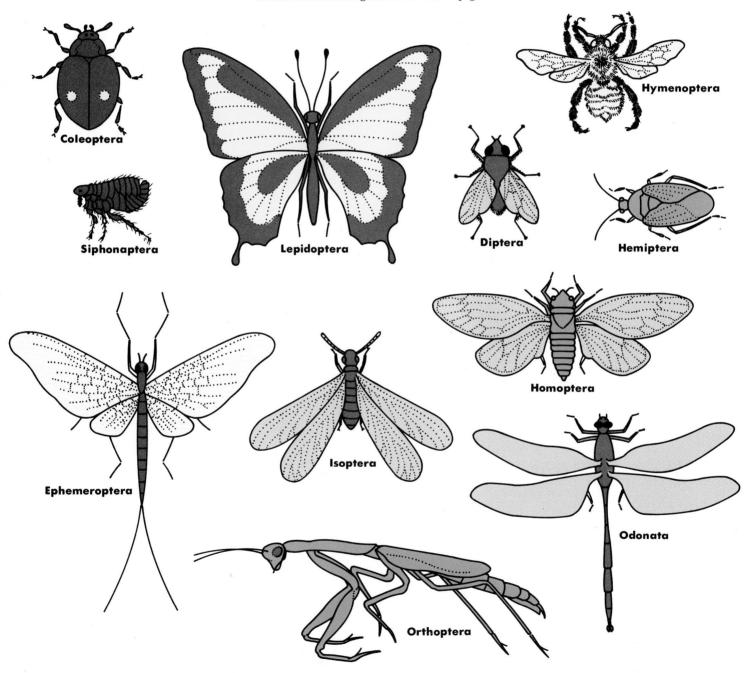

This sampling of butterflies includes examples of some of the rarest insects in the world. The displays at left and right contain specimens from Malaysia, New Guinea, Australia, and Micronesia. Those in the center once fluttered in Peru, Brazil, Colombia and Jamaica.

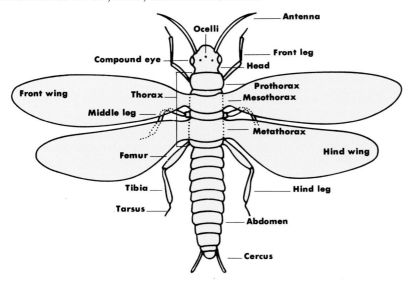

**J**

Figure J: The anatomical parts of a generalized insect are depicted above.

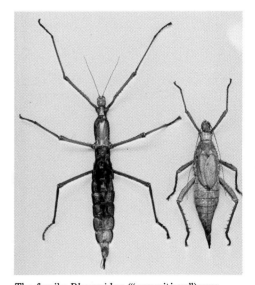

The family *Phasmidae* ("apparitions") was perhaps named by someone who couldn't believe his eyes. These macabre creatures are over 6 inches long.

## Structure

Since the structure of the various insects differs widely, it would be misleading to present the anatomical parts of a generalized insect in great detail. But for identifying the grosser structures on the majority of insects, the parts shown in the diagram above will generally be accurate, or at least recognizable if not interpreted too literally. In any case, it is a good place to begin your study of insect parts.

For related projects and crafts, see the entries "Ant Farms," "Beachcombing," "Dioramas," and "Wildlife."

### Bibliography

Borrer, D. J. and DeLong, D. M., *A Field Guide to the Insects of North America North of Mexico.* Houghton Mifflin Co., 1970.

——, *An Introduction to the Study of Insects.* Holt, Rinehart and Winston, 1970.

Jaques, H. E., *How to Know the Insects.* Wm. C. Brown Co., 1947.

Lutz, Frank E., *Field Book of Insects.* Doubleday & Company, Inc., 1935.

Needham, J. G. and Needham, P. R. *A Guide to the Study of Fresh Water Biology.* Holden-Day, 1962.

Oldroyd, Harold, *Collecting, Preserving and Studying Insects.* Weidenfeld & Nicholson, 1970.

Swain, R. B., *The Insect Guide,* Doubleday, 1948.

Zim, Herbert S. and Cottam, Clarence, *Insects.* Western Publishing Company, Inc., 1951.

The dead leaf butterfly (*Kallima inachus*), ranges from India to Formosa. At rest, its wings fold to mimic a dead leaf with astonishing realism.

947

*Inge Nissen came to the United States from Denmark. A free-lance designer whose work has been featured in many magazines and yarn company publications, she teams jewelry designs with some of the crafts that make use of "soft" materials —weaving, knitting, crochet, macrame, and needlepoint. The jewelry shown here is an example of such a combination. Inge has a craft shop in New York City where she sells her own work and that of other designers.*

# JEWELRY
# Baubles, Bangles, and Hardware

If you associate jewelry with precious stones and costly metals, an adventurous new world awaits you—an exotic realm of delicate yet bold jewelry made from yarn, beads, and feathers—including some fancy footwear. Learn how to transform coconut shells into earrings and pins; turn hardware into armware, and old spoons and forks into fashionable rings and bracelets. On the more traditional side, there are instructions here for making an elegant bracelet and necklace from precious—and not-so-precious—stones and metals. Also included are Craftnotes that identify the most useful jeweler's tools and findings—those tiny prefabricated fastenings—and tell you how to use them and where to buy them.

### Jewelry, Lapidary and Metalwork
## Feather jewelry

Combining feathers, yarn and wooden beads is one way to make "soft" jewelry that is quite a change from most ornamentation. I kept these designs simple to give the beauty of the feathers full play. Feathers are available at hobby shops and display supply houses; beads could come from dime stores or craft houses.

### Fringed Feather Necklace
The big, fringed necklace (opposite) is made by attaching beads and feathers to tiers of crocheted scallops. Choose yarn, beads and feathers in your favorite colors (perhaps to coordinate with a special outfit), or, if you like, use muted colors like those I chose to point up the softness of the materials.

To make this necklace, you will need: one ball of heavy four-strand mercerized crochet cotton in brown; 35 small wooden beads with holes large enough to accommodate two thicknesses of the cotton; 18 feathers approximately 3 inches long (I used spotted turkey feathers); white household glue; and a crochet hook, size G.

The necklace consists of a crocheted foundation chain that ties around the neck and five tiers of a decreasing number of scallops. It is finished with two hanging chains (Figure A; see Crochet Craftnotes, Volume One, for an explanation of abbreviated crochet terms and stitches). Beginning with the foundation chain, ch 130. To fasten off, break off yarn, leaving a 1-inch end; bring end through loop of last stitch and pull taut.

**A**
Figure A: This detail shows the crocheted foundation chain, the five tiers of scallops, and two hanging chains. The beads shown are attached during the crocheting process.

*First tier:* Ch 13, drop loop off hook and pull it through one bead; with crochet hook pick up loop. Skip 46 ch on foundation chain, sc in next ch; * ch 13, pull loop through one bead as before, skip 6 on foundation chain, sc in next chain; repeat from * 4 times, ch 13, fasten off as for foundation chain (5 scallops made).

*Second tier:* Ch 13, pull loop through bead, sc in center ch of first scallop of first tier, * ch 13, pull loop through bead, sc in center ch of next scallop; repeat from * 3 times, ch 13, fasten off (4 scallops made).

*Third tier:* Ch 13, pull loop through bead, sc in center ch of first scallop of second tier, * ch 13, pull loop through

bead, sc in center ch of next scallop; repeat from * 2 times, ch 13, fasten off (3 scallops made).

*Fourth tier:* Ch 13, pull loop through bead, sc in center ch of first scallop of third tier, * ch 13, pull loop through bead, sc in center ch of next scallop; repeat from * once; ch 13, fasten off (two scallops made).

*Fifth tier:* Ch 13, pull loop through bead, sc in center ch of first scallop of fourth tier, ch 13, pull loop through bead, sc in center ch of second scallop, ch 13, fasten off (one scallop made).

Finish with ch 13, pull loop through bead, sc in center ch of scallop of fifth tier, ch 13, fasten off (this forms two hanging chains).

Opposite: the base of this feather-fringed necklace is worked in one simple crochet stitch; the spotted turkey feathers are inserted and glued into the beads later.

Figure B: Follow the diagram at right for placement of additional beads and the feathers. A drop of glue is applied to each quill in order to secure it.

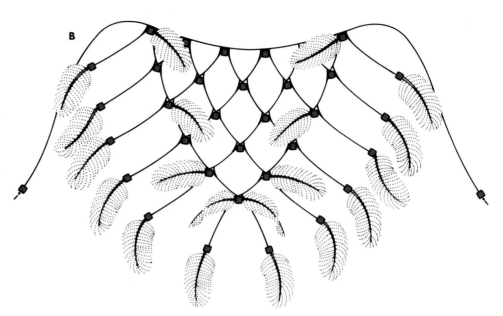

Earrings this light and delicate are a pleasure to wear. The chains are crocheted in cotton yarn; wooden beads and feathers are added later.

Slip one bead on each end of the foundation chain (Figure B) and one on the end of each of the hanging chains, then insert a feather in each of these beads. To do this, knot the yarn close to the last ch below the bead, trim end, apply a dot of glue to the feather quill to secure it and insert the quill in the bead. Insert additional feathers in beads, as shown, applying glue to secure them.

### Feather Earrings

In this project, my goal was to make earrings with a delicate look. You could match the necklace shown on page 949, using the same yarn, beads and feathers.

To make one pair of earrings, you will need: one ball of fine, three-strand mercerized crochet cotton in beige; ear wires with drop loops (see Craftnotes, page 953); eight wooden beads with holes large enough to accommodate three thicknesses of the crochet cotton; eight feathers approximately 2 inches long (such as the pheasant feathers used here); white household glue; and a crochet hook, size F.

For each earring, crochet two strands with 25 chains each. Fasten off each strand by breaking off the yarn 1 inch from last chain; bring end through loop of last chain and pull it taut, forming a knot. Pull both strands through the loop in the ear wire, and adjust the length. Slip ends through beads, and insert a feather in each bead. Knot the yarn close to the last chain; trim end and apply a dot of glue to secure.

### A Butterfly for Your Foot

For fun—and foot—I arranged pheasant feathers around a large yarn-covered ring trimmed with beads. With some tiny bells added to the tie strands, an elegant butterfly-like foot ornament was created.

To make one butterfly ornament you will need: one ball of heavy four-strand mercerized crochet cotton in orange; 26 wooden beads with holes large enough to accommodate two thicknesses of the crochet cotton; two small brass bells; approximately sixteen 1½- to 3-inch-long feathers; a plastic or metal ring 1¾ inch in diameter; crochet hook, size G; white household glue; and a tapestry needle with a large enough eye to accommodate one thickness of the crochet cotton.

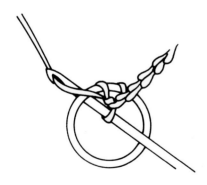

**C**

Figure C: To work a single crochet around the ring, put the hook through the ring, loop the yarn under the hook, and draw the loop through the ring (2 loops on the hook). Complete the stitch as directed in the Craftnotes, Volume One, page 30.

*Start with the first tie:* Leaving a 3-inch end, ch 45. * Work 3 sc around ring (Figure C). Drop loop off hook and pull it through one bead. Pick up loop on hook; work 3 sc around ring, pull loop through 3 beads. Repeat twice from *; make 3 sc around ring, pull loop through one bead, 3 sc around ring. One-half of the ring should now be covered. For toe loop, ch 20; fold chain in half and work 1 sc in each of first 3 ch of the loop. Beginning with 3 sc around ring, cover the second half of the ring like the first half, ending with 3 sc around ring. Join yarn to first tie by working 1 sc in each of the 3 ch closest to the ring. Ch 42 for the second tie. To end off, break off the yarn leaving a 3-inch end; bring the end through the loop of last stitch and pull it taut, forming a knot.

Wear this exotic butterfly foot ornament and you are sure to be the center of attraction at any party. For more sedate occasions, tie it around your neck as a pendant. The tiny brass bells at the tie ends assure you of music wherever you go.

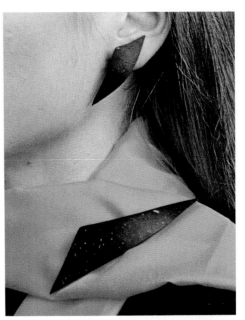

Follow Inge Nissen's methods for preparing pieces of coconut shell, and you will certainly find it difficult to convince people you are not wearing jewelry made from the finest wood.

*Finishing:* Thread the end of each tie through the needle. Attach a bell to each by wrapping the end around the ring of the bell several times. Then weave about 1 inch of the end back into the tie using the needle. Trim the end close to the tie and rub in a bit of glue to secure it. Insert a feather into approximately every other bead, forming a butterfly-wing-like shape on each side. When the feathers have been arranged to your satisfaction, remove them one at a time and apply a small amount of glue to the quill tips; reinsert in the beads.

## Jewelry, Lapidary and Metalwork
# Coconut jewelry

Working with unusual media has always intrigued me, and I decided to experiment with coconut shell. The earrings and pin shown above right are the result.

The following are needed to make coconut jewelry: pieces of the outer shell of a coconut; shellac, furniture oil or wax; medium- and fine-grade sandpaper; a jeweler's saw or jigsaw; a small vise (optional); tracing paper for patterns; rubber cement; a clean rag. In addition, you will need white household glue or clear cement; a pin back for the pin and a pair of ear wires with cups (Craftnotes, page 953).

Drain the coconut and break the shell with a hammer. Prepare the shell pieces by removing as much coconut meat as possible. Then wash the pieces thoroughly with soap and water; let dry completely. Using medium-grade sandpaper, rub off the inner membrane and the hairy outer surface. Finish with the fine-grade sandpaper.

Make paper patterns by tracing the full-size patterns (Figure D), or draw your own designs. Cut the patterns out along the outlines, and rubber-cement them to the outer surface of the shell pieces (reverse the second earring pattern). Using a jigsaw or jeweler's saw, cut out the shapes following the edge of the pattern. (You may find it easier to hold the pieces steady if you clamp them in a vise.) If you make a mistake, simply peel off the pattern and rubber-cement it to another piece of shell. When you have cut out the shapes, sand the edges smooth, progressing from medium- to fine-grade sandpaper. With the rag, apply several coats of shellac, or rub in furniture oil or wax. Glue the findings to the back and allow to dry.

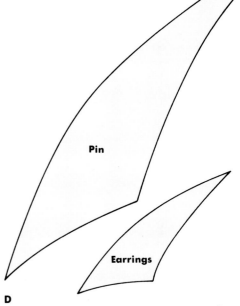

Figure D: Trace these full-size patterns to make the coconut pin and earrings pictured above.

951

# JEWELRY CRAFTNOTES: TOOLS

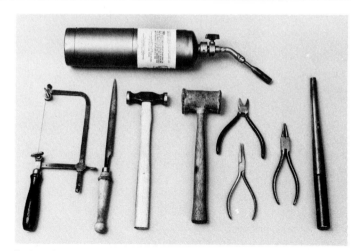

Basic tools used in jewelry making include: Top: propane blow torch. Bottom (from left to right): jeweler's saw, 6-inch half-round file, planishing hammer, rawhide mallet, (top) diagonal wire cutters, (bottom) chain-nosed pliers, round-nosed pliers, ring mandrel.

Your own hands and fingers can accomplish much in the jewelry-making process, but additional strength and dexterity will sometimes be required. In general, jewelers' tools are smaller and more precise than equivalent tools used in wood-working. Take good care of them and use them only for the tasks for which they were designed. The photograph shows the basic tools and equipment used in jewelry making.

## Pliers
Jewelers use small pliers for bending, twisting and curving metal. Round-nosed pliers with ⦂ jaws, chain-nosed pliers with ● jaws (pictured above) and half-round-nosed pliers with ◓ jaws are the three main types. To avoid unwanted marks and identations on the metal, put adhesive tape over serrated jaws.

## Files
A file is used to refine and smooth edges. A 6-inch half-round file is a basic and versatile tool. The round side of the file is used to smooth inner surfaces and curves; for flat, outer surfaces and wire ends, work with the flat side. To use a file, exert pressure on the forward stroke and release pressure on the return.

## Hammers and mallets
These are used mainly to change the shape and form of the metal in some way. The rawhide mallet, in conjunction with a wood or metal form, is used to bend and form broad curves and shapes. To flatten metal and remove any unwanted bumps, place it on a flat steel surface, such as an anvil or a steel mending plate, and strike it with a planishing hammer, which is flat at both ends. A ball pein hammer has two different striking surfaces, each used to obtain a different effect. To texture a piece of metal, place it on a steel surface and tap it with the rounded end of such a hammer. The flat end of the ball pein hammer is similar to that of the planishing hammer, and is used in the same way.

## Wire cutters
For cutting lengths of thin metal wire or chain, use wire cutters as you would scissors. Diagonal wire cutters are preferred because they are capable of greater accuracy when used in hard-to-reach places.

## Jeweler's saw
For metal too thick or heavy to be cut with wire cutters, it is necessary to use a saw. A jeweler's saw consists of a frame and a replaceable blade. When placing the blade in the frame, compress the frame slightly so the blade will be under tension. To cut, support the metal on a block of wood and exert pressure only on the downward stroke. Be sure to keep the saw blade vertical and at right angles to the metal.

## Propane blow torch
If you are planning to make major alterations in the surface or shape of a piece of metal, it must be softened, or annealed, by the application of heat. In most cases, a simple, inexpensive propane blow torch will supply a sufficient amount. In addition to the torch, you will need a large asbestos pad (at least 12 by 12 inches) to protect the work surface. A charcoal block placed on top of the asbestos pad will help concentrate the heat. Place the metal to be annealed on top of the charcoal block or asbestos pad. When working with any type of torch, avoid wearing loose-fitting clothing and make sure long hair has been tied back. Ignite the torch with a striker (an open flame such as a cigarette lighter or a match can be dangerous). Pass the flame back and forth over the metal until it reaches a dull red or pinkish color. (Working in a subdued light makes the color change more apparent.) Allow the metal to air-cool until the pink glow has subsided; then use an old pair of pliers to pick up the metal and drop it in a container of cold water to cool it completely.

## Mandrels
A ring or bracelet mandrel is a thick-walled, hollow steel cylinder or oval form. It is the base around which a piece of metal is pounded into a curved shape. Because it is tapered, the metal can be formed in any required ring or bracelet size, depending upon its position on the mandrel. As you pound, the mandrel can be steadied in two ways, depending upon the type. Short mandrels are held by a special vise, which has a protrusion over which the mandrel fits. Long mandrels are placed in a vertical position on a sturdy table. One hand is wrapped around the mandrel and the metal to be curved, while the other hand holds the mallet.

## Sources of jewelry tools and findings
Some of the tools and findings shown on these two pages are available at craft and hobby shops. The following mail order sources carry a more complete supply, and will send you a catalogue and price list on request:

Anchor Tool and Supply Company, Inc.
Box 265, Chatham, N.J. 07928

Allcraft Tool and Supply Company
100 Frank Road
Hicksville, N.Y. 11801

# JEWELRY CRAFTNOTES: FINDINGS

Jewelry findings are small articles made of metal, usually used for attaching and connecting. A few of the more useful findings are pictured here. Findings occasionally have moving parts (as in spring rings, earring wires, pin backs, cuff link backs and some tie clips). Those with no moving parts include chains, jump rings and tips for stones.

Although many craftsmen prefer to construct their own findings, manufactured findings are available in many designs and kinds of metals and at different price levels, which depend on the metal used. Each metal has advantages and disadvantages: Nickel or brass findings plated with a yellow or white metal, along with copper findings, are the least expensive. The eventual discoloration of brass and copper can be prevented with a coating of lacquer, clear nail polish or plastic spray, but the protective coating will wear off and must be renewed occasionally.

Gold and silver are the two most popular jewelry metals. Although they are costly, many craftspeople prefer them because they are the easiest to work with. Because it is less expensive than gold, silver is the usual choice of the handcrafter, with gold being used mainly by professional manufacturers. If your craft or hobby shop doesn't have what you need, write to the suppliers listed opposite for a catalogue and a current price list.

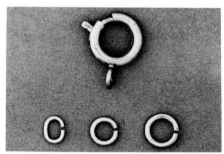

**Jump rings**

A jump ring is a short length of wire formed into an oval or circle. They are sold singly or by the dozen, and are used to connect lengths of chain to each other and to other findings, such as spring rings. They are also used to suspend pendants from a chain or neck ring. To attach a jump ring, open it up by grasping each end of the ring wire with chain-nose or round-nose pliers and twisting in opposite directions. Insert one end in the part you wish to be connected and twist the jump ring closed again.

**Spring rings**

Spring rings, which can be opened and closed with a fingernail, are sold singly or by the dozen and are used as clasps for necklaces, bracelets and other chains. Using a jump ring as joiner, attach the tiny round extension of the spring ring to the last link at one end of the chain. At the other end of the chain, attach another jump ring; the spring ring will connect with this to open and close the chain.

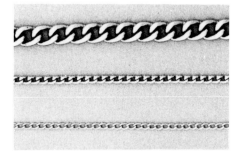

**Chains**

Chains are used alone or as a foundation for necklaces and bracelets, and are available in many styles and sizes. They are sold by the foot. Use a wire cutter to obtain the length you need for individual projects.

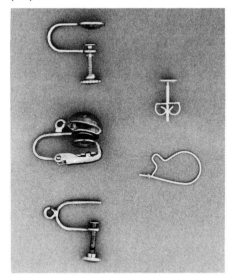

**Ear wires, screws and clips**

Sold by the pair, ear wires, screws and clips are available in many styles for both pierced and unpierced ears. For pendant-type earrings, use the drop-loop type and suspend the ornament from the loop. Earring findings with cups are used to make stationary, button-type earrings. Use two-part epoxy or other strong glue to secure the ornament to the cup. (Advanced jewelry crafters use solder.)

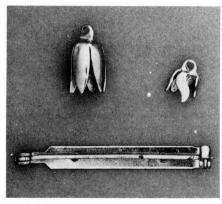

**Pin backs**

Available in several lengths (usually from ¾ to 2 inches). Pin backs have a flat base that is simply glued or soldered to the back of the ornament. Make sure to position the pin back slightly above the center of the ornament, so the pin will hang properly.

**Tips for stones**

Use these tips as a simple, uncluttered means of turning a stone, precious or non-precious, into a pendant. Using chain-nosed or round-nosed pliers, pry open the prongs of the tip and fit it over the top end of the stone, to which you have applied the glue. Pinch the prongs closed and let the glue dry. Using a jump ring, suspend the stone from a chain or neck ring.

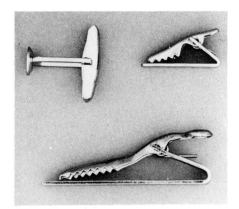

**Tie clips and cuff link backs**

To use these findings, simply glue the back of the desired ornament to the tie clip base or the cup of the cuff link back.

*Stephen Wrynn teaches jewelry making and design at the Craft Students League of New York City. He studied at the School of Visual Arts, and reproduces antique neck chains and bracelets for the Metropolitan Museum of Art gift shop in New York City.*

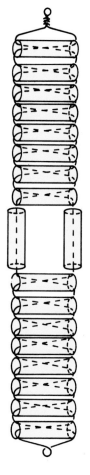

**E**

Figure E: This diagram shows how wire is threaded through fiber plugs to make a bracelet.

---

**Jewelry, Lapidary and Metalwork**
# Hardware store jewelry

Jewelry made from odds and ends of hardware is just-for-fun: fun to design, easy to make, amusing to wear. To me it is like a puzzle game—putting unlikely bits and pieces together for unexpected combinations. While you're at the hardware store buying the materials for either of the bracelets described here, take a look around at the other bins and boxes; design possibilities are everywhere.

### Chain Bracelet
The materials required to make the chain bracelet at right in the picture below are: harness swivel snap approximately 2 inches long; ¾-inch-diameter metal ring; 36-inch-long ball (or beaded) chain with coupling; wire cutters.

To make the bracelet, place the swivel snap and the ring about 5 inches apart on a flat surface. Then simply thread the chain alternately through the ring and the ring of the swivel snap, passing the chain through each three times, until the length of chain is used up. Snap the chain ends closed with the coupling. Place the bracelet on your wrist and fasten. If necessary, adjust the size by cutting off a length of chain at one end.

### Fiber-plug Beaded Bracelet
For one bracelet (at left in picture below) to fit a 6-inch wrist, you will need: eighteen 1-inch-long fiber plugs—the kind used to anchor screws in walls; 24- or 28-gauge copper wire; one No. 6 copper jump ring; one copper spring ring; round-nosed pliers (see Craftnotes, pages 952 and 953).

Start with a 4-foot length of wire. At the center of the wire, make a small loop by twisting the wire around one jaw of the pliers. Then thread the wire ends through the plugs, crisscrossing them, and following the path shown in Figure E. For larger wrists, add more plugs, as needed. Use the pliers to squeeze the wire ends together at the middle of the last plug. Form a loop from the double wire and secure by wrapping the ends several times around the base of the loop (Figure E). Trim the ends with wire cutters, and attach a spring ring to one end loop and a jump ring to the other with the pliers.

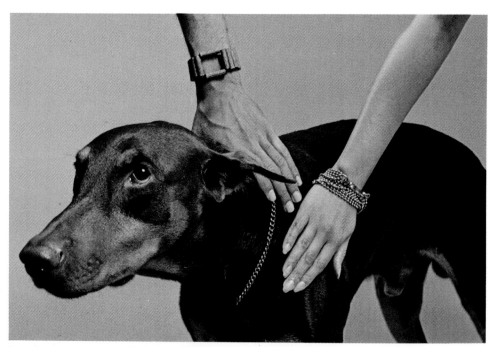

You will enjoy making these hardware bracelets as much as Jubal enjoys the attention lavished upon him by the wearers. Directions for making the fiber-plug-beaded bracelet (left) and the chain bracelet (two are shown at right) are above.

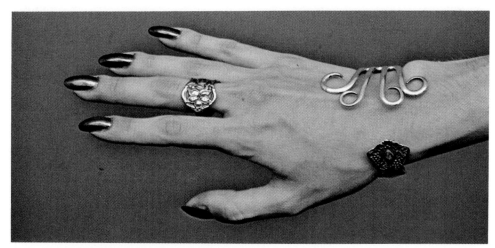

1: Use round-nosed or chain-nosed pliers to curl flattened tines for the fork bracelet. Spread the tines slightly outward, curling two in one direction and two in the other.

Cutlery was transformed into this unusually beautiful silver jewelry by Stephen Wrynn. Follow the directions on this page for shaping a fork into a bracelet and a spoon into a ring.

### Jewelry, Lapidary and Metalwork
# Jewelry from cutlery

A family heirloom or a flea-market find can quickly be hand-shaped into a gift that will be treasured for years. For an extra touch of individuality, you can have initials or a date professionally engraved at a small additional cost. To make either the spoon ring or the fork bracelet shown above, you will need: a silver spoon or fork (sterling is best since it is easier to shape, but silver-plated cutlery may be used); a rawhide or wooden mallet; a ring or bracelet mandrel for shaping (see Craftnotes, page 952). A wooden dowel with a diameter equal to that of the wearer's finger may be substituted for a ring mandrel; a baseball bat may be used as a bracelet mandrel.

If you are using a silver-plated spoon or fork, the base metal underneath the silver plating will be very hard. In order to bend and curve it into shape more easily, you will first have to soften the metal by heating or annealing it. For this you will need a propane blowtorch and an asbestos pad, charcoal block, striker, an old pair of pliers, and a container of cold water. The process is described in the Jewelry Craftnotes on page 952.

### Fork Bracelet

For the fork bracelet, you will need round-nosed pliers and a flat steel surface, such as an anvil or steel mending plate, in addition to the equipment listed above.

Anneal the fork if necessary. When it is cool, place it, tines down, on the flat steel surface. Use a rawhide or wooden mallet to flatten out the hump at the base of the tines, then curl them with the pliers (photograph 1). Pound the fork into a bracelet shape, using the bracelet mandrel or baseball bat as a support (photograph 2). Remember to leave sufficient space between the ends of the bracelet—about 2 inches—to allow the wearer to slip it on and off. If the fork has been annealed, use silver polish to remove any discoloration the heat of the torch may have caused. Slide the bracelet on sideways, and squeeze it closed.

### Spoon Ring

To make the spoon ring, you will need a jeweler's saw and a half-round file in addition to the equipment listed above.

The ring is contoured in much the same way as the fork bracelet (photograph 2) was, with a ring mandrel or dowel substitute forming the shaping guide. First pound the handle of the spoon into a ring shape with the mallet, then form it into a spiral. Cut off the excess at the bowl end (Figure F), leaving approximately ¼ inch of overlap, and using the jeweler's saw. Smooth the cut end with the file (Craftnotes, page 952), and, placing the ring on its edge on a wood surface, tap the cut end downward to close the ring into a circle. Polish if necessary.

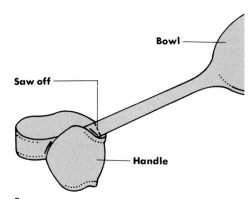

2: Holding the fork in place on a bracelet mandrel, strike it repeatedly with the rawhide or wooden mallet to form a circle. Work slowly and carefully to avoid forming an uneven or bumpy curve.

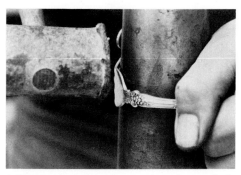

**Bowl**

**Saw off**

**Handle**

F

Figure F: The bowl end of a spoon is sawed off at the point indicated (dashed line) after the spoon has been shaped into a spiral.

Stephen Wrynn secured a polished malachite in a simple pronged wire setting in order to obstruct the beauty of the stone as little as possible. After making the setting, suspend the stone from a length of chain or the neck ring described opposite.

## Jewelry, Lapidary and Metalwork
# Stone pendant and neck ring $ ▨ ⚹ ⚱

Stones that can be used for jewelry can be obtained in a number of ways—and they needn't be cut, tumbled, polished, precious or semi-precious to be beautiful (see Lapidary). Many interesting pebbles, crystals and minerals can be found on beaches, on the road, and even in your own backyard.

Setting a stone in a cage or in wire prongs are two of the simplest of all mounting methods and neither requires many tools. All you need is round or square wire (sold by the foot or by weight, depending on the amount); round-nosed or chain-nosed pliers; wire cutters; and two-part epoxy glue. The thickness of the wire you should use will depend on the way you plan to set the stone. For the cage setting, use 16- or 18-gauge wire; the prong-type setting requires a thinner wire, such as 20-gauge. Choose wire that goes well with the color of the stone. For the pendant at left, I liked the way the silver wire and green stone looked together; but I would team copper wire with an orange or brown stone, as shown below left.

The main purpose in mounting a stone is to enhance its beauty. The stone may be plain, in which case a fairly elaborate cage may be constructed. But many stones have such intrinsic beauty that covering any part of them is a shame. In such cases, "less is more" and the prong-type setting is more appropriate. If you plan to use silver or gold wire, I advise experimenting with inexpensive wire before you make the final setting. For either type of setting, start with a 1-foot length of wire.

To make a cage, wrap the wire around the stone, using your fingers to get the general shapes. Then use the pliers to make tighter, smaller curves and bends and to form a loop at the top for hanging. Trim off any excess wire.

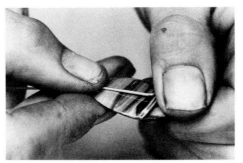

3: Starting at the center back of the stone, near its base, begin shaping the first of the four prongs by bringing the wire across the back to one edge.

4: After forming the first pair of prongs, bend the wire at right angles to them, so the wire lies along the center back.

5: The completed prong setting is shown next to the stone for which it was made. Variations in stones mean each setting will be different.

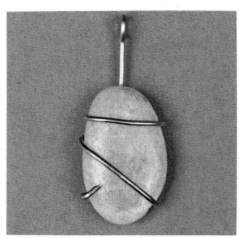

A stone used in making jewelry need not be precious in a cash-value sense, as this beach pebble wrapped in a cage of copper wire illustrates.

The prong setting resembles a human figure with arms, hands, legs and feet—used to hold the stone securely. Make the bottom pair of prongs (legs with upturned feet) first. Beginning at the center near the bottom of the stone, bring the wire across the stone's back (photograph 3). With the pliers, form the first prong by bending the wire about ⅛ inch toward the front of the stone. Bend the wire back along itself, forming a double thickness prong. Bring it back across the bottom center of the stone and repeat the prong-forming process on the other side. Then bring the wire back to your starting point. This completes the bottom pair of prongs. Now, bend the wire down along the center, forming the spine of the figure (photograph 4). Form the top pair of prongs (arms and hands) in the same way the bottom pair was formed. Bend the wire at a right angle to the arms and trim to 1 inch with the wire cutters, forming the neck of the figure. Make a small loop for the head at the end of the wire, from which the pendant will be suspended. The completed prong setting and the stone for which it was made are shown in photograph 5. Make final adjustments to tighten the setting, if necessary. Then, following the manufacturer's directions, apply two-part epoxy glue along the inside of the spine, arms, and legs. Carefully insert the stone in the setting, and allow the glue to dry. Slip a chain of the same type of metal used for the setting through the top loop, or make a neck ring as described opposite.

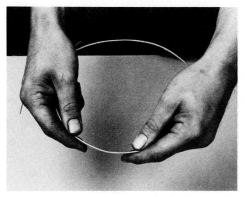

6: Use your hands to form the wire into an oval shape, with the ends about 2 inches apart.

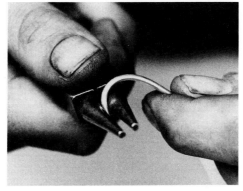

7: Use round-nosed pliers to bend the ends of the neck ring outward, forming hook-like shapes.

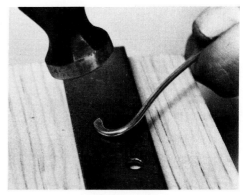

8: Flatten the hook ends with a ball pein or planishing hammer. The steel mending plate shown or an anvil is used for a hammering surface.

**Neck Ring**

To make the neck ring shown opposite, you will need: 19-inch length of 10- or 12-gauge round wire; chain-nosed or round-nosed pliers; ball pein or planishing hammer; flat steel surface, such as a steel mending plate or anvil, on which to hammer; a file (Craftnotes, page 952).

Curve the wire into a round or oval shape (photograph 6). Since the wire is sold in lengths which have been cut from a large coil, and already has a curved shape, it is easy to obtain a uniform curvature. I prefer a slightly oval shape that dips down in front because it conforms to the body shape and therefore "sits" well on the neck. Form an outward-pointing hook at each end of the ring (photograph 7), and hammer these hooks flat (photograph 8)—they will not be interlocked. At this point, I usually strengthen the entire length of wire by pounding it gently with the hammer, flattening it slightly in the process. If you decide to strengthen the wire in this way, it will require some reshaping as you go. Finally, smooth the ends of the flattened hooks with the file (Craftnotes, page 952), and slip it on the stone pendant. Place the ring around the neck, adjusting its curvature and the space between the hooks so the fit is comfortable and secure.

**Jewelry, Lapidary and Metalwork**
# Wrapped wire bracelet  $ 🗵 🚶 🔬

This simple, elegant unisex bracelet can be made in pairs for a couple to wear. I used silver wire for the bracelet and gold wire for the wrapping wire; the two wires could be of the same metal, or any combination you prefer.

To make one bracelet, you will need: 6-gauge wire, the length equal to the circumference of the wrist minus 1½ inches; 1 foot of 20-gauge wire for wrapping; bracelet mandrel (a baseball bat may be substituted); rawhide or wooden mallet; ball pein or planishing hammer; pounding surface, such as a steel mending plate or anvil; file; and two-part epoxy glue.

Using the mallet, form the bracelet around the mandrel as you did the fork bracelet (photograph 2). I used solid silver wire, which is soft enough for me to bend without annealing. However, I recommend that you anneal any wire before attempting to curve it (Craftnotes, page 952). Flatten the bracelet ends with a planishing hammer or the flat end of a ball pein hammer, pounding them on a steel surface (photograph 8). Smooth and round the ends with the file, exerting pressure on the forward stroke only. The next step is to form a spiral of thin wire by wrapping it around the center section of the bracelet (Figure G). Beginning about ¾ inch from the bracelet's center, make evenly-spaced wrappings until the wire is used up. Carefully taper the ends of the wrapping wire with the file. Following the manufacturer's directions, apply two-part epoxy glue at each end of the spiral and at intervals on the inside of the bracelet. Let dry; polish if necessary.

For related crafts and projects, see "Beadwork," "Lace," "Lapidary," "Macrame," and "Silvercraft."

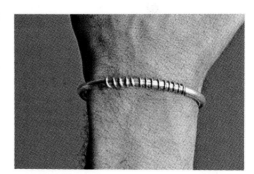

Wrap a length of thin wire around a length of thicker wire for a basic bracelet that might be worn by either a man or a woman.

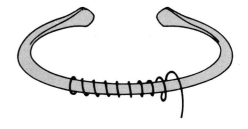

**G**
Figure G: Here thin wire is twisted around heavier wire at the center of the formed bracelet.

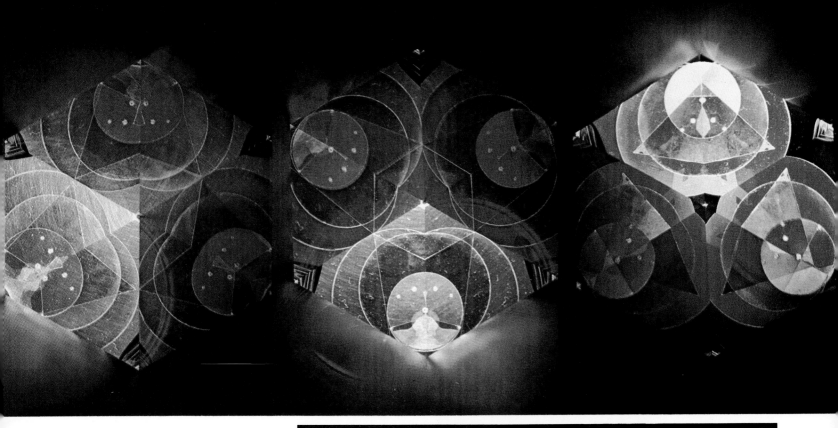

# KALEIDOSCOPES
## Science at Play

*Judith Karelitz is an artist and educator, and has been a kaleidoscope fancier since the age of four. As an artist she has been involved with color, light and optics; her primary medium is polarized light. The Karelitz Kaleidoscope, a polarized-light sculpture, is in the Permanent Design Collection of the Museum of Modern Art in New York. Judy's work has been shown at a number of galleries and museums, and two of her kaleidoscopes are patented.*

Say it slowly: ka*lei*do*scope. The word itself—based on three Greek words meaning *beautiful, a form,* and *to see*—is almost as pleasing to the ear as its images are to the eye. (On page 967 you can see the syllables of the word actually create a kaleidoscopic pattern.) Invented by Sir David Brewster in 1816 and patented a year later, this early educational toy has been teaching and charming viewers of all ages ever since.

### Multiple Reflections

The scientific principle behind kaleidoscopes and related toys is that of multiple reflections: The reflected image of any object, when placed before another mirror, is reflected in turn by that mirror.

In the late seventeenth and early eighteenth centuries, small religious shrines used this principle. Inside a wooden pavilion, tiny replicas of saints or the Nativity scene were placed in front of angled mirrors that gave added dimensions to the compositions. Today you can see the same idea at work in store windows when a mannequin, placed before a series of mirrors, is endlessly reflected. And if you have ever found yourself face-to-face with hundreds of twins in an amusement-park mirror maze, you were part of the science of optics at play.

### The Kaleidoscope

A basic kaleidoscope consists of a tube, an eyepiece, a capsule containing objects to be viewed, and two or three reflectors inside the tube running its length and inclined toward each other at an angle. The degree of that angle determines the number of images created. The formula is simple: Divide 360 degrees by the number of degrees in the mirrored angle to find out how many images you will see. (Photographs 1, 2, and 3). An angle of 60 degrees will give you a symmetrical pattern reflected by the mirrored surfaces to produce a six-sided image. What you see is part of the object (or the whole object, depending on its size and shape) together with its mirror images reflected in the mirrored surfaces (Figure A).

The pattern changes when the kaleidoscope is turned because the objects in the

Can you believe that a kaleidoscope with colorless shapes floating in a clear fluid created the magnificent rainbow above? What's more, the design can be held constant while the colors change or both the colors and the design can change. Polarized light is part of the secret behind this Karelitz Kaleidoscope, a light sculpture on display at museums, but the artist isn't telling any more than that.

1: Two mirrors meeting in a 90-degree angle produce a four-sided image (360 degrees in the circle divided by 90 degrees equals four images).

2: Two mirrors meeting in a 45-degree angle produce an eight-sided image (360 degrees in the circle divided by 45 degrees equals eight images).

3: Two mirrors meeting in a 60-degree angle produce a six-sided image (360 degrees in the circle divided by 60 degrees equals six images).

capsule being viewed are free to move about. Point the tube upward and the objects fall to the bottom of the capsule and a smaller part of them is reflected; point it downward and different, larger patterns are formed. Turn the kaleidoscope clockwise and the images tend to disappear into its center; turn it counterclockwise and they move out again.

### What's a Teleidoscope?

A toy related to the kaleidoscope, and often mistaken for one, is the teleidoscope. A *ka*leidoscope has a capsule at one end of the tube containing bits and pieces of such materials as colored acetate or beads; the *te*leidoscope has a lens in place of the capsule so the object or scene toward which you point the tube is reflected again and again.

The most ordinary things are transformed when seen through a kaleidoscope or one of its variations. Call it science, call it magic—it's a new way of seeing and exploring your world.

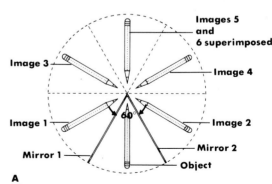

A

Figure A: The principle behind the kaleidoscope is that of multiple reflections. The reflected image of an object, when placed before another mirror, is reflected in turn by that mirror.

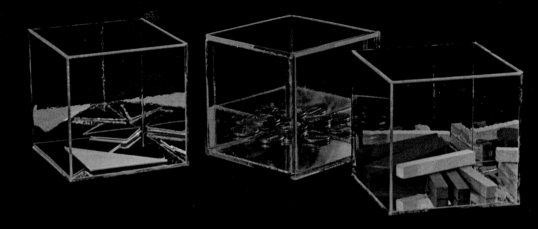

The kaleidoscopic cube with removable lid has many uses. A few, lower left to top right, are: terrarium, photo cube, flower vase, shake-up toy, penny bank and rattle. Can you think of more?

Toys and Games
# Kaleidoscopic cubes

$\$$ ⊠ 👥 🔔

Put an object in a kaleidoscopic cube and it will appear as four identical objects, as if by magic. The optical effect results from a 90-degree angle formed by two adjacent mirrored sides. The cube is put together in such a way that you can remove the top and change the object any time you choose. A flower in the cube will stay fresh for days without water; a single blossom will look like a whole bouquet. A photograph of a friend will appear four times over. Or you can use the cube as a penny bank and see your money grow much faster than it ever did before, right before your eyes. Ray Sherman, an architectural model maker, designed similar cubes with colorful wooden sticks and cardboard shapes inside. The pattern they make is different each time you shake the cube, and the rattle adds to the fun.

## The Materials

This cube is made of clear and mirrored sheet acrylic, which I have found is safer and easier to use than glass mirrors or shiny metal. Such acrylic plastic is sold under several brand names including Plexiglas, Lucite, Acrylite and Perspex. Look for suppliers in the Yellow Pages of your phone book under "Plastics." The mirrored acrylic I use has a blue protective coating over the mirror backing—which proved an attractive finish for the outside of those surfaces. If you prefer, you can spray the three opaque sides of the cube with paint after it is assembled. If you paint, mask the transparent sides carefully with paper and masking tape.

Ask the acrylic supplier to cut the pieces to the proper size for you. There will be an additional charge for this service, but it is worth it. (You can cut the pieces yourself with a power saw, but a special fine-toothed blade is needed.) Buy acrylic ⅛ inch thick and have six pieces cut for each cube you want to make, one each in clear and in mirrored acrylic, in these three sizes: 2¾ inches square, 3 inches square, and 2¾ by 3 inches. Leave the protective paper on the pieces until the cube is assembled (this will forestall scratches). Number the pieces in the order in which they will be joined:

No. 1: 2¾ by 3 inches, mirror  No. 4: 2¾ inches square, clear
No. 2: 2¾ inches square, mirror  No. 5: 3 inches square, clear
No. 3: 3 inches square, mirror  No. 6: 2¾ by 3 inches, clear.

## Sanding

Before you assemble the cube, smooth the edges and remove any saw marks by scraping them with the flat edge of a scissor blade (photograph 8, page 962). For a more professional finish, you can smooth the edges with sandpaper, being very careful not to scratch the faces of the plastic. Tape wet-or-dry sandpaper to a flat surface, wet it, and slide the plastic edge across the sandpaper (photograph 4). Start with grade 400, and then go to grade 600 (fine) for final smoothing. Hold the piece straight and do not rock it from side to side—this would result in a rounded edge and an imperfect fit. (Judy's hint: Holding two equal sides together as you sand makes it easier to keep the edges straight.) Sand a little at a time, then stop and check the edge. It is important that you sand only enough to smooth the rough edges, and not enough to change the size of the piece. Although you should sand the edges before assembling the cube, wait until the cube is formed for the polishing, since the solvent used to join the seams will not work on a polished surface.

### Assembling the Cube

Piece No. 1 will be the bottom of the cube, with its mirrored side up. Pieces 2 and 3 will be two sides, meeting in a right angle, with their mirrored faces on the inside. Pieces 4 and 5 will be the two additional sides. The two shorter sides should face each other and rest on top of the bottom piece; the bottom edges of the larger sides should be flush with the bottom of piece 1. Hold these pieces together with masking tape. Piece 6, the top piece, is not joined to the others but is kept removable so objects in the cube can be changed. This piece should snap into place between the extended top edges of pieces 3 and 5 (photograph 5). If it does not snap into place easily, sand the edges very lightly until it does.

### Applying the Solvent

The bottom and side pieces, still held in position with masking tape, are fused, rather than glued, with a solvent that softens the acrylic plastic at its edges until the two surfaces flow together. This solvent can be applied with a hollow-needle applicator or an artist's paintbrush (photograph 6). First peel back a bit of the protective paper, then apply the solvent, following the manufacturer's directions carefully. Do not smoke while using the solvent. Try to get a thin, even flow of solvent from the top to the bottom of the joint—tilting the cube and allowing the solvent to run down from the top corner is a good way to get a smooth, uninterrupted flow. Press the pieces together, and let the joints dry for several hours before proceeding to the next step.

### Polishing

Once the cube is assembled, you can leave it as is or polish the exposed edges to a high shine. If any of the edges are still rough or uneven, sand them or scrape them with a scissor blade (photograph 8, page 962). If you have a power buffing wheel, use this to polish the edges with a buffing compound made for use with plastics. Leave the protective paper on after the cube is assembled until you finish buffing the edges. You can also polish the edges with a non-abrasive toothpaste on your fingertip or on a cotton ball. Use just a little and keep the paste out of the seams as much as possible. Buff with a soft cloth. When edge-buffing is completed, remove the protective paper and clean off any fingerprints or dust by wiping the cube with rubbing alcohol on a soft cloth or by washing it in a solution of mild soap and water. Do not use nail polish remover or commercial window cleaners—these will cause small cracks or crazing. Antistatic cleaners and polishes made especially for acrylic plastics are also available.

### Terrarium Cube

This cube is the same as the one above, except in size. Use ¼-inch-thick sheet acrylic, and have one clear and one mirrored piece cut in each of these three sizes: 8½ inches square, 9 inches square, and 8½ by 9 inches. Number the pieces as follows and join them in order:

No. 1: 8½ by 9 inches, mirror     No. 4: 8½ inches square, clear
No. 2: 8½ inches square, mirror     No. 5: 9 inches square, clear
No. 3: 9 inches square, mirror     No. 6: 8½ by 9 inches, clear.

Follow the directions given above for assembling and finishing the kaleidoscopic cube, then plant a miniature garden inside. The cube will act as a terrarium and just a few plants, mirror-multiplied, will make a lush little indoor garden that will require very little water. Leave an open space in the center of the garden so that the mirrored bottom can show through as a reflecting pool.

4: Sand the edges of all six sides on wet sandpaper before assembling the cube.

5: The top piece snaps into place and is not permanently attached to the rest of the cube.

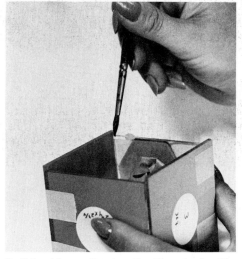

6: Cube sides are fused, rather than glued, with plastic solvent applied with a paintbrush.

A child's world takes on new dimensions when seen through this Hue View.

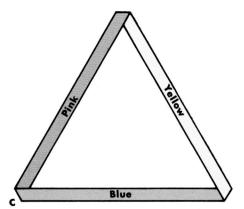

Figure B: Have the plastics supplier cut the three strips of acrylic at a 60-degree angle.

Figure C: The three strips will form a triangular tube. Be sure the angled edges meet each other exactly in the sequence shown above.

## Toys and Games
# The Hue View

The Hue View®, which I designed and named, is a variation on a variation of the kaleidoscope. The basic 60-degree teleidoscope gives you a six-sided view of the world around you as reflected in its three shiny sides; the Hue View does that and adds another dimension, that of color, with only three strips of reflective colored acrylic that can be transparent or opaque.

### Easy If You Know How
This toy looks very easy to make and it is—but there's a secret that will help you make it right. When your supplier cuts the three strips of ⅛-inch-thick acrylic, have him cut them at a 60 degree angle as shown in Figure B. This will slant both long edges of each strip. (Take the drawing with you to show him exactly what you want.) I suggest you have the strips cut 10 to 12 inches long and slightly less than 2 inches wide. This makes an easily grasped tube and is economical: if you use only one color, you can cut two complete optical toys from one square foot of acrylic—one for you and one for a friend.

For the viewer pictured on this page, I put together one strip each of yellow transparent, bright pink transparent and medium blue transparent acrylic. Other effects can be achieved by using only one or two colors or a different color combination, but this is my favorite.

Do not sand the cut edges before assembling the sides, as this might distort the angle. Place the strips exactly as shown in Figure C, and hold them together with rubber bands or masking tape (photograph 7) at both ends and in the center.

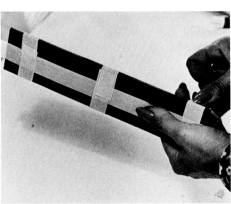

7: Strips must be held together firmly in the triangular tube shape while the solvent is applied and allowed to dry. Use masking tape or rubber bands at both ends and in the center.

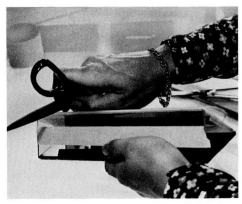

8: When the tube is completely dry, remove rough spots and saw marks from exposed edges by scraping them with a blunt edge of a scissors blade. Then smooth with wet sandpaper.

Blow out any dust particles from the inside before applying the solvent (page 961). Use an artist's paintbrush for this and load the brush with enough solvent to keep it flowing down the entire inside length of the tube. Any blobs or skips will affect the symmetry of the image seen through the tube and will be visible from the outside. Let the tube dry for a few hours; then scrape cut edges with a scissor blade (photograph 8), and smooth them with wet-or-dry sandpaper. Sand both ends with a circular motion, tilting the tube slightly to round the edges and eliminate sharp corners for safety's sake. Start with grade 400 and finish with grade 600. Polish the edges as directed for the cube (page 961) if you want a bright shine.

### Now the Magic Begins
Look through the colorful viewer at your fingers, a porch railing, the television screen, books on a shelf, the newspaper. Hold the tube steady and scan the scene around you. Watch it change shape and color. You can even make a gray day rosy, green or blue by looking at the sky through the long sides of the tube.

## An Alternate Way

If you cannot have the strips cut at the angle shown in Figure B, you can still make a viewer that will give satisfactory results. Have the three strips cut with square edges and place them side by side with a 3/16-inch space between. Use short pieces of masking tape to keep the pieces from shifting. Then use colored tape to join them together along their lengths (Figure D).

Remove the masking tape holding the strips steady and fold the acrylic strips into a triangular tube shape with the colored tape on the outside. Move the sides into position so that the inside points meet at each corner. Secure the third side with tape (Figure E). Cut off any excess tape with a single-edge razor blade.

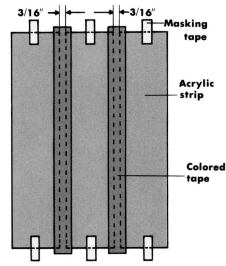

Figure D: If you cannot have the strips cut at the angle shown in Figure B, lay three square-edged strips side by side, 3/16-inch apart, and join with two lengths of colored tape.

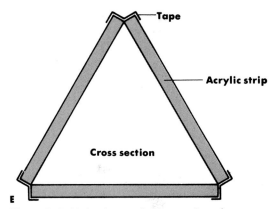

Figure E: Fold the three strips into a triangular tube (tape outside), making the inside corners meet as shown. Tape the third joint.

The same old world just doesn't seem the same when seen through the lens of a teleidoscope. Did you recognize this as a passing yellow cab?

## Toys and Games
# The teleidoscope

The teleidoscope goes one step beyond the viewer on the opposite page. It is the same reflective triangular tube; this time it is made of black acrylic plastic and placed inside a cylinder. The latter could be a container that originally held long fireplace matches. (Outside, this teleidoscope looks exactly like the kaleidoscopes on page 965.) A 2-inch-round clear acrylic sphere at one end acts as a lens to bring faraway sights into close range (Figure F). Because the inner tube forms three 60-degree angles, the image will be six-sided.

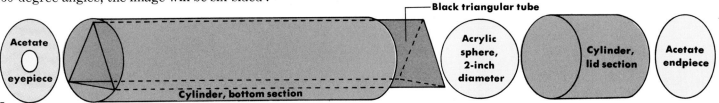

Figure F: This teleidoscope is a reflective triangular tube inside a cylinder with a clear sphere at one end acting as a lens. All inside parts must make tight contact to produce a sharp image.

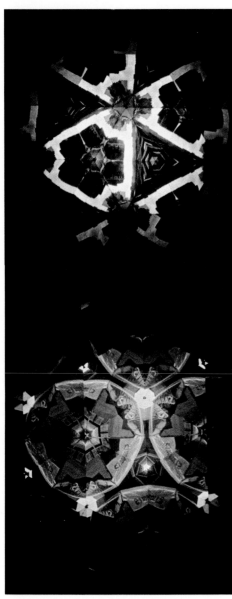

Above are two more city street scenes showing an office building and pedestrian traffic signal in the top photograph and a hot-dog vendor's umbrella in the bottom photograph, as viewed through the magic eye of a teleidoscope.

### The Inside

Make the basic triangular tube using three strips of ⅛-inch-thick opaque black acrylic. (Black acrylic is the most reflective, so if only clear acrylic is available, spray the strips on their outer surfaces with black paint (photograph 9). The length and width of each strip will depend on the size of your particular cardboard match container. To determine the width you need, measure the inside diameter of the cylinder and have each strip cut seven-eighths of that diameter. Use the bottom section of the cylinder to get this measurement, as it is slightly smaller than the lid. Measure as accurately as possible, and if you must approximate, round off to the *smaller* figure. You can always pad a smaller triangular tube with masking tape or rubber bands (photograph 10), but you can't make a large one smaller.

Poke out the top and bottom of the cylinder and save for later use. You will find they fit into shallow grooves on the inside, and these will be used to hold the eyepiece and endpiece that you will cut. Measure the length of the cylinder between these two grooves, subtract 2 inches to allow for the ball at the end, and have the acrylic strips cut to that length.

Pad the acrylic sphere with masking tape (photograph 11) to fit tightly inside the shorter end of the cylinder (formerly the lid of the match container). If the difference between the size of the sphere and the inside diameter of the cylinder is substantial, cut a ring of cardboard and tape this around the sphere, adding more masking tape if needed.

9: If only clear acrylic is available, spray the three cut strips with black paint on the side which will be the outside.

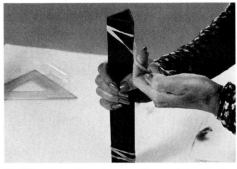

10: The triangular tube must fit snugly inside the cylinder; if it is too small, pad it with masking tape or rubber bands.

### Eyepiece and Endpiece

Cut the eyepiece and the endpiece from heavyweight clear acetate, using the top and bottom end pieces of the cylinder as patterns. (If the top end is made of acetate, use it as is.) You will find they vary slightly in size, and one end cannot be used as a pattern for both eyepiece and endpiece. Tape the end circle to the acetate and cut around it, moving the circle and holding the scissors still to get a smooth line (photograph 12, below.) For the eyepiece, center a round gummed label (¼ to ¾ inch) over the smaller of the two acetate circles and spray-paint the acetate black. Remove the label; you will have an eyepiece which looks like a flat doughnut.

11: The lens sphere must also fit snugly. If it is too small, pad it with masking tape or a ring of cardboard taped to make it fit.

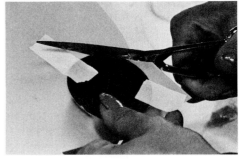

12: For kaleidoscope diffuser, tape circle from lid section to translucent paper and cut a disc, moving the paper instead of the scissors.

## Putting It Together

Start with the shorter end of the cylinder and poke the clear acetate endpiece into the groove. This can be tricky—get one section into place, then gently nudge the rest of it with a ruler or the eraser tip of a pencil. Drop the sphere into the cylinder, making sure it fits tightly against the cylinder wall. Otherwise its weight will dislodge the acetate and the sphere will fall out. Fit the doughnut-like eyepiece into the groove in the longer section. Finally, put the black triangular tube inside and close the outer cylinder with transparent tape where the two sections meet. Finish the outside with adhesive-backed paper, spray paint, or a glued-on section of a favorite poster or print.

**Toys and Games**
# The kaleidoscope

$ ▨ ♙ 🖌

The kaleidoscope is much the same as the teleidoscope, except that a capsule holding bits and pieces of paper, beads, flowers or whatever you choose is substituted for the clear lens sphere. The capsule end can be rotated to change the images (Figure G). All inside parts must make firm contact for a sharp image.

In addition to the elements needed for the teleidoscope (except the sphere), you will need a diffuser to blur the background and soften the light when you look through the tube. Cut this from 10-mil thick matte-finish acetate, waxed paper, vellum or tracing paper, using the end piece as a pattern (photograph 12). Cut a narrow strip (no more than ½ inch depending on the thickness of the capsule contents) from cardboard and tape this into a ring shape. It must fit tightly inside the lid section and can be padded with masking tape if necessary. To close the capsule after filling it, cut another tight-fitting disc of 10-mil thick clear acetate and put it between the ring and the triangular inner tube. This can be removed if you want to change the contents of the capsule—in this way, you need make only one viewer, but, in sequence, can have as many kaleidoscopes as you please.

Put the pieces together as shown in Figure G and cover the outside of the cylinder in two separate sections (not taped together) if you want the end piece to rotate freely. You can tape the sections if you don't want to change the contents—to change the image you will rotate the entire kaleidoscope.

Hold the kaleidoscope up to the light and be prepared to be spellbound by the endless number of beautiful patterns you can create from very ordinary things.

The outside of a kaleidoscope or a teleidoscope can be decorated with adhesive-back paper (left), a section of a poster or silk-screen print (center), or spray paint (right).

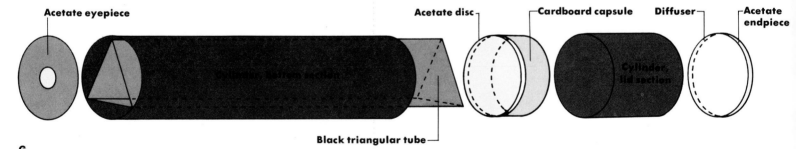

Acetate eyepiece — Acetate disc — Cardboard capsule — Diffuser — Acetate endpiece

Cylinder, bottom section — Cylinder, lid section

Black triangular tube

**G**

Figure G: The kaleidoscope is made much the same as the teleidoscope. However, in place of the lens sphere, there is a capsule at one end to hold objects to be viewed.

## Bits and Pieces

A word about the bits and pieces—they should be free to move from side to side, but should not be so loose that they fall forward and block the movement of the other pieces. Vary them in size and weight so they won't clump together and fall to the bottom of the capsule. The old-fashioned kaleidoscope usually had only transparent pieces; you can add opaque pieces such as twigs or pins for an interesting design. Experiment with your favorite things—you may not recognize them when you see them through the kaleidoscope. A few of many fascinating possibilities are shown on the following pages. These photographs show the contents of four kaleidoscopes and just a few of the infinite images they can create.

The primitive image, right, was created by these few contents: Five pieces of translucent acetate, each a different shape and color, plus five large and small safety pins (one open and bent).

The old-fashioned image, right, was created with clear and colored glass beads and discs, bits of colored beach glass, two straight pins and pieces of colored and striped acetate.

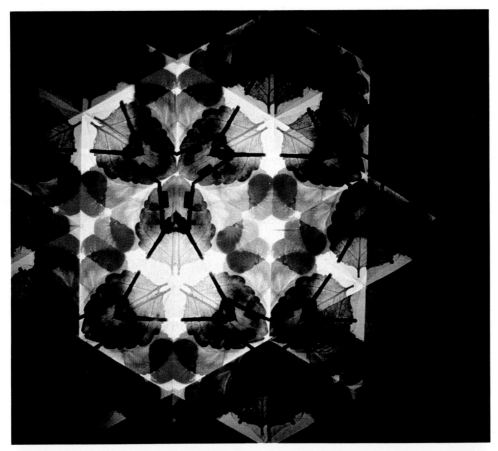

The muted pink and green image, left, was created by four plant leaves of varying sizes and one flower petal, all pressed between clear tape, plus one small twig.

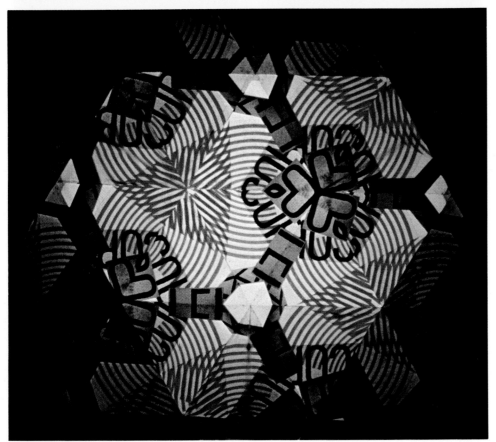

The optical-illusion image, left, was created by the word kaleidoscope (press-on letters on translucent acetate) cut into syllables, plus large and small shapes of striped acetate.

This canvas-covered kayak is a modified version of the famous Eskimo sealskin kayak. It is wider, less tippy and more stable than a traditional kayak, but still a relatively speedy craft.

# KAYAKS
## Go Like an Eskimo

Kayaks are the slim, waterproof canoes Eskimos rely on for survival in icy arctic waters. In their traditional form, light frames made of split driftwood are lashed together with rawhide, and then covered with sewn sealskins. When wet, the wood frames swell, tightening the skins like a drum. A skirt, made of whale bladder or a similar waterproof material and tied with a drawstring, is fastened to the cockpit in which the paddler sits. In rough seas, the Eskimo tightens this skirt around him to keep the water out. Should the kayak capsize, the Eskimo rights it with a sweep of his double-bladed paddle—or *pautik*—a technique known as the "Eskimo roll." It is a lot safer than trying to swim ashore in frigid waters.

Not all kayaks are designed for rolling or for dodging arctic ice floes. They can be —as is the case with the one we built shown opposite—somewhat less nimble but safer, and still be fun to use. In impromptu races, we have had no trouble beating several canoes, proving that our kayak still retains some of the speed inherent in the Eskimo original.

European explorers got their first glimpse of Eskimo kayaks in the tenth century, when Greenland was discovered. About 400 years later, Europeans began making copies of the Greenland kayaks. Although the traditional Eskimo sealskin kayak is still being used in arctic areas of Alaska, Canada, Greenland and Siberia, today's Eskimos might have difficulty recognizing some modern kayaks as descendants of their original design. Sealskins have been replaced by canvas, molded plywood, aluminum and fiberglass. Hull shapes and dimensions have been altered to make a kayak better suited to a special task. Thus modern kayaks built for whitewater slalom racing have relatively short hulls for maneuverability, blunt bow and stern keel lines to reduce resistance to turning, and rounded gunwales (the line where the deck meets the hull), to minimize the effect of water on the deck during leans or going through rolls or waves. By contrast, flat-water racing kayaks have long, sleek hulls that give them speed and directional stability, and a low profile to minimize wind effects.

Some experiments with kayak designs were not too successful. A Swedish version, developed in the early 1900s, had a sharp narrow bow for cleaving the waves and a wide, flat rear end designed to ease the passage of water underneath. When the waves came head on, it did well; when they came from behind, it did badly. The foldboat or folding kayak, made of rubberized canvas stretched over wood framing, was popular during the 1950s. But it proved no match for the stronger fiberglass that has largely replaced it as a covering on commercial kayaks.

### Modern Versions

The kayak most widely used today is the all-purpose or touring kayak. Like the traditional arctic kayak, it is double-ended (both ends tapering to a narrow point), and long in relation to its width and beam. Both types may range up to 20 feet in length but are rarely more than 21 inches (for the arctic model) to 28 inches wide (for the touring model). With their relatively slim hulls and light weight, they are quite speedy. Unfortunately, the same qualities also make a kayak very tricky to handle. Learning to use one can be like learning to ride a two-wheel bicycle.

That is why we modified our kayak to make it easier and safe to handle. Our 12-foot, 4-inch-long by 32-inch-wide craft is shorter and wider than traditional designs. Its plywood bottom board strengthens the framing and, by lowering the center of gravity, improves the stability. It also makes the boat easier to build. At the same time, the extra weight and beamier construction do make the boat less nimble than a kayak built for racing or for whitewater runs. And it has no skirt or flap to keep the water out when capsized. So don't try this boat in whitewater or on rough open seas; it is not designed for such work.

We covered our kayak with canvas rather than sealskin. Canvas may not make a better skin for the craft but it is readily available, and we liked the idea of saving the lives of some seals.

*Bill Becker (left) and Bill Hopkins (right) collaborated on designing and building the kayak pictured opposite. Both are scientists who pursue boat building as a hobby. Bill Becker is a mathematician and computer expert who has been designing and building boats since his high school days. Marine biologist Bill Hopkins is also an accomplished draftsman, wood carver, carpenter, boat mechanic and fisherman.*

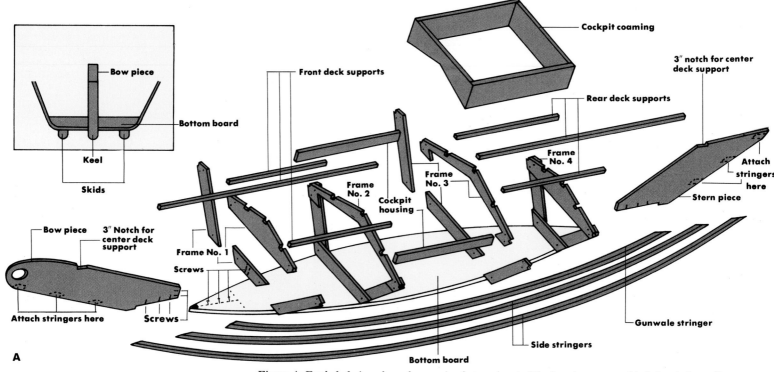

**A**

Figure A: Exploded view shows how major frame pieces of the kayak are assembled. Inset shows the positioning of the halfround keel and skids, which are attached after the canvas is in place.

## Materials Needed for Kayak

2-by-8-foot panel of ½-inch exterior plywood (bottom board)

2 9-foot lengths of 1-by-8-inch No. 2 pine (bow, stern and frame pieces)

8 13-foot lengths of ¾-by-¾-inch clear pine (for stringers, gunwales, and deck braces)

1 14-foot length of ¾-inch half-round (keel)

2 13-foot lengths of ¾-inch half-round (to cover gunwale seams)

3 10-foot lengths of ½-inch half-round (to cover deck seams)

1 8-foot length of 1-by-6-inch pine (cockpit coaming)

2 2-foot lengths of 1-by-2-inch No. 2 pine (cockpit housing sides)

### Fasteners

4 2-inch, No. 6 flathead brass screws

4 2-inch, No. 8 flathead brass screws

100 1½-inch, No. 8 flathead brass screws

16 1-inch, No. 6 roundhead brass screws

30 ¾-inch, No. 2 roundhead brass screws

24 3/16-by-2-inch plated steel bolts with nuts

48 plated washers for 3/16-by-2-inch steel bolts

5 boxes ½-inch aluminum or copper tacks

### Miscellaneous

1 gallon of wood preservative (you must be able to paint over it).

1 gallon marine paint to go over canvas

1 5-by-16-foot section of heavy (grade 13) canvas

## Building the Kayak

To make this kayak, it helps to have had some woodworking experience. But a beginner, working carefully with the drawings and accompanying instructions, can manage the job if he allows enough time for it. It took us a full two weeks to complete. Figure A shows how the structural frame is assembled, and the accompanying list gives the materials needed for the kayak. The tools needed are: a crosscut saw; saber or keyhole saw; power or hand drill and various sizes of drill bits; claw hammer; screwdriver; countersink for screws; square with level built in; tape measure; 4 C-clamps, each with at least a 2-inch opening; miter box; small adjustable wrench; large shears (for cutting canvas); sawhorses (or two chairs will do); wood rasp; pocket knife; and sandpaper in assorted grits.

The first step in construction is to cut out the bottom board, Figure B. On the 2-by-8-foot piece of plywood, mark off an 8-foot-long center line 8 inches in from one edge of the long side. Divide this line in two by drawing a perpendicular line, 16 inches long, at the halfway or 4-foot mark. Position a ¾-inch-square wood strip or stringer, 13 feet long, that you will use as a drawing guide for the curved bottom line as in Figure C and photograph 1. With the stringer clamped as shown and bent so the outside of the stringer nearly touches the end of the 16-inch perpendicular center line, drive a nail just inside the stringer to stabilize the stringer's bent position temporarily. Then draw a line along the outside of the stringer, making sure it passes through the end of the center line. Unclamp the stringer, flip it over, re-clamp on the other side of the center line, drive the nail, and draw the curve for the opposite side of the bottom board. Before cutting out the bottom board, draw the center lines for each of the four frame locations, spacing them as indicated in Figure B. Then cut out the curved lines marked on the bottom board with a saber or keyhole saw, being careful not to cut inside the lines. Set the bottom board aside.

Figure D shows the patterns for cutting the bow, stern and frame pieces from two 9-foot lengths of 1-by-8-inch pine. Note that the dimensions of the frame pieces for frame Nos. 1 and 4, and those for Nos. 2 and 3, are the same. The curved portions of the bow and stern pieces may be drawn freehand. Cut out the frame pieces as indicated. Using the bow piece as a guide to the width, center it on each end of the bottom board, fore and aft, and mark and cut out 2-inch notches as in Figure B. The ½-by-2-inch extensions shown on the bottoms of the bow and stern pieces in Figure D will fit into these notches; cut carefully to get a tight fit.

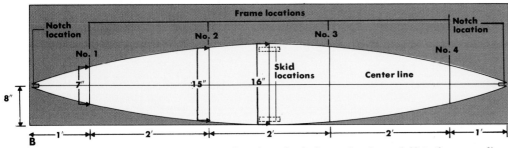

**Figure B:** Bottom board is cut from a 2-by-8-foot piece of ½-inch exterior plywood. Note the perpendicular lines marking the center lines for each frame position, and the notches cut into each end of the bottom board. The bow and stern pieces will fit into these notches.

1: Place plywood for bottom board on sawhorses, clamp as shown here, and then draw the curve for the cutout of the first side as in Figure C.

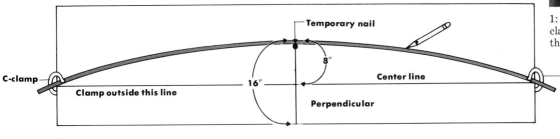

**Figure C:** With a wood strip clamped as shown, draw the line for the cutout of the first side of the bottom board along the outside of the curved strip. Then clamp the strip in curved position on the other side of bottom board center line and draw the curve for the second side.

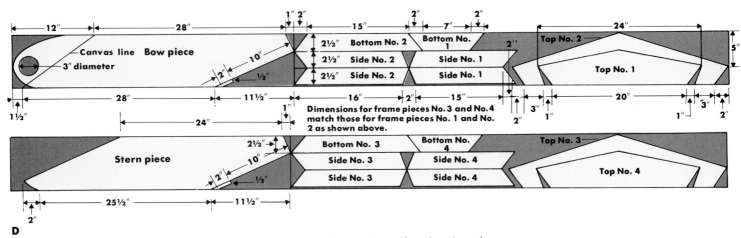

**Figure D:** Follow these dimensions in cutting out the frame, bow and stern pieces. Note that pieces for frame Nos. 1 and 4 match, as do those for frame Nos. 2 and 3. Use saber or keyhole saw to cut out the circle and the curved portions in the bow and stern pieces.

## Beginning the Assembly

With the bow, stern and frame pieces cut out, you are ready to begin assembling. All wood fastening for the kayak should be done with waterproof glue and brass screws. The screw holes for each outer piece of wood should be predrilled and countersunk to allow the screws to fit snugly and flush. For the larger screws, drill partway into the attached wood with a bit diameter smaller than that of the screw threads to avoid splitting. Remember to screw through plywood but never into it, as the screws will tend to pull out of the plywood.

Apply glue to the joining surfaces of the bow piece and the bottom board. Then, using a square to make sure the bow piece is perpendicular to the bottom board, fit the bow piece extension snugly into its notch centered on the bottom board's center line. Attach the bow piece to the bottom board with three 1½-inch No. 8 flathead brass screws, spaced about 2½ inches apart (Figure A). Attach the stern piece to the bottom board in the same manner.

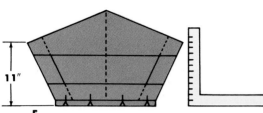

**E**

Figure E: Bottom board is fastened to each frame with four screws running through board into frame. Screws are equally spaced on either side of center line, leaving center line open for attachment of the keel later. Use square to measure the height of each gunwale from the bottom.

Next, fasten all the bottom frame pieces to the bottom board, centering each on the line previously marked for it (Figure B). Use glue and four 1½-inch No. 8 screws driven through the bottom board into each frame piece as in Figure E. Fasten the bottom of frame No. 1 to the end of the bow piece, Figure A, with glue and two 1½-inch, No. 8 flathead screws. Fasten the bottom of frame No. 4 to the stern piece in the same way.

Starting with frame No. 1 (Figure A), temporarily clamp the frame pieces together as in photograph 2. Use a square to assure that the height of the side frame pieces on either side is the same, Figure E, and that the peak in the top frame piece is directly above the center line on the bottom board. Then drill holes for the 3/16-by-2-inch plated or galvanized steel bolts that will join the bottom, side and top pieces of frame No. 1, as in photograph 3 and Figure A. Use two bolts to join each side piece to the top piece, one to join each side piece to the bottom piece. Remove the clamps, apply glue to all joining surfaces, and bolt the frame parts together, inserting a plated washer under each nut and bolt head. Repeat the procedure for the remaining three frames.

2: With C-clamps holding bottom, side and top frame pieces together, check with square to make sure the gunwale on each side is the same height, and the peak in the top frame piece is directly above the bottom center line.

3: Drill two holes for the plated 3/16-inch bolts where the top frame pieces join the side frame pieces. Drill one hole where the side frame pieces join the bottom frame pieces. Use plated washers under each nut and bolt head.

4: If the cut stringer does not fit flat against the bow piece, use a rasp to shape the end of the stringer for a perfect fit. Be sure to follow the same procedure when you are fitting the other end of stringer against the stern piece.

**Attaching the Stringers**

The technique of fastening the side stringers to the frames is to start with the bottom stringers and work up, alternating sides after fastening each one to avoid deforming the bow and stern pieces. You fasten each stringer to the two middle frames (Nos. 2 and 3 in Figure A) first, then to frame Nos. 1 and 4, and finally to the bow and stern pieces. Start by marking each frame at the heights shown for the two lower side stringers in Figure F. Then glue joining surfaces of bottom stringer and frame Nos. 2 and 4, and fasten the stringer to these frames with one 1½-inch No. 8 screw at each frame location. Use the same procedure to fasten the stringer to frame Nos. 1 and 4.

To fit a stringer against the bow and stern pieces, each end of the stringer must be faired—that is, cut on an angle that will insure a flat fit. To do this, first clamp a 1-by-3-by-8-inch block of wood to the bow piece at the appropriate height for the stringer as indicated in Figures A and G. Mark the point where the stringer will meet the bow piece. Then, holding the stringer underneath the block of wood, use the block of wood as a guide for the saw as you cut through the mark previously made on the stringer, Figure G. Test the cut stringer against the bow or stern piece to make sure it fits perfectly. If not, file it, as in photograph 4, until it does. Then drill a pilot hole for a 1½-inch No. 8 screw in the angled end of the stringer (not too close to the thin end), and glue and screw the stringer to the bow piece. Repeat the fitting and fastening procedure where the other end of the stringer fits against the stern piece. Next, in sequence, attach the bottom stringer on the opposite side, the middle stringer on the first side, and the middle stringer on the opposite side, fitting and fastening each as you did the first bottom stringer.

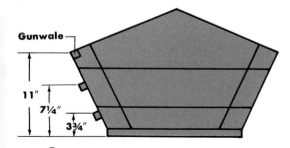

**F**

Figure F: Mark each frame at the heights shown for the bottom and middle side stringers, on both sides of the kayak. Fasten the bottom stringer first, then the middle stringer, following the procedures described in the text.

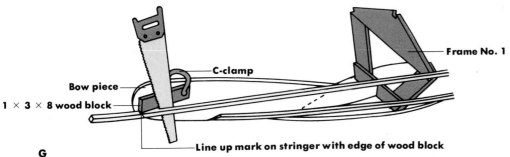

**G**

Figure G: To shape the ends of the stringers so they will fit flat against the bow and stern pieces, use a wood block to hold the stringer against the bow piece at point where the stringer will attach to the bow piece. Hold the saw flat against the block which forms a cutting guide.

The top stringer (the gunwale) on each side fits into notches cut into the outer edge of the upper piece of each frame (Figure A). These notches should match the curvature of the stringer as it passes across each frame. To assure this, clamp the top stringer to the stern and bow pieces so that the stringer lies on top of each frame and is flush with its outer edge. Mark where the inside of the stringer crosses each frame and follow these marks in cutting a ¾-inch-deep notch in the outer edge of each frame. Repeat the procedure on the opposite side. If stringers do not fit snugly in these notches, file the notches until they do. Then, starting with the center frames, glue and screw each stringer into its notches, and then to the bow and stern pieces as you did the bottom and middle stringers.

**Making the Deck Braces**

Six deck braces support the kayak's canvas skin (Figure A). Of the two in the center, one runs from a center notch in frame No. 2 through a center notch in frame No. 1 into a notch near the top of the bow piece. The other runs from a center notch in frame No. 3 through a center notch in frame No. 4 into a notch in the top of the stern piece. Of the four side deck braces, two fit between frame Nos. 1 and 2 and two between frame Nos. 3 and 4. They fit in notches cut halfway between the frames' center lines and the gunwales as indicated in Figure A.

Since the frames and the bow and stern pieces are already in position, use a section of ¾-inch-square stringer to measure lengths of deck supports from the center of frame No. 2 to the end of the bow piece notch, and from the center of frame No. 3 to the end of the stern piece notch. Cut the 3-inch-long notch in the bow piece for the forward center deck support so that the deck support that fits into it will have a slight upward curve. The 3-inch-long notch in the stern piece for the rear center deck support is cut parallel to the top of the stern piece.

Cut the four side deck supports to fit between frame Nos. 1 and 2, and Nos. 3 and 4, as in Figure A. These will fit at the midpoint between the center line in the top of each frame and the outer edge of the top stringer that forms the gunwale. Mark this midpoint on each side of each top frame piece. Then, centering a section of stringer over these marks, make marks on each side of the stringer for the notches. Use the end of the stringer as a template to mark the depth of each notch.

Saw out all notches marked on frame, bow and stern pieces. Predrill holes for 1½-inch No. 8 flathead screws through each deck support, one hole where a deck support fastens to a frame, two where it fastens to a bow or stern piece. Countersink these holes for screw heads. Then glue and screw the deck supports in place.

**Cockpit Housing and Coaming**

Although the cockpit coaming (the raised enclosure surrounding the cockpit) is installed after the boat has been covered with canvas, it should be cut out, assembled and test-fitted in place before the canvas goes on. From an 8-foot length of 1-by-6, cut the two sides and two end pieces shown in Figure H. The depth of these pieces is 5⅝ inches (the actual width of a 1-by-6). Note that the angled cuts made in the bottom of the No. 1 end piece match the angles on the bottom of the top piece of frame No. 2. Hold the bottom of end piece No. 1 against the bottom of the top piece of frame No. 2 and trace the lines for cutting. This cutout area is needed to provide more leg room for the paddler to get into and out of the kayak. The four cutout coaming parts are sanded and then butt-joined as in Figure H, by drilling two ¼-inch diameter holes in each corner and gluing and doweling as shown.

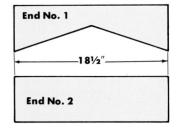

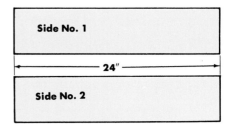

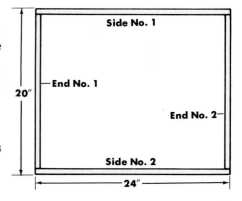

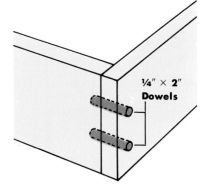

**H**

Figure H: Cut the boxlike cockpit coaming pieces from an 8-foot length of 1-by-6, then glue and dowel them together. Trace angled cuts for the bottom of end No. 1 from bottom of frame No. 2.

973

5: Test-fit the assembled cockpit coaming by placing it between frame Nos. 2 and 3 and centering it on the center line of both frames. Draw lines where each coaming side meets a frame piece. These will mark the position for the two cockpit housing pieces (Figure A) you will install next. Coat plated boltheads and nuts with rustproof primer as insurance against rusting.

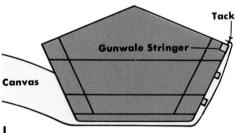

Figure I: Canvas is tacked to gunwale with tacks going into top of the gunwale stringer. Then canvas is pulled up the other side, where it is tacked to the top of the gunwale stringer on the second side. The technique of stretching and tacking the canvas is explained in the text.

## Test Fitting the Coaming

Test the assembled coaming by fitting it into place between frame Nos. 2 and 3 with the coaming level and the center line of the end pieces aligned with the center line of the frames, as in photograph 5. Draw a line down each coaming side where it meets a frame piece. The resulting four lines will mark the position of the two pieces that form the sides of the cockpit housing (Figure A). Remove the coaming and set it aside. Then cut the cockpit housing pieces from 1-by-2-inch-by-2-foot pine, using the distance between frame Nos. 2 and 3 to determine the length of each piece. Use glue and two 1½-inch No. 8 screws to attach each cockpit housing side piece to the frames it fits between, aligning the side pieces along the penciled marks.

With the basic framing assembled, go over the whole interior and exterior with sandpaper, rounding off any sharp edges that might scrape hands or legs or abrade the canvas skin. Use rasp and sandpaper to round the edges of the bottom board (Figure A, inset) so the canvas will fit smoothly over the bottom. Then apply two coats of a wood preservative (we used pentachlorophenol), allowing it to dry thoroughly between coats. Finally apply a coat of marine paint or varnish.

## Covering with Canvas

For this job you will need the help of a friend who can stretch the canvas while you are tacking it. The bottom and sides of the kayak are covered with a single piece of canvas. Spread a 5-by-16-foot piece of canvas under the boat so that its length parallels the length of the kayak and one edge of the canvas laps over the gunwale stringer on one side, as in Figure I. Tack the canvas edge to the top of this stringer at the midpoint of the kayak with a ½-inch aluminum or copper tack. Then, with your partner stretching the canvas so that it fits smoothly along the gunwale, tack the canvas to that gunwale stringer every 6 inches. Work from the middle of the kayak to within 3 inches of the stern, then from the middle to within 3 inches of the bow. Remember to keep the canvas stretched taut (not curved or irregular) as you tack. Now go back and fill in with additional tacks between the first ones, first at 3-inch intervals and then at 1-inch intervals.

With the first side tacked, bring the canvas from under the boat up over the gunwale stringer on the untacked side, and have your partner pull the canvas taut while you tack the canvas to that gunwale stringer. Start tacking in the middle as you did before. Work from the middle toward first one end and then the other, but stop 3 inches from each end. Start with 6-inch spacing, then fill in with 3-inch and then 1-inch spacing. Again, have your partner try to keep the canvas as taut as possible.

Next, turn the boat upside down on sawhorses and trim off the extra corners of canvas on the first side and the excess canvas on the second side. Have your partner stand at the front of the kayak and pull the free end of untacked canvas toward him and to the left so that it fits smoothly over the bow pieces. Tack it to the front of the bow piece, tacking every 6 inches and working from the top (actually the bottom of the upended boat) down. Using the bow piece as a guide, slit any excess from the tacked canvas. Then apply glue to the tacked canvas and, with your partner pulling the other side of untacked canvas toward him and to the right until it is smooth over the bow piece, tack this through the canvas covering to the front end of the bow piece. Remember to space your 6-inch intervals halfway between the tacks holding the first piece of canvas. Trim off any excess as before. Fit, glue and tack the loose pieces of canvas to the stern piece in the same way you did those for the bow piece.

## Covering the Deck

To cover the deck, cut the remaining canvas into six pieces as shown in Figure J. When cutting, allow ¾ inch for the canvas to overlap the gunwale stringer, another ¾ inch for canvas to fit around the inside of the cockpit, and another ¾ inch where the canvas center sections will be overlapped as in Figure K. Glue and tack canvas into the side of the gunwale stringer, around the inside of the cockpit housing, and along the center of the deck supports as shown. Space tacks 1 inch apart.

The next step is to shrink and paint the canvas. Shrinking is done by wetting the canvas thoroughly with hot water. Let it dry, then repeat the process. When it has dried thoroughly the second time, apply a coat of marine enamel.

## Adding the Trim and the Keel

All the tacked seams are covered with wood halfround trim that is cut to size and then painted with one coat of marine enamel before attaching. Cover the seams along the side of each gunwale stringer with ¾-inch halfround, using glue and 1-inch, No. 7 screws spaced 1 foot apart. Cover the deck seams with ½-inch halfround, glued and screwed with ¾-inch, No. 7 screws spaced 1 foot apart.

The next step is to cut out the keel, shape it, give it one coat of marine enamel, and attach it to the kayak. A single piece of ¾-inch halfround clear pine running from the canvas line on the stern piece under the bottom up to the canvas line on the bow piece forms the keel (see inset, Figure A, page 970). The halfround is flexible but it will need some help in order to bend smoothly around the ends of the bottom board and up over the bow and stern pieces.

With the boat upside down, lay the halfround along the center line of the bottom board, mark the areas that will need to be bent and note the approximate outlines of the curves you will need. Then remove the halfround and hold the areas to be bent over the spout of a tea kettle filled with boiling water. Steam these areas for 15 minutes or so until you feel them become pliant, then bend them into the curves you will need. The curves do not have to be exact; the glue and screws will draw the halfround tight against the bow and stern pieces. With the curves set, paint the keel, and allow paint to dry thoroughly. Then apply glue to the flat side of the halfround, and screw the keel to the bottom board with one 2-inch No. 6 flathead screw going through the bottom board into each frame. Then press the bent ends of the halfround up over the bow and stern pieces, and trim and taper each end so that it fits smoothly onto these pieces where the canvas covering ends. Fasten these curved sections of the keel to the bow and stern pieces with glue and 1-inch No. 7 screws spaced 6 inches apart. To keep the kayak from tilting on its side and to protect the bottom canvas from abrasion, add two skids as shown in Figure A inset and Figure B. To make the skids, cut two 4-inch lengths of ¾-inch halfround and round off the front and back edges of each piece. Give these a coat of marine paint and, when that is dry, fasten them through the canvas into the bottom board with glue and two 1-inch, No. 7 screws to each skid, as in Figure A inset.

With the keel and skids in place, coat them and the already painted canvas with two additional applications of marine enamel, following the manufacturer's instructions on drying time between coats.

Next, stain the cockpit coaming you had set aside and then give it two coats of spar varnish. When dry, glue and screw it into position in the kayak using 1½-inch No. 8 screws. Use three screws, equally spaced horizontally, through each coaming end into the abutting frame. Use two screws, widely spaced, through each coaming side into the cockpit housing piece it fits against.

## Using the Kayak

Although this kayak tracks better and is more stable and less tippy than a traditional design, getting into or out of it requires a bit more care than you would apply to entering or leaving a stolid rowboat. To get in, the ideal arrangement is to have the boat in shallow water with someone holding it steady. Place hands on either side of cockpit. Move one foot into the center of the cockpit area. Then, staying low, carefully move the other foot alongside the first one. Using your arms to brace you on either side of the cockpit, gradually lower your body into sitting position, keeping your weight centered in the kayak as you slide your legs under the front of the cockpit frame. To get out, reverse the procedure by using your arms, braced on either side of the cockpit, to lift your body up and back until you can draw your legs back into the cockpit and up into a standing position.

We recommend that you buy the double-ended ("feathered") paddle you will need; it would be difficult to make one. When paddling, try to balance the strokes on either side but put most of your effort into pushing on the upper blade that is out of the water. You will find that this is less tiring than devoting a lot of energy to pulling the lower blade through the water.

If the canvas covering gets torn, it can be patched with a piece of canvas glued over the tear and then painted with marine paint.

For related projects and entries, see "Canoeing," "Sailmaking and Repair."

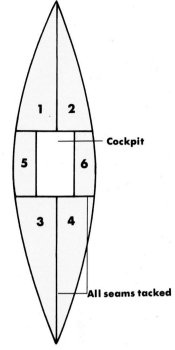

**J**
Figure J: From the canvas left over after covering the sides and bottom, cut six pieces to cover the deck. Allow an additional ¾ inch for canvas to overlap gunwales and cockpit sides and at the seams over the center deck supports.

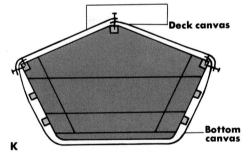

**K**
Figure K: Sections of canvas covering the deck lap over and are tacked to the sides of the gunwale stringers. At the center deck supports, one section of canvas laps over the other and both are then tacked to the top of the deck support.

# KILNS
## The Potter's Fire

*Nancy Baldwin is a potter known for her work in raku, sawdust and salt firing. She has designed and built many kilns with her husband, an engineer, in Northport, New York, where she conducts summer workshops. During the winter, she teaches adult education classes in hand-built and wheel-thrown pottery. She studied pottery making at the Brooklyn Museum School, Greenwich House Pottery in New York City, and the Penland School of Crafts in North Carolina. Her work has been exhibited on Long Island at the Long Island Crafts Guild, the Benson Gallery, Bridgehampton, and Gallery North, Setauket; in New York City at the Fairtree Gallery and with Artists/Craftsmen of New York.*

A kiln is essentially an oven designed for firing and thus hardening pottery. Its invention may have resulted from an accident almost as fortuitous for mankind as the discovery of fire. In the kiln, fire and heat transform clay from a dry, fragile, crumbly substance made of earth, water and air into a tough, durable ceramic with the ability to withstand shock, contain liquid, and in general serve useful and decorative purposes. The fired clay pot is counted the primary utilitarian artifact of almost every known culture. Mundane vessels used to hold water and food in former civilizations are ensconced in museums, proof that kilns are as old as man.

A kiln (pronounced *kill*) can be simply a pit dug in the ground and filled with twigs and branches. An earthenware pot placed on top of the branches, then covered with straw or dung, can be fired effectively as the wood burns; primitive peoples in some parts of the world still use this method to fire beautifully crafted pottery. In more advanced civilizations, heat can be generated in a kiln either by the combustion of fuel or by electricity. Modern kilns are designed and constructed in hundreds of different ways, following a few basic firing principles.

### Updraft, Downdraft

Potters talk about updraft and downdraft kilns as the two major types using fuel. If you have ever built a fire in a fireplace, you have seen the updraft principle in action. As the logs burn, they draw on oxygen in the air of the room and send smoke and heated air up the chimney. The ancient updraft kiln diagrammed at the right was devised by Greeks and used well into Roman times. It was constructed of adobe brick; the fuel—wood—was stoked through the tunnel entrance into the igloo-shaped firing chamber. The pots were placed under the dome and the chimney draft hole was at the top. The heat could be controlled, though not very precisely, by the rate of stoking and by altering the size of the chimney hole, but it was impossible to control the flames as they raced through the firing chamber.

In ancient times, potters discovered that clay became stronger if it was fired at a very high temperature. All subsequent developments in kiln design and construction resulted from attempts to contain, increase and control the heat in the firing chamber. Some of the most efficient and innovative kiln designs came from the Orient where ceramic art reached heights of refinement, notably during the Sung dynasty in thirteenth century China. In one ancient Chinese design for a downdraft kiln, the floor of the firing chamber was built on a long incline with the draft hole at ground level at the far end, opposite the fuel port. This caused the heat to rise and increase gradually before being drawn down and out the draft hole. Today, downdraft kilns incorporate the idea of drawing the heat through the firing chamber on a curving path, then down and out a flue hole near the base, then up a chimney. The word *kiln* is of Japanese origin and once connoted the geographical region from which a traveling potter came with his specialty.

The outline of a large pot is dimly visible through the flames of Nancy Baldwin's gas fueled salt kiln. The pebbly, orange-peel texture that salt imparts to the surface of a pot shows in the photograph of one of Ms. Baldwin's large pieces on page 987.

*Beth Forer combines the talents of linguist, designer and potter, having studied Russian and ceramics at the University of Michigan and industrial design at Pratt Institute in New York. Experienced in all aspects of pottery making, she has a special interest in raku and salt firing. She serves as a consultant on clays and glazes for Firehouse Ceramics, a company in New York that supplies clay to potters.*

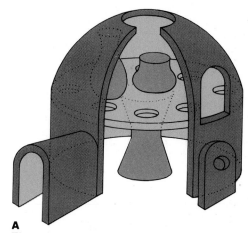

**A**

Figure A: An updraft kiln designed thus was used by the Greeks and Romans of antiquity to fire many of the kinds of pots preserved in museums today. Built of adobe brick, it was fueled with wood. A pedestal supports the perforated firing platform that allows heat to circulate throughout the chamber.

1: Small electric kilns like the one on top suit the needs of a homecrafter in ceramics or enameling. Size has little relevance to firing temperature; the small kiln might fire to the same temperatures as its big brother below.

3: Electric coils set into grooves in the rings provide a radiant heat source in the small electric kiln. The shelf spacers that prop open the rings are among the several kinds of kiln accessories that potters use to create shelves and other supports for stacking pots.

2: Large electric studio kilns have automatic temperature controls to facilitate the firing process. Constructed of removable stacked rings of heat-resistant material covered with stainless steel, they accommodate large loads and big pieces. In the center kiln, two rings have been removed to show a large pot ready for the first biscuit, or bisque, firing.

## Types of Kilns

Most modern kilns, whether fueled or electric, are constructed of special bricks made of refractory materials that can withstand intense heat without disintegrating. The most controlled firing conditions are achieved in large commercial kilns heated by either gas or electricity, which individual potters can rent. But potters often prefer to design and construct their own kilns. Electric kilns commonly used by studio potters and home crafters are pictured above. (See also "Enameling," Volume Six.) Like the electric oven, they work on the principle of radiant heating rather than the combustion principle used in the sawdust and raku kilns described on pages 980 to 985. Electric kilns are safe and easy to use indoors so long as adequate electric current is available and ventilation is adequate. The large kiln costs several hundred dollars and would be suitable for a group of potters to share in a craft studio. It is segmented so the kiln can be made larger or smaller to accommodate firings of different sizes. A small electric kiln such as the one pictured on top of a large kiln (photograph 1) would better suit the needs of an individual potter or enameler working on a small scale. The heating elements, electrical coils set into the rings, are basically the same for all electric kilns, regardless of size.

Most large studios and pottery schools prefer gas fueled kilns since they are more economical to operate than electric. Too, gas kilns are more suitable when a so-called reduction atmosphere is sought to remove oxygen from the clay for special beautiful effects. A salt kiln, which gives another special effect, is also usually gas fueled. In the salt process, at certain times during the firing the potter throws ordinary salt into the kiln through holes, usually removable bricks provided in the sides of the kiln for this purpose. The salt vaporizes, causing an orange-peel texture to form on the surface of the pots (see Craftnotes photograph, page 987). Salt is destructive in the kiln, however, tending to encrust the firebricks and kiln accessories. A wash of alumina hydrate prolongs the life of kiln walls and elements.

## The Fire and the Clay

Fire has a power and a chemistry all its own. It can be creative or it can be destructive, and for this reason, potters consider it both friend and foe. The results of a kiln firing, even under the most controlled conditions, are as unpredictable as they are unexpected. This owes not just to the fire but to all of the variable elements that go into the craft of making pottery. (See "Ceramics," Volume Four and "Pottery," Volume Thirteen.) There are many different kinds of clays, each of which strengthens at a different temperature range. In order to use a kiln properly, the potter must know the properties of the clay he is using. There are also many kinds of glazes (see Craftnotes, pages 986–987) that melt in different firing ranges and thus must be matched with the clay. Clays and glazes that require a high firing temperature are called "high-fired," while those requiring a relatively low temperature are called "low-fired."

Electric kilns can be set so they turn off automatically when the desired temperature has been reached, but in almost all kilns (sawdust and raku are the exceptions) potters use pyrometric cones, pictured at right, to monitor the progress of the firing. These numbered cones are formulated to melt at specific temperatures, as the chart at right shows. General temperature ranges are given for the three over-all categories of clay: earthenware, stoneware and porcelain.

When clay is purchased from a supplier, the firing range is usually indicated on the package by the numbers of the cones to be used. For example, a stoneware clay may call for firing between Cone 8 and Cone 10. When firing this clay, the potter would set three cones, 8, 9 and 10, into a wedge of the same clay and set it inside the kiln in front of a peephole. When Cone 8 melts and bends, as the one at the left in the picture, this indicates that the lowest temperature in the firing range has been reached and warns the potter that the firing is almost finished. When the middle cone bends slightly it means that the firing is completed and the potter must begin to decrease the heat. If the third cone melts, the pottery is probably overfired.

## Biscuit and Glaze Firing

Almost all pottery undergoes two firings. The first, called the biscuit, or bisque firing, strengthens the already dried clay pot so it is safer to handle during glazing (see Craftnotes, pages 986–987). Biscuit firing is a slow process whether you use an electric or a fueled kiln. An average biscuit firing takes 8 to 12 hours. The kiln is then turned off and left closed to cool slowly for at least 6 hours. In a kiln like the large electric studio kiln, a peephole plug is removed after about 6 hours of cooling. If there is not much coming from the hole, the top is propped open slightly and the kiln is left to cool for several hours more.

Biscuit-ware can be stacked for firing one on top of another in the kiln since unglazed pots do not stick together. But when these pots have been glazed and are fired for the second time, they must be placed so they do not touch each other, and the kiln shelves must be coated with a chemical solution, called kiln wash, that prevents sticking. If the bottoms are glazed, the pots must be supported by stilts.

## Oxidation and Reduction

When combustion occurs with plenty of air, the fire consumes oxygen in the air in a process known as oxidation. In a kiln, this occurs naturally and is usually marked by a clean, smokeless flame. The process of reduction, however, occurs when the fire, deprived of sufficient oxygen from air, seeks it out and robs it from the clay and glazes (thus causing their oxygen content to be reduced). Potters in ancient China were the first to discover that beautiful colors resulted from reduction firing.

A reducing atmosphere is easily achieved in a fueled kiln simply by cutting down on the air supply by regulating openings of the burner port and exhaust hole. This creates a smoky condition indicating an excess of unburned carbon. To achieve reduction in an electric kiln, combustible material could be introduced, but this is not recommended as the heating elements in the kiln might be damaged.

In both sawdust and raku firing, described on the pages that follow, the reduction process creates beautiful variations in colors and tones. In raku, reduction is achieved simply and dramatically by putting a hot pot, taken directly from the kiln, into combustible organic material for a short time.

4: Pyrometric cones are placed inside a kiln during the firing as temperature gauges visible through peepholes. Cones are numbered according to the temperature of their melting points and can be purchased to measure a wide range of firing temperatures, as shown in the chart below.

### Temperature Equivalents for Orton Standard Pyrometric (Large) Cones

| CONE NUMBER | | TEMPERATURE EQUIVALENT | |
|---|---|---|---|
| 022 | | 1112°F | |
| 021 | | 1137 | |
| 020 | | 1175 | |
| 019 | | 1261 | |
| 018 | | 1323 | |
| 017 | | 1377 | |
| 016 | | 1458 | |
| 015 | Low-Fire | 1479 | Earthenware |
| 014 | | 1540 | |
| 013 | | 1566 | |
| 012 | | 1623 | |
| 011 | | 1641 | |
| 010 | | 1641 | |
| 09 | | 1693 | |
| 08 | | 1751 | |
| 07 | | 1803 | |
| 06 | | 1830 | |
| 05 | | 1915 | |
| 04 | | 1940 | |
| 03 | | 2014 | |
| 02 | | 2048 | |
| 01 | | 2079 | |
| 1 | | 2109 | |
| 2 | | 2124 | |
| 3 | Mid-Range | 2134 | Earthenware and Stoneware |
| 4 | | 2167 | |
| 5 | | 2185 | |
| 6 | | 2232 | |
| 7 | | 2264 | |
| 8 | | 2305 | |
| 9 | | 2336 | Stoneware and Porcelain |
| 10 | High-Fire | 2381 | |
| 11 | | 2399 | |
| 12 | | 2419 | |

5: The pots above illustrate two finishes that can result from sawdust firing. The pot at left by Anna Deudne was rubbed with yellow ochre and burnished with a spoon before firing. Nancy Baldwin's lidded black box was burnished with a spoon and fired to blackness without any coloring agent. Both pots have been polished—one with wax (left), the other with linseed oil—after firing.

6: After an area of ground of 25 inches square has been leveled, bricks are laid without mortar to form the solid floor of the kiln.

7: Building the unmortared brick walls for the kiln is accomplished quickly as a group effort. Spaces between bricks are necessary to let air in for the fire.

Nancy Baldwin and her students constructed this sawdust kiln with two basic materials: ordinary salvaged building bricks and sawdust. A sheet of scrap metal is used as a cover. The long smoldering of sawdust in this kiln produces earthy tones and black textures, like those on the pots at left.

## Ceramics
# Construction of a sawdust kiln $ ☒ 👫 🏄

A sawdust kiln fires at a relatively low temperature, so it is possible to make the kiln of ordinary red building bricks rather than special firebricks. The bricks I used were salvaged from an old house with the owner's permission. First, lay a base of bricks on a leveled area of ground approximately 25 by 25 inches (8 bricks) square (photograph 6). These bricks should be set into the earth securely and evenly. Then simply build a box of unmortared bricks on this base, laying them row upon row, leaving a ¼-inch air space between every few bricks (photograph 7). The sawdust kiln can be built to accommodate only one small pot, if you wish, or large enough to hold several small pots or one enormous pot. The air spaces are important because they allow air to enter the kiln during firing and this insures an even, continuous burning of the sawdust. As you can see from the photograph above, the completed kiln walls are about 34 inches (8 bricks) high.

Sawdust is a good fuel for two reasons: First, it often can be obtained free with a bit of ingenuity; and second, for all its simplicity, it can produce unique lusters and tones on pottery. I found that to obtain free sawdust, it is best never to call a lumberyard beforehand and ask for it; rather, go there in person with several large plastic bags. Go directly to the area where wood is being sawed and volunteer to sweep up. In most places you will be welcome. With a bit of reconnoitering beforehand, you may be able to discover what time of day the sweeping is usually done and appear at the right moment. Sawdust can be fine or coarse and each gives a slightly different result to the finished pot. Finer sawdust is denser, so it allows less oxygen to reach the pots. The result is a darker, sometimes totally black finish like the box in photograph 5. By mixing coarser chips with the fine sawdust, you may get pots with mottled earth tones like the one at left in photograph 5. I say *may*, as any potter would, simply because the firing is always unpredictable, even in the most sophisticated of kilns. No matter how hard we try to control results with glazes and other finishes there are no guarantees that what we want is what we will get. In fact, it is best not to set your heart on one particular result; that is part of the excitement and mystery of the potter's art.

8: A twig marks a spot 6 inches above the base of the kiln. That is the depth of the first layer of sawdust on which the pots will rest.

9: Fill the pots to be fired with sawdust and, if they have lids, put them on before setting the pots carefully on the 6-inch-deep bed of sawdust.

10: Space the pots evenly on the sawdust, leaving several inches of space between them.

## Firing with Sawdust

We prepare the sawdust kiln for firing by first placing a twig marker inside (photograph 8), about 6 inches from the bottom; we then fill the bottom of the kiln with sawdust up to that marker. I like to mix in some coarser wood chips and pack the fuel down slightly—but only slightly. Do not pour the sawdust from a height. Keep it confined to the kiln as much as possible when pouring. The pots will be placed on the first layer of sawdust, but first they must be filled with sawdust too (photograph 9). Remember that unfired pots are fragile, so don't pack them tight or they might break. If your pot has a top, put it on after filling the pot, then place the piece upside down on the sawdust. As you can see in photograph 10, we place pots 2 or 3 inches apart and about 3 inches in from each side. The pot placed in the middle will often become the blackest, since it is farthest from the air supply. Cover the pots with a second layer of sawdust about 6 inches deep above the tallest pot. Again, mix in some coarser chips. I usually fire one layer of pots in this kiln; but it is easy enough to add a second layer by putting a 4-inch layer of sawdust between layers of pots. I rarely fire more than two layers at a time.

## Toasting the Kiln

When you build a kiln with a group of people, as we have done, one can experience a feeling of kinship and ritual. It is said that the ancient Japanese potters bowed respectfully to the kiln before beginning the firing. The day we built this sawdust kiln, we paid our respects to the kiln god with a little ceremony.

After arranging circles of newspapers on top of the last layer of sawdust (photograph 12), we shared a slice of bread, each of us breaking off a bit and placing the remainder in the center newspaper ring. We then set a candle in the slice of bread, drank a toast, and lit the candle (photograph 11). The flame ignited the paper ring and then all the rings caught fire. As the paper burned down, it ignited the sawdust which began to smolder in only a few minutes. Sawdust must smolder, never catch fire and flame. The large piece of sheet metal that we used to cover the sawdust kiln pictured opposite was obtained at a junkyard. It is set over the kiln as soon as the sawdust begins to smolder and should extend several inches beyond the bricks on all sides to protect the kiln in case of rain. You need a space at least 6 inches deep between the top layer of sawdust and the sheet metal. If you are firing on a day when there is little wind, or if the weather is damp, add an extra layer of bricks around the top rim of the kiln to allow more air to feed the sawdust fire. The sawdust will burn and smolder for many hours, sometimes for as much as a day or more. When it has burned away completely, the firing is finished. The temptation to pluck the pots from the ashes will be great, but it is better to allow them to cool for several hours, until they are cool enough to touch with bare hands. Otherwise, they might crack and you might get burned. Waiting is tantalizing, but fun in its own way, as you will find out.

Sawdust firing is not intended to produce utilitarian pieces. These pots are more fragile than any other kind of pottery and cannot hold soil (for plants), water or food. Many beautiful objects can be made, though, if this is kept in mind.

11: The group that builds the kiln toasts the kiln god and his often unpredictable fire.

12: Circles of twisted newspaper provide a quick way to kindle the sawdust beneath. (A candle placed in the center of a slice of bread has been lit in a ritual gesture that ignites the paper circles.)

13: A metal garbage can with rows of holes punched around the sides can serve as a sawdust kiln for firing one or two pieces. After igniting, put the lid on but leave it ajar.

## A Sawdust Kiln in a Garbage Can

Though it is usual to make a sawdust kiln with bricks, I also use a metal garbage can occasionally to fire one or two pieces at a time (like the large plate in photograph 13). An ordinary galvanized can with a lid works well. To allow air to enter the can and keep the sawdust burning, you must punch out two rows of holes 1 inch apart, the top row 6 inches below the rim of the can. The holes are easily made by laying the can on its side and driving a metal punch or large spike through from the inside.

Fuel and load the can the same as recommended for the brick kiln: Fill the bottom 6 inches with sawdust, place your pot on top (fill it if hollow) then cover with another 6 inches of sawdust to just below the holes. Ignite with paper and when the sawdust is smoking, put the lid on at an angle—do not push it down tight.

## Re-lighting and Extinguishing

In either type of sawdust kiln, the fire might go out if there is not enough breeze to provide air circulation. If the sawdust stops smoking, remove the lid and re-light it, using more newspapers. If the day is particularly still, more air space at the top will help; in the brick kiln, add another layer of bricks around the top.

There is a possibility that the sawdust might catch fire and flare up on a windy day. If you see flames at any time inside the kiln, extinguish them with sand. Keep welding gloves and a bucket of sand handy. Do not use water or you will render the sawdust useless as fuel and ruin your pots. The sand will put out the flames but allow the sawdust to continue smoldering and firing the pots. Flaming does not necessarily mean spoiled pots. Sometimes the fire will mark the pots with flame licks that can be very beautiful.

## Preparing Pots for the Sawdust Kiln

Pots to be fired in sawdust are never glazed, but they must be very dry or they will explode during firing. Use prepared Red-Art clay (available in hobby shops) to form the pots. Whether you form the pot by hand or on a wheel, allow it to dry leather-hard. That means the clay is rigid but still somewhat workable on the surface. By burnishing the surface of the dried clay with the back of the bowl of an old spoon, using a circular motion, a faceted effect is imparted to the pot. A fresh leaf can be burnished into the clay with the spoon and its impression will be burned in during firing. If you use a silver-plated spoon, some of the silver will wear off during the burnishing; some potters think the silver gives a special tone to the clay when this happens. The clay can also be colored by rubbing it lightly with a finger dipped in yellow ochre, a colorant used in glazes (see Craftnotes, pages 986–987). After the pot has been air-dried and treated, it should be oven-dried at about 140 degrees Fahrenheit for 6 to 8 hours before it is fired.

After being fired and cooled, pots should be polished with a chamois, then waxed and polished to bring up their luster. Using a paste wax (transparent car wax, boot polish, or jeweler's compound), rub a thin coat of wax on the pot with your finger. (Not too much; you can always add more but you can't take too much away.) Buff it by hand or with an electric buffer (photograph 14). As an alternative, a finished pot can be rubbed with linseed oil if a deeper color is desired. The small black box (photograph 5) was fired, then rubbed two or three times over a 24-hour period with linseed oil and polished on a buffing wheel. Burnishing is a meditative, quiet kind of work, nice to do alone or with a few friends.

14: Fired pots that have been waxed can be burnished on a powered buffing wheel, as at right, or simply rubbed by hand to bring out the deep lusters and light-catching reflections.

Raku-fired pots made by Rita Sharon display typical variations of grays and blacks, as well as the famous raku crackle especially apparent on the glazed pot centered in the bottom row.

This raku box by Nancy Baldwin demonstrates the potter's sophisticated use of glazes. The box was first covered with white slip (liquid clay) then overpainted with clear glaze. The decorative circles were painted with copper carbonate. (Craftnotes, page 986). Smoked areas and crackle are results of the oxidation-reduction process (pages 979, 984-985).

Nancy Baldwin's outdoor raku kiln has acquired the well-used look that only years of service can give. Designed and built by her, it is constructed of firebricks made especially for kiln use and is fueled with propane gas. Since the bricks are unmortared, the kiln can be disassembled at any time.

**Ceramics**
# A raku kiln

The word *raku*, meaning "enjoyment" or "pleasure", describes a unique method of firing pottery that originated in Japan during the sixteenth century. Raku is often associated with the Tea Ceremony, a ritual expressing the principles of simplicity and harmony with nature implicit in the philosophy of Zen Buddhism. The potter who fires in the raku method is present during every moment of the creative process and is as much an element in the drama as the clay, fire, water and air. A raku-fired pot has a natural, elemental appearance, a kind of raw beauty that contrasts sharply with that of pots decorated and fired under more elaborate and controlled conditions. We see the lick of the flame and the infusion of smoke in the cracks that air and water inflict on the surface of the hot clay and glaze during the brief but dramatic firing process. If you like, a raku piece can be glazed and fired within one hour from start to finish. Firings in most other kinds of kilns take several hours, with the process sometimes lasting for days.

The pots for raku are formed from a special raku clay—a stoneware body with about ⅓ grog (a course ground mixture of fired clay) added to make it porous. Pots are first dried and bisque-fired at cone 04 temperature in an electric kiln (page 978) before firing in the raku kiln. While experienced potters delve into the subtleties of raku and discover a surprising range of possible artistic expression, a beginner can find no better introduction to the potter's art than in building an outdoor raku kiln and firing simple pieces.

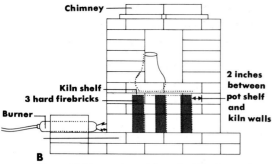

**B**

Figure B: Front view of the raku kiln shows the firebrick construction and the placement of a brick-supported pot shelf in the firing chamber. The gas burner is placed about 4 inches from the burner port.

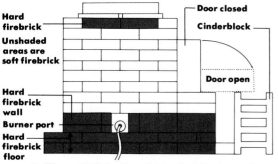

**C** Figure C: Side view of the raku kiln shows the burner port (left) and the cinder block that supports the door when it is open.

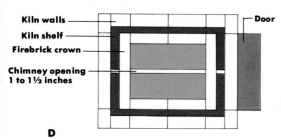

**D**

Figure D: Top view of the kiln shows what is actually the chimney top. Heat escapes through the 1-inch-wide center slot between the two kiln shelves held atop the structure by a crown of firebricks.

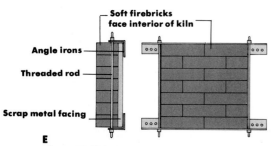

**E**

Figure E: Side view (left) shows a kiln door constructed of firebricks and scrap metal clamped together with L-shaped angle irons, top and bottom, and threaded rods held in place with nuts. The front view of the door (right) shows how the angle irons extend beyond the side edges to serve as handles. The bricked side faces into the kiln.

My outdoor kiln is simply constructed of unmortared firebrick; the fuel I use is propane gas. There are no temperature gauges to worry about but the propane gas tank must always be used with a pressure regulator; the gas company will install this regulator in accordance with proper safety regulations and set it at about 11 pounds of pressure. Just be sure the tank is kept a good distance from the kiln during firing so it does not get hot. Before you construct a raku kiln, however, you should know that local ordinances sometimes prohibit the use of such a kiln because smoke results from the reduction process described below. Away from such population centers, there is no better place for raku than in the open air on a breezy day, surrounded by trees and sky.

### Raku Materials and Tools

The kiln pictured on the preceding page and in the diagrams at left is my own variation of a basic design. It can be made smaller or slightly larger, but for my own purposes this is a convenient size to accommodate a group of six people all firing their pieces during a single day. It accommodates two or three pots at one time, depending on the pot size. It is built of about 50 hard firebricks and 150 soft firebricks, K-23, and requires three kiln shelves (two for the chimney, Figure D, and one to serve as the inner platform on which the pots are placed, Figure B). The door facing is a metal plate purchased at a junkyard. As with the sawdust kiln, there must be tiny air spaces between the bricks at every level to allow air to enter during firing.

A burner which attaches to the fuel tank hose can be purchased from a manufacturer of kilns and kiln equipment such as New England Ceramic in Danbury, Conn.; Alpine in El Segundo, California; and Charles Hones, Inc., in Baldwin, New York. Special long-handled raku tongs (photograph 15) are also needed. I am lucky enough to have a son who is a blacksmith and he makes tongs for me in his nearby forge. Smaller ones can be purchased at a ceramic supply house. The side-door opening on my kiln is, I think, safer and easier to work with than a top opening would be. The door was built of soft firebricks, a metal plate, angle irons and threaded rods (Figure E). The door is supported underneath by bricks and is braced to lean against the mouth of the kiln. When open, the door rests on a cinder block (Figure C). One person can manage to open and close it alone, but it is easier if two people work together.

The over-all cost of a kiln the size of mine with all the necessary equipment is about $200, less if you are a good scrounger and handy at improvising equipment. Major expenditures are for the bricks, gas burner and fuel regulator. Most potters rent the propane tank and buy replacement cylinders of gas as needed.

### The Firing Process

The gas burner is supported by firebricks and is placed with the nozzle about 4 inches outside the burner port in the side of the kiln (Figure B). I turn the burner on and ignite the gas with a spark lighter. The flame should have a 4-inch blue cone with a yellow flag on the end that enters the kiln, hits the hard firebrick wall, and sends the heat circulating around the pots and up through a slot at the top of chimney (Figure D). The kiln door must be closed during firing. It is opened only to insert or remove pots. Some persons put their pots in a cold kiln and heat them up slowly, especially the larger ones, but most pots are placed in a red hot kiln. It takes the kiln about 2 hours to heat up from cold to red hot if it is dry. A wet kiln takes much longer. After the firing is over, the fire is out and the kiln has cooled, cover it with a large auto plastic, tied down, to keep the kiln dry between firings.

A simple test for the right temperature can be made by placing a raw, glazed pot inside the kiln at the outset. When the glaze becomes shiny or looks melted and the kiln is glowing red hot, it is safe to assume that the kiln is hot enough. The excitement I find in raku firing comes from being in intimate contact with the pot during its birthing, in seeing the transformation take place from the moment when I put it into the kiln and begin the oxidation-reduction process (page 979). All along the way, the pot acquires color and texture not only because of what I do to it, but also because of what Mother Nature does to baffle and outsmart me. She always has something new to say about how the finished pot will look.

The process begins with the forming of the pot (see "Ceramics", Volume Four, and "Pottery", Volume Thirteen), and the applying of glaze or color (see below and Craftnotes, page 987). The bisqued pot is allowed to warm and the glaze dry on top of the kiln; then it is placed in the kiln with tongs for the firing.

The organic smoking materials that smoke the clay to effect color changes in the glaze are dried leaves, pine needles and straw in tubs that can be covered with garbage-can lids. These should be arranged near the kiln, no more than a couple of yards away. (Some potters use sawdust for a reduction material, but I dislike it because it tends to become imbedded in the hot glaze, creating too much blackening of the pot.) Nearby, I also have a tub of water, with a cushion of sand on the bottom, and a pile of dry sand. The water and sand are both cooling agents. For fast cooling, I use water. For slower cooling, I bury the pot in sand. If you use a pile of sand on the ground, mark the place where you have buried the pot with a twig so that you won't forget where it is and step on it by mistake.

### Colors and Crackle

Delicate variations of gray and black characterize most raku pottery but other interesting colorations can be achieved. A dramatic effect can result from rubbing the clay with coloring oxides as was done with the mask below (photograph 19). Still another variation is the typical raku crackle apparent on several of the pots on page 983. This effect is the result of fast cooling and shrinking of the glaze while the clay remains hot, when the pot is taken from the hot kiln. If the oxygen-reduction process follows, the cracks are blackened by the smoke. You can actually hear a small tinkling sound as the crackle forms when you hold the pot in the air with tongs. If you wish a very fine crackle, and if the pot is not delicate, it can be plunged into water before reduction. If you try this, you do risk cracking the pot. It is best to allow it to cool in the air until tinkling is heard, then plunge it into the smoking material.

Photographs 15 through 19 below illustrate the basic steps in the reduction process. A pot that is placed in the smoking leaves can be turned slowly with tongs (or by hand if you wear heavy-duty leather welding gloves). The purpose of this is to make sure that the smoke reaches all the surfaces that you wish to be darkened. After reduction, the pot must be either buried in sand or immersed in water to cool it completely and stop the reduction-oxidation process.

There are many variables in the firing of raku. The weather, for example, affects all firings. Firing in cold weather affects the crackling process. Rain or fog keeps the temperature in the kiln down; and glazes can emerge smoky on a damp day. A clear, dry day is ideal for firing.

Because sawdust and raku pots are fired at relatively low temperatures, they are not water-tight and should not be used to hold anything edible. It is only at higher temperatures that all of the possibly poisonous metallic oxides are burned out of both clay and glazes. So enjoy your sawdust and raku pots for their beauty and spiritual values rather than for their utility.

For related entries, see "Ceramics", Volume Four, "Enameling", Volume Six and "Pottery", Volume Thirteen.

15: As a hot piece of pottery is lifted from the glowing kiln with long-handled tongs, fast cooling causes surface cracks, called crackle, to form on the glaze.

16: The oxygen reduction process begins when the hot pot is plunged into combustible material—leaves and straw in a metal tub in this case. If the heat actually ignites the material, as above, sprinkle on a little water, then put a lid on top with tongs to smother the flames.

17: The smoke coming out around the lid of the tub indicates a reduction atmosphere that will produce a variety of special raku colorations on glazed or unglazed pots.

18: A ceramic mask that was rubbed with yellow ochre and fired is now reduced in the tub of smoking leaves and straw. Areas that come into closest contact with the combustible materials blacken.

19: The final dramatic colorations on this haunting ceramic mask by Suzanne Reissman demonstrate one of many effects possible with raku.

A ceramic glaze is a thin layer of clear or colored glass that adheres to the surface of a piece of pottery. (See also "Enameling," Volume Six, and "Ceramics," Volume Four.) By altering the glaze formula (its recipe) and the firing method used, a large variety of textures and colors can be achieved.

Although there is an almost infinite number of possible glaze recipes, all contain three basic substances:
1. Flux, the ingredient that helps make the glaze melt at a given temperature.
2. Silica, glass former and the hardening agent.
3. Clay, the "bones and meat" of the glaze that helps hold and later fuse the glaze onto the pot.

In addition, metallic oxides (or carbonates, which are almost the same but of lesser intensity) can be used to add color to the glaze. One oxide can give widely differing results depending on the amount used, the glaze formula, the clay it is used on, and the firing technique. But with experience and experimentation, results can be predicted in a general way. For example, cobalt oxide or cobalt carbonate almost always gives some shade of blue, though black can also be achieved depending on the formula. Iron oxide produces yellows, browns and reds; manganese gives browns and blacks; chrome gives greens, browns and pinks. Tin oxide is often used, not as a colorant but to give opacity and whiteness to a glaze.

Different firing techniques, too, change the color achieved with any single glaze. The glaze is applied as a liquid that quickly dries to a powder; it will melt at a specific temperature, turning into a thin layer of glass. By altering the firing temperature, a matte or a gloss surface can be achieved with the same glaze. By altering the formula itself, a higher or lower melting point can be established.

Other firing conditions that greatly affect glazes are oxidation and reduction (see page 979). Either can be achieved at high or low temperatures. Oxidation, a burning process, can be effected in almost any kiln, but reduction, lowering the oxygen content of the clay, can only occur in a kiln burning such fuels as gas, propane, or wood—not in an electric kiln.

## Mixing glazes

Mixing a glaze is something like making cake frosting. A specific set of ingredients is combined in a bowl with water to form a liquid the consistency of thick cream. This mixture is applied to the bisque-ware—clay that has been fired at a rather low temperature so the clay is strengthened but is still porous. Then the pot is fired again at the temperature appropriate to the glaze.

There are hundreds of ingredients to choose from, some being more common than others. The list below is a sparse one of bare essentials, but even with these ingredients, hundreds of glazes that will turn to glass at various temperatures can be devised.

## Basic glaze ingredients

To make a starting glaze, you will need whiting (a flux), kaolin (a clay), flint (silica or glass), and feldspar (a flux containing elements of both clay and silica). All of these ingredients—and the colorants mentioned above—come in powder form and can be purchased by the pound. Five pounds of each would be an adequate supply for a beginner.

White lead, red lead and borax are frequently used in fluxing and coloring low-fired ware. Unfritted lead is poisonous, so it should be used with great care; **never use it on dinnerware.** Anyone working with lead should seek advice and guidance from a potter experienced in glaze chemistry and the proper use of chemicals.

Fritting is a process that can make soluble substances, such as lead, insoluble, and thus safer to use. A frit, acting as a flux, is often listed among the ingredients in a glaze recipe (see below), usually for low-fired ware.

## Equipment

A gram scale such as the one pictured above is the most accurate means of mixing glaze ingredients, but it is expensive. A simple kitchen scale can be substituted. The standard basic glaze recipes are calculated on the basis of 100 grams. After the ingredients have been mixed, you will need a measuring cup for pouring the glaze over the ware, a screen (40- to 80-mesh) for straining lumps out of the mixed glaze, and a rubber baker's spatula for pushing glaze through the screen. At all times, observe these basic and important safety precautions: Never eat or drink anything in the area where glazes are being used. Avoid inhaling chemical dust.

# CERAMIC GLAZES

### Glazing procedure

1. Combine all dry ingredients in a bowl.
2. In a second bowl, add a small amount of water. The right amount will come with practice, but in general begin with less than you think you will need.
3. Sprinkle the combined dry ingredients into the water, stirring and adding more water if you need it until the glaze has the consistency of thick cream.

4. Strain the glaze through the screen into a plastic bowl, like the one pictured, using a spatula to break up lumps. Depending on the glaze, it might need to be strained more than once.
5. Apply the glaze to the bisqued pot. Experimentation will acquaint you with the glaze. Sometimes one glaze will give two completely different colors on the same pot in the same firing, depending on the thickness of the application. Usually, unless some predetermined variation is intended, an even coat is the best. The easiest application method is to dip the entire pot into the glaze bucket. It is usually best to glaze the inside of the pot first, so that spills and drips can be wiped from the outside before the final glaze is applied on the outside. This can be done by filling the pot with the glaze and simply pouring it out. (See "Ceramics," Volume Four.) Brushing on the glaze is another application method (this can be used when a decorative pattern is desired, as shown in the photograph opposite). But often brush strokes remain even after the firing and a perfectly even coat is difficult to achieve. The third and most common application method: Simply pour the glaze over the outside of the pot.
6. Be sure when mixing glazes to write down each ingredient and its amount as you add it to the formula. With this record, you will avoid making a mistake if you want to try the same glaze again.

### Glaze recipes

Two of the most commonly used clays are: earthenware (the reddish clay from which flower pots are made), a low-firing clay that would allow for low-fired bright yellows and reds; and stoneware, a high-firing clay that gives earthy tones under high-fire reduction conditions. Firing temperatures for these basic clays are given in the cone chart on page 979. Glaze recipes suitable for both types of clay, including raku, are given below. All measurements are given in grams based on a total of approximately 100 grams. Glazes can be test-fired on small pieces, such as the tiles shown below.

Rita Sharon's small pot, above left, has been freshly coated with a high copper content "calico" glaze. The same pot is shown, right, after raku oxidation-reduction firing.

### Simple raku glazes for beginners

Glen Lewis white, a good crackle glaze:
    80 grams of Gerstley borate (natural)
    20 grams of F4 feldspar

Add to above for: Blue lustre
    2 grams of copper carbonate
    ½ gram of cobalt carbonate

Add to Glen Lewis white for: Red and Yellow lustre
    2 grams of copper carbonate
    8 grams of vanadium stain

### An earthenware glaze (cone 04)
Base:
55 grams of lead monosilicate*
25 grams of frit 3134
20 grams of flint

Colorant (center tile, above):
    10 percent red iron oxide

Colorant, medium blue (tile at right, above): 2 percent cobalt carbonate

Clay fires from cone 09 to cone 3.

*a frit, not a poisonous lead

### A stoneware glaze (cone 6)
Base:
    30 grams of Cornwall stone
    26 grams of kaolin
    20 grams of frit 3110
    15 grams of whiting
    10 grams of flint
     8 grams of lithium carbonate

Colorant, chrome black (gunmetal tile at left in center photograph):
    1 gram of copper carbonate
    3 grams of yellow ochre
    4 grams of vanadium stain

Clay fires from cone 4 to cone 10.

### Commercial glazes

Ready-mixed glazes are available in a wide variety of colors, and if you do not wish to go deeply into the subject of glazes, this is a sensible alternative. However, such commercial glazes are about twice as expensive as the dry ingredients. Also, since they come mixed with water, they have a shorter life than the dry chemicals which remain usable for years if kept dry and cool in sealed containers. The mixing of glazes never ceases to be something of a mystery, even for experienced potters who have taken courses in glaze chemistry. But only by mixing your own ingredients can you learn how all of the potter's elements really work together.

This decorated porcelain box by Nancy Baldwin was glazed and fired in a salt kiln; the salt produced the fine orange-peel surface texture.

# Ancient Craft to Modern Sport

*Andrea Bahadur and Mark Skwarek, partners in the Go-Fly-a-Kite Store in New York City, have collected handmade kites from far corners of the world, helping to introduce many exotic variations in the process. They are craftsmen in their own right and have taught kitemaking at New York's New School for Social Research, in city parks, and at the New York Kite Festival.*

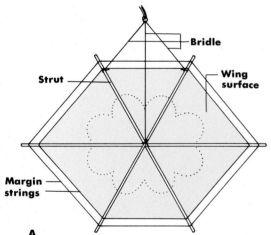

**Bridle**

**Strut**

**Wing surface**

**Margin strings**

**A**

Figure A: Basic to most kites are the struts (support pieces), the wing-surface, the margin strings, and the bridle, which is attached to the tether or flying line.

Almost since time began, man has wanted to fly. Long before he had the science to make a glider he could ride on, he made one—the kite—that could carry him up and away in his imagination. Kites have never lost their power to fascinate, and throughout the world, on wind-struck days, people gather to enjoy the sight as these little gliders catch and ride the wind.

Far from being but toys of childhood, kites are made and flown by adults as well as their offspring, and just what type of kite gains national popularity, and how it is flown, can be a fascinating study in itself. In India, for example, the fighter kite rules the skies. This kite, pictured opposite, was designed for mock battles and in some Indian villages there are skirmishes every day. The true fighter's flying line is glass-coated and the object is for one pilot to steer his kite so its line crosses and cuts that of his opponent's kite, setting it free. In the grander contests, staged between entire villages, the kites are of noble proportions and require team handling. (In this case, when one is loosed, the battle turns into a cross-country race as both teams and, frequently, the crowd join to follow the kite—the winner claiming it when it comes to rest.) Instructions for this kite begin on page 998, but the glass-coated line used for classic battles in India is dangerous and is not recommended for this use.

In Japan, the kite is part of the nation's art heritage, as well as its sporting life. In the past, it was not unusual for a craftsman to spend days making one. Fewer artisans now take up this craft, but even today in some of the remote villages, one will see kite artists at work.

**Construction and Materials**

Making a kite carries some of the excitement of flying one, and on the pages that follow you will find instructions for building several types. These vary greatly in design, and you may want to try them all. While kites differ in appearance, there are several factors common to all which are essential to a successful design.

The basic elements of the kite are the wing surface; the struts, which, along with the margin strings, form the frame; the bridle, which holds the kite at an angle to the wind; and the tether or flying line by which the kite is steered, usually attached to a loop on the bridle (Figure A). The materials used for these parts must be both lightweight and strong, especially those used for the wing surface. Thin plastic films, nylon, Dacron and certain polyesters and non-woven fabrics are excellent, as are the traditional rice paper and reinforced tissue paper. Just which is best is often determined by the design of the kite in question. The sled kite (page 991) can be made from a leaf bag of plastic. The Greek kite (page 992) and Indian fighter kite (opposite and page 998) should be made with colored art or Madras tissue; the dragon kite (page 996) requires rice paper and crepe paper. You will need thin bamboo sticks for some of these kites, and you can carve your own, following the Craftnotes that are given on page 995.

Kites vary in complexity of design as well as in appearance. Of those shown here, the sled is the easiest to make, taking only a few minutes to construct. This is an excellent first project for child or adult. The Greek kite, also easily executed, is beautiful as well—the one shown here was a prize-winner at the 1973 Canadian National Exhibition. The dragon and Indian fighter kites are somewhat more exacting, and you may want to try your hand at one of the others before going on to construct either of these.

Every year there are numerous kite-making contests and fly-ins across the country, where devotees meet to compete and trade notes on new techniques. The large festivals are attended by adults who have enjoyed the sport for years, as well as by children out to test their wings for the first time.

For outdoorsmen, flying a handmade kite is an enticing prospect. Here, devotees admire an Indian fighter kite as it soars above the crowd.

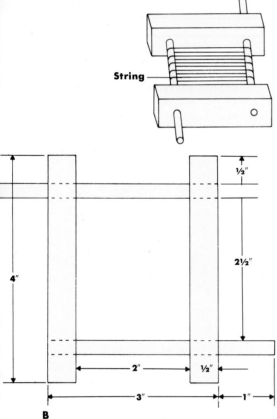

String

½"

2½"

4"

2"

½"

3"

1"

**B**

Figure B: The offset reel, used to hold the kite line, is made from two 4-inch lengths of 1-by-½-inch scrap wood and two 4-inch handles of ¼-inch dowel. Drill holes in the side pieces and glue the offset handles in place.

## Preparations

Before first launching a new kite, you will want to check the wind and weather conditions, find a good site, and gather your equipment. This includes the right types of line, a line-reel, and gloves, if the wind is strong or the kite large.

Kite line, like fish line, has a tested strength that is usually marked on the spool —20-pound-test, 30-pound-test and so on. Any kind of line may be used with a small kite, but nylon and Dacron are preferred, since they are lighter and stronger than cotton. The pull on the line that dictates the tested strength needed will depend upon the size of the kite's wing surface and the angle at which it is flown, as well as on the strength of the wind. So for each of the kites described here, we have recommended the kind and strength of string to use. For convenience and maneuverability, the line is usually wrapped on a reel. The simplest reel is nothing more than a smooth wooden dowel, but you can easily make a larger, more convenient reel (Figure B). You may eventually want to invest in a deepwater fishing reel and a short fishing rod for even greater control in handling the kite, but such equipment is expensive, and for most purposes the reel shown is adequate.

To make the offset handle reel, you need two wood scraps, each about 4-by-1-by-½-inches; two 4-inch lengths of ¼-inch dowel; and some glue. Use the wood scraps for the side pieces, the dowels for handles. Drill holes through the side pieces with a ¼-inch bit, coat one end of each dowel with white glue, and tap the dowels into place (Figure B).

Before deciding whether to fly a kite, or which one to use, check wind conditions. These are classified as follows. *Light breeze:* velocity 3 to 7 miles per hour; will carry smoke and cause leaves to rustle. *Medium breeze:* velocity 8 to 12 mph; will make a flag wave and scatter dry leaves. *Strong breeze:* velocity 13 to 20 mph; will make trees sway and toss. If there is no tree movement at all, the wind is probably not strong enough for kite flying, and if trees are whipping around, it is too windy. If there are thunderclouds, watch out. Lightning is dangerous for kite fliers because the kite line, if wet, may conduct electricity.

Choose a kite and kite line suited to the wind condition, and take this into consideration in deciding how to launch the kite, too. You will find that you can launch a kite from your hand in a medium breeze simply by tossing the kite in the air and playing out more line as it gains altitude. In a light breeze, have a friend hold the kite about 100 feet away from you, and as he releases it, reel the line in quickly. After the kite responds, give the line some slack as the kite climbs. In a strong breeze, the kite may rise quickly, pulling the line along with it, then level off as you stop the line from unreeling. If this happens, the kite will probably nosedive and then turn in a loop. As it climbs out of the dive, take up the slack until you are in control again. Eventually, the kite will climb above the ground wind to the upper wind, which is stronger and steadier.

## Launching and Landing

Choose a kite site that is well away from buildings, trees and power lines—a kite touching a power line might conduct electricity. Fields, playgrounds and beaches are ideal. If the breeze is light and unsteady, try to start from a hilltop; and stay clear of wooded areas where branches might tear the wing surface.

Landing the kite is usually much easier than getting it launched, but there are a few tactics to keep in mind. Reel the line in slowly as you bring the kite down the last hundred feet or so, and if it levels off, give the line some slack to prevent a nosedive. If the kite is fragile, have a friend walk along under the line for the last hundred feet and catch the kite before it touches the ground.

## Making a Good Thing Better

If the kite does not fly as well as you would like, you may be able to set it right by altering the bridle or adding a tail. The sled and Greek kites should require no adjustments. The fighter and dragon kites may. If one of these kites zigzags as it climbs, the line is attached too near the tail of the kite. If the tail end flaps, the line is attached too near the nose. Tying a new attachment loop on the head or tail leg of the bridle changes the angle of flight and will counteract these faults. If the kite continues to wobble, adding a tissue-paper or crepe-paper tail will steady it.

## Toys and Games
# A lofty sled

The Scott sled—invented by an Ohioan, Walter Scott—is a particularly easy kite to make. The frame consists of two dowels taped to the wing surface; the kite is kept open during flight by wind pressure alone. The sled can be made as large or as small as you want, but all the parts should be kept to the relative proportions shown here so the kite will fly properly.

You will need: two birch dowels, ⅛ inch in diameter and 18 inches long— available at hardware, kite and hobby stores; two toothpicks cut to a length of 1½ inches; transparent tape; cotton string; and a sheet of plastic 18 by 24 inches. For the kite shown here, a trashcan liner of 1-mil plastic or a leaf bag is fine. If you decide to enlarge the kite substantially, making it, say, two or three times bigger, 2-mil polyethylene should be used. This can be obtained at hardware stores. Finally, you will need permanent ink (not water-based) markers for making a design on the wing surface.

Begin by cutting the plastic to size (Figure C), then sketch in your design. The geisha figure here, drawn by a Japanese artist, is scaled for easy enlargement and reproduction. If you prefer, create your own design. Make sure, however, to complete this step before going on with the construction. Once the decoration is done, tape the toothpick pieces in place on the two outermost wing tips, then tape the dowels in place (photograph 1).

Cut a 5-foot piece of string for the bridle. Gently pierce the taped corners to make holes for the string, and, after threading one end of the string through each hole, tie each end around a toothpick. Finally, make two knots to act as a loop in the center of the bridle (Figure D), and trim off any excess string.

The sled is a top-notch flier when the breeze is light and steady. If the wind gusts, however, it may collapse. Try to keep the center billowed out until the kite climbs high enough for the steadier upper winds to keep it sailing. The sled should be flown on a 20-pound-test line.

1: The frame for the sled is a simple one—an 18-inch dowel taped on either side of the design. Bevel the dowels at each end or sand them smooth to protect the plastic.

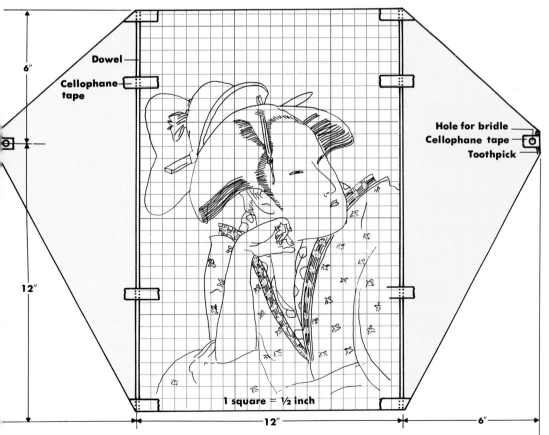

**Dowel**

**Cellophane tape**

6″

12″

12″

1 square = ½ inch

6″

**Hole for bridle**
**Cellophane tape**
**Toothpick**

**C**
Figure C: Using this as your pattern for the sled kite, cut the plastic to the dimensions shown. Enlarge the design onto the kite (see page 57, Volume One), then cut and attach two 18-inch dowels.

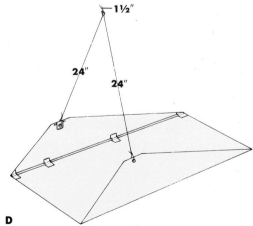

1½″

24″          24″

**D**
Figure D: Attach the bridle by passing the ends of the string through holes made in the plastic. Adjust the string to the length shown and secure it around toothpick reinforcements. At the center of the bridle string, make a loop for attaching the tether line.

The airborne Greek kite looks like a giant flower, bursting with color and trailing clouds of flutter-strips. For all its drama it can be made easily and quickly.

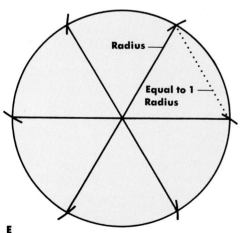

**E**

Figure E: A trick of geometry is used to make a pattern for the 6-spoked Greek kite frame. Use a compass to draw a circle. With the compass set to the same radius, draw six arcs intersecting the circumference of the circle. Connect the arcs with three lines drawn through the center of the circle.

**Toys and Games**

# The Helen of kites

¢ ⊠ 👫 🐢

The beautiful Greek kite, also known as the Toro or barndoor kite, has a six-sided wing surface stretched over three crossed struts. The struts are notched to fit together forming six spokes which are held in place by two rows of string that run around the kite's perimeter. This frame is then covered with tissue paper which is glued to the inner string.

## Materials

You will need: three dowels, 36 inches long and 3/16-inch in diameter; 4-ply cotton string; and white glue for the frame. Brightly colored 20-by-30-inch art tissue paper is ideal for the wing surface. A single-edge razor blade, or craft knife, and a compass with pencil attached, are the only other materials needed.

## Construction

Begin by making the frame. The three dowels must be measured and cut exactly so they intersect in their centers to form six equal angles. A geometric device—dividing a circle into six equal parts (Figure E)—will be helpful here.

Using your compass, make a pattern by drawing a circle with a 4-inch radius on plain white paper. Place the compass point on the circumference, and keeping the compass set to the 4-inch measurement, draw an arc on the circumference (Figure E). Move the point of the compass to this intersection and draw a second arc.

Repeat until the circle is divided into six equal parts and then draw three lines through the center of the circle, so each line connects two opposite arcs. The dowels will be laid over these three pattern lines. But first you must notch the dowels to fit together in the center, and to hold the two perimeter strings.

To do this, mark each dowel at its center, 1½ inches in from each end, and 2 inches in from each end. Using the craft knife, cut shallow grooves at the two end marks, and then carve a notch at the center mark. Each dowel should now be scored at five points: the midpoint, 1½ inches in from both ends, and 2 inches in from both ends. Note that, while two of the dowels have the center notch on one side only, the third is carved out on both sides (Figure F). In following this step, be sure to keep the notches very shallow, as the dowels may break otherwise. Fit the dowels together at the center grooves, and tie them securely with string (photograph 2).

Place the frame over the spoke pattern and tie the margin lines around the frame perimeter. For the inner margin, tie string around one of the grooves spaced 2 inches from the dowel end. Run the string around the frame, making a knot around each groove, and adjusting the struts as you work so they line up with the pattern spoke lines. Tie the second string around the 1½-inch score-marks of the frame, making knots and adjusting the struts as before (photograph 3). Make sure the lines are taut and the dowels straight, then secure the string in each groove by squeezing a drop of glue over it. Let the glue dry before you attach the tissue paper.

The wing surface of the Greek kite is a hexagon of tissue paper that is glued to the inner margin string of the frame. The tissue must be stretched smooth, without tucks, tears or wrinkles, and it requires gentle handling throughout.

Start by gluing two sheets of the tissue together along their 30-inch edge. Overlap the sheets by about 1 inch so you get a sheet that is 30 by 39 inches. Follow the pattern for the tissue (Figure G) to get the general shape, and size it by laying the frame on top of the tissue and cutting around it. Leave 1½ inches all around

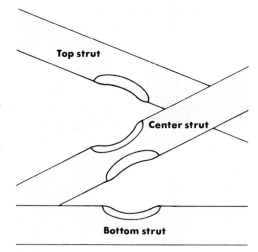

**F**

Figure F: For joining the frame struts, cut two shallow grooves in the center strut and one groove in each of the outer struts. Fit the grooved dowels together as shown.

2: Secure the three struts with lashing, winding string tightly around their intersection point. Tie a square knot to secure the lashing. The grooves will keep the sticks from slipping out of place.

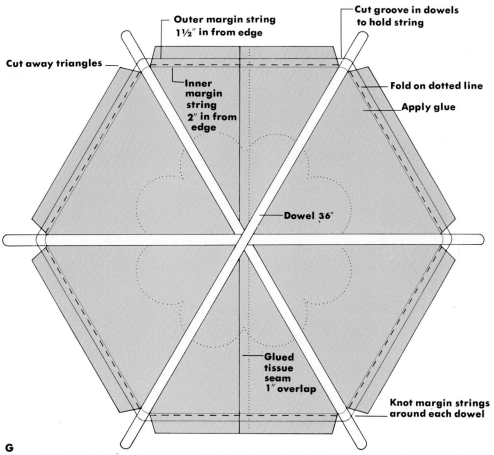

Outer margin string 1½″ in from edge

Cut groove in dowels to hold string

Cut away triangles

Inner margin string 2″ in from edge

Fold on dotted line

Apply glue

Dowel 36″

Glued tissue seam 1″ overlap

Knot margin strings around each dowel

**G**

Figure G: To get the tissue shape you need for the wing surface, lay the frame over the tissue and cut around the outer margin string, allowing 1½ inches extra all around for folding.

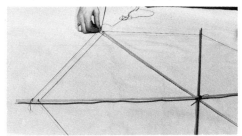

3: Tie two margin strings around the perimeter of the frame. Loop one string around the inner groove in each dowel and knot it firmly. Repeat for the outer margin string. All six sides should be of equal length.

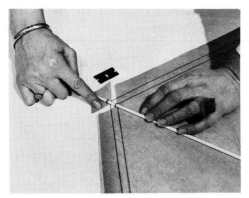

4: Cut away a triangle of tissue at each corner, being careful not to sever the margin strings. When folded, tissue should not overlap sticks.

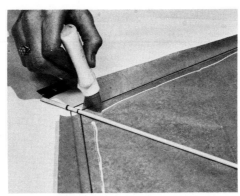

5: Apply a thin line of white glue just inside the inner margin string of the frame taking care to not glue tissue to the struts.

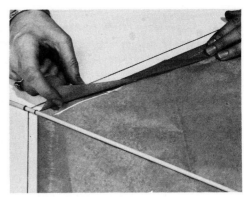

6: Fold the edges of the tissue over the inner margin string on each side and glue flutter strips over the outer margin string.

the outer margin string for folding and gluing the tissue around the inner margin string. Cut away a triangle at each corner to allow for the fold (photograph 4). Then apply glue just alongside the inner margin string (photograph 5), and fold the tissue edges over the string (photograph 6). Do *not* cover the outer margin string.

We attached short strips of tissue to the outer margin string to give the kite a fluttering edge. To do this, simply fold the end of each strip over the outer string and hold it in place with a drop of glue. The strips are approximately ½ by 8 inches, and packing paper, which is already cut to these dimensions, makes an ideal fringe.

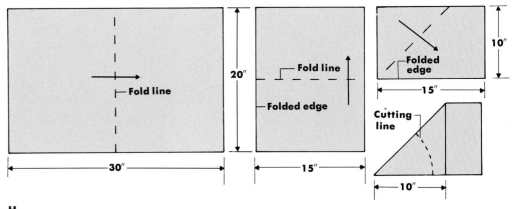

**H**

Figure H: To make the flower decoration, start with a 20-by-30-inch sheet of tissue, folded as shown. When you cut along the dotted line, the folded tissue yields a symmetrical, 8-sided decoration.

### Dressing Up the Kite

The center of the Greek kite is decorated with a colorful, stylized flower. To cut out this 8-petaled version, follow the fold pattern (Figure H), folding the tissue three times in all and then cutting an arc through all the folds. Open the tissue, center it on the kite and glue it in place. You can add narrow strips of tissue to the center, as we did, to make a bustle, cutting these the same length as the fringing strips, or using packing paper. Glue them in small bunches to the center of the flower.

### Before Take-off

The Greek kite has a three-legged bridle, made from two pieces of string, one long and one short. The bridle must be tied to two adjacent upper and lower struts; the center strut, notched on both surfaces, is the weakest of the three (Figure I).

Use a 40-inch length of string for the long piece. Tie to the top strut 2 inches in from the end (Figure I). Measure off 36 inches and tie the other end of the string around the nearest bottom strut. Make this knot just at the edge of the tissue. Make two holes in the center of the decoration, and tie a shorter (24-inch) piece of string around the intersection of the dowels, passing it through these holes.

**I**

Figure I: The bridle for the Greek kite consists of three 18-inch legs made from two pieces of string. The 36-inch string is tied to two adjacent upper and lower struts and is divided into two equal sections by the 18-inch string. The latter is attached to the frame at the center intersection of the three struts.

Measure off 18 inches and tie this string to the center of the long string. All three legs of the bridle should now be 18 inches in length (Figure I). You can check these measurements by pulling the knot to the center of the kite. To make adjustments, slide the knot along the long bridle string. Make a loop to hold the ground line.

The Greek kite has a large wing surface and you will not need to add a tail to make it fly properly. Check wind conditions before flying the kite: Use a 20-pound-test line in a medium breeze, a 30-pound-test line on a windy day.

# CRAFTNOTES: KITEMAKING

### About bamboo and how to get it
Bamboo, a treelike grass with a hard, woody stem, grows in tropical regions, but the things made from it have become popular worldwide. You may be able to get an adequate supply of ready-cut bamboo from old bamboo shades or screens. Old fishing poles or bamboo furniture will be a source for bamboo you can split and carve to size. Another possible source is your carpet dealer—bamboo poles are sometimes used to hold rugs.

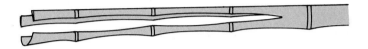

When the pole has been halved, cut out the inner surface of the rings with a sharp knife. Then split each half into three or four sections, each ¼ to ⅜ inch in width.

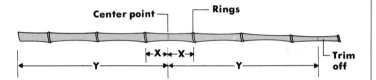

### Trimming bamboo
The split bamboo that will be used should be trimmed so the rings on either side of the center are equidistant from it. Finding the two rings nearest the center of the pole, halve the distance between them to find the midpoint. Using this as the center, measure the bamboo to the desired length and cut off the ends with a hand saw. Use the knife or sandpaper to smooth the rings until they are as nearly flush with the straight grain as possible.

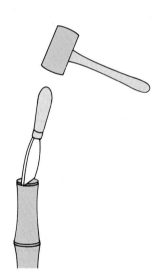

### Splitting bamboo
Start with a pole 4 or 5 feet long and about ¾ inch in diameter. The enlarged rings, or knuckles, spaced along the pole are harder than the straight grain and are difficult to split.

Use a wide wood chisel to split the pole into half-sections, standing the bamboo vertically on a hard surface and holding it upright with a vise. Hold the chisel so that it cuts into the end grain and spans the top diameter. Tap the chisel lightly with a hammer or mallet to start the split. Once it is begun, pressing on the chisel downward with your hand will continue the split. When you get to a ring, however, you may have to use the hammer again to drive the chisel through the harder wood. If this happens, be careful that the chisel does not slip and go across the grain at these points, as that would create a bump on the stick.

### Tapering bamboo
The ends of a split bamboo stick can be tapered to a width of about ⅛ inch. Hold the stick in the center and carve toward the end, cutting away from yourself and turning the stick after each stroke. Continue until the stick is tapered evenly. Finish by smoothing with sandpaper.

When bent, the bamboo should form a smooth, regular curve. Hold one end of the stick in each hand, and gradually move your hands closer together. If there are irregularities in the curve of the stick, use sandpaper to take down the high spots.

The Thai dragon takes to the skies with mock ferocity, as if dragons were meant to fly—and twist and whirl—in a dazzle of grace and colors.

# Serpent in the sky

The Thai dragon kite has a triangular head, painted to look as fierce and forbidding as possible, and a 20-foot-long snaking tail. The dragon will wriggle and twist as it flies but its long tail makes it a stable navigator and all the gyrations just add to the fun. The head has three struts for support—bow, spine and tail-piece (Figure J); the tail floats free and can be made from crepe paper.

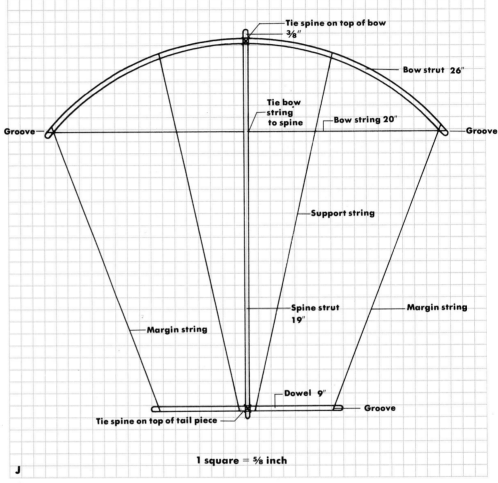

Figure J: To make a pattern for the frame of the Thai dragon kite pictured at left, enlarge this pattern as described in the Craftnotes, page 57, Volume One.

## Materials

For this kite you will need: one 26-inch length of bamboo, cut to be about 3/16 inch thick in the center and tapered at both ends; one 19-inch length, 3/16 inch wide, and ⅛ inch thick; a birch dowel, ⅛ inch in diameter and 9 inches long; a 20-by-20-inch sheet of rice paper, available at stationery and art supply stores, and a package of crepe paper. (To split, trim and taper bamboo, see Craftnotes, page 995). If desired, you can substitute fiberglass rods for the bamboo and sheet Mylar or Tyvek for the rice and crepe paper. These are available in small quantities at kite and hobby shops and sporting goods stores.

## Construction

To make the kite frame, start by enlarging the pattern in Figure J. Begin construction of the frame by starting with the bow. One-quarter inch from each end of the 26-inch bamboo length, cut a shallow groove (1/16 inch deep) going completely around the stick. The bow string will be attached here. Mark the exact center of the

7: Fit the spine over the bow and lash the two lengths together. Wrap the string around the intersection several times, knot it and fix it with a drop of glue.

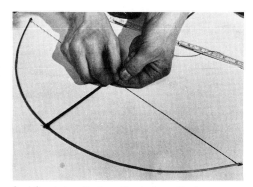

8: After tying the bow line to keep the bow flexed, center it on the spine and tie it with a small piece of string. This will hold the bow in place while you tie the margin strings.

9: Measure the margin strings with a rule, and adjust them until both are the same length. If these strings are uneven the kite will be lopsided and will not fly properly.

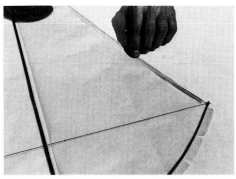

10: Place the rice paper design face down. Apply glue along the edges of the paper, and fold them over the margin strings. Then fold paper over the bow and glue in place.

bow to indicate its intersection point with the spine. Cut a 24-inch piece of string and knot one end of it around one of the bow grooves. Now carefully curve the bow to fit the curve in the pattern. Bend the bamboo until the ends are about 20 inches apart, and knot the free end of the string around the groove at the opposite end of the bow.

For the spine, cut shallow grooves ⅜ inch in from each end of the 19-inch bamboo length, for attachment to the bow and tail-piece. Place the groove at the top of the spine *over* the center of the bow strut, and lash the two pieces together (photograph 7). Then lash the center of the bow string to the spine (photograph 8).

Score the 9-inch birch dowel with a groove ¼ inch in from each end to hold the margin line. Mark the center of the dowel; put it under the spine so its midpoint rests in the groove cut out of the spine and lash the two pieces together.

Tie margin strings to each end of the bow, fastening each string tightly and securing it with glue. Run the margin strings to the grooves of the dowel and make temporary knots. Measure the strings as shown in photograph 9 and adjust them until they are equal in length. Knot the strings securely, fixing all knots with a drop of glue and letting them dry. Cut off excess string.

To get the shape of the wing surface (Figure K), lay the frame on top of a sheet of rice paper. The bow and the dowel should lie flush against the paper; the spine will not touch it. Using the frame as an outline, and working with a single-edge razor, cut around the outside of the bow, margin strings and dowel, allowing 1 to 2 inches extra tissue for folding around the margin strings and bow. Cut narrow triangles out of the bow edge section of the paper so it will make a smooth fold.

**Designing the Dragon**

Paint the head of the dragon on the rice paper, using crayons, permanent-ink markers, or bamboo brushes and black ink. If you like, you can enlarge the pattern shown (Figure K).

To secure the wing surface to the frame, place the rice paper, design face down, on a flat surface and apply glue in a strip along the sides of the paper. Put the frame, spine down, over the paper and fold the sides over the margin strings and bow (photograph 10), gluing it to the bamboo at the top. Do not glue the lower edge of the wing surface as the tail will be attached to this edge. Attach the two support strings in position (Figure J).

Crepe paper, to be used for the tail, comes in sheets 20 inches wide and 10 feet long. Leave the paper folded when you take it out of the package, and cut off two 9-inch-wide pieces. Glue these strips together end to end into a 20-foot strip, unroll the paper tail and taper it to a point. Glue the top of the tail to the bottom of the kite.

In order to attach the bridle, turn the kite face up, and make a pair of holes at the top, one on each side of the spine (Figure L), where you will attach the short leg of the bridle. Measuring 16 inches down from the top, make another pair of holes on either side of the spine to secure the long leg of the bridle. Tie the bridle strings (Figure L), and make a small loop where the lines meet.

Fly this kite in a medium breeze with 20-pound test line.

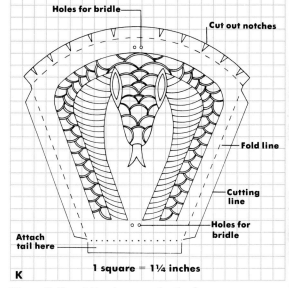

Figure K: To cut the rice paper for the dragon wing surface, place the frame over the paper and trace around it, leaving an adequate margin for folding it over the frame. Then enlarge the serpent head design (see Craftnotes, page 57, Volume One).

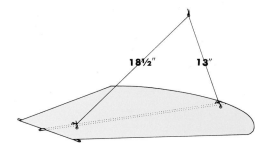

Figure L: Attach the short string of the bridle near the top of the kite, making a knot around the spine. The longer string is attached at the bottom and the two are joined with a knot and loop.

## Toys and Games
# A tricky fighter

The Indian fighter kite, pictured in the air on page 989, looks simple, but it is a challenge to build—and fly. The bamboo must be properly flexed so that the strings and tissue are stretched taut, and the frame must be perfectly symmetrical. If it is even slightly off-balance, the kite will be uncontrollable in the air.

### Materials
You will need: one split bamboo stick, 33¼ inches long, 3/16 inches wide at its widest and tapered to ⅛ inch at both ends; and a second stick, 23 inches long and ⅛ inch wide. These are made by splitting bamboo poles (see Craftnotes, page 995). The best covering for this kite is colored art tissue, available in dime and kite stores. You can also use 5-mil Mylar.

### Construction
The bow is the most important part of the kite. Enlarging the pattern (Figure M), draw the curve of the bow on a piece of 30-inch-square paper. Taper the ends of the bamboo for the bow (Craftnotes, page 995). Holding each end of the bamboo, flex the bow and lay it along the curve. Gradually smooth and trim the bamboo until it fits the curve exactly when you bend it.

Make straight, ¼-inch-deep notches in each end of the bow, cutting into the end grain, and wrap a piece of strong thread tightly around the bamboo just above each notch to prevent the bow from splitting at the ends.

The Indian fighter kite, when properly made and properly launched, rules the skies. To launch this kite, first flex the spine, loose the kite and give it plenty of play as it spins and then ascends.

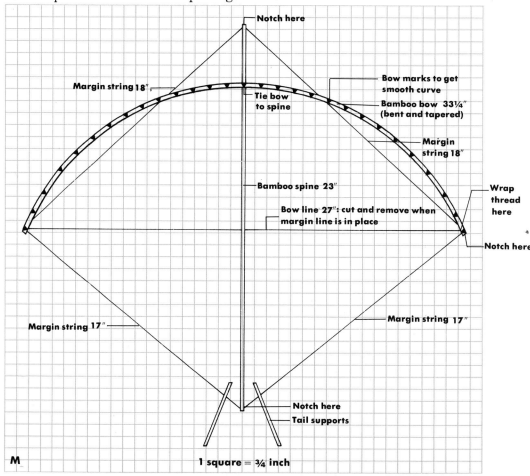

Figure M: To make the frame pattern, enlarge the pattern above on a piece of paper at least 30 inches square (Craftnotes, page 57, Volume One). Mark the bow, as shown on the grid, and draw a smooth curve through these marks. Then draw lines for the spine and tail pieces on the graph. Bend the bow piece until it fits the curve on the graph. Cut two 4-inch strips of thin bamboo to use as tail supports.

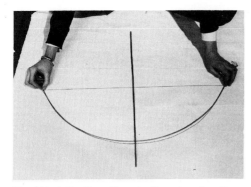

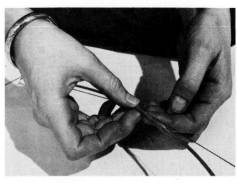

11: Attach the flexed bow to the spine. Lay it on top of the spine, so the center of the bow intersects the spine 3½ inches from the top of the spine. Lash the bow in place on the spine.

12: Measure along the margin string. The two bottom sections should be equal; so should the top. To adjust, tilt the bow and slide the margin string through the notches.

13: Where the string crosses inside the curve of the bow, pull it out to the bow and tape it in place. The pieces of tape on each side should be kept an equal distance from the spine.

Put one end of a 30-inch string into one of the notches and knot it around the end of the bow. Bend the bow until its curve fits the pattern and the ends are about 27 inches apart; then tie the other end of the bow line to hold the bow in this shape. Mark the spine strut 3½ inches from the top, and cut ¼ inch into the grain at each end. Lay the center of the bow over the mark in the spine (photograph 11) and tie the two pieces together. Tie one end of an 8-foot string around the notch in the top of the spine. Run the string from spine-top to bow-notch to spine-bottom to opposite bow-notch and back to the spine-top, slipping it into each notch and knotting it firmly. When you are sure the margin line will hold, remove the cross-line holding the ends of the bow.

Next, measure the string running from the ends of the spine to each end of the bow (photograph 12). The distance should be equal on both sides, about 17 inches for the bottom section and 18 inches for the top section. Make necessary adjustments and put a drop of glue on the string at each notch. Then tape the string to the outside curve of the bow (photograph 13).

The surface of the Indian kite has a reversible design made by gluing together sheets of colored tissue. One such design is shown in Figure N. Glue sections A, B, C and D together, noting that you will need an extra section D.

Lay the frame on top of the tissue wing surface with its bow uppermost. Applying glue along the perimeter of the tissue, fold it over the outline of the string and frame. To support the tail section, lay two very thin 4-inch-long strips of bamboo on top of the tissue paper tail (Section D, Figure N). Cover the bamboo and tissue with a thin layer of glue and overlay it with the extra tail section "D" to reinforce the area. To make the initial piloting easier, add a crepe paper tail. Remove it by stages as you gain experience to maximize maneuverability.

Attach the bridle as shown in Figure O, and test the balance of the kite by holding the loop of the bridle. If the kite tips to one side, it will not fly properly. Add tape to the outermost point of the bow on the light side until the kite is properly balanced.

Near the nose of the kite is a point of stress where the string and the tissue meet the bow, and this should be strengthened with a piece of cellophane tape to prevent the tissue from tearing away. Also use tape to reinforce the tissue at the points where the bridle holes are located, and at the tip of the nose.

Just before you fly the kite, flex the spine. Holding the nose in one hand and the tail in the other, bend the spine toward the bridle. Launch the kite from your hand, playing out 3 to 4 feet of string. It will begin to spin in a circle, and as it reaches the upward part of its turn, give the line a firm tug and play out more string as the kite continues to ascend.

The fighter is a frisky, eccentric kite, and it takes a while to get the knack of flying it. If the fighter dives, slacken the string until the nose turns up again, and then pull steadily in to send the kite upward. Once you have the knack, with a little practice you will have the fighter responding to the slightest tug of your hand—darting from side to side or soaring straight up in the air. Fly this kite only in a light to medium wind, using lightweight 4-ply cotton line.

For related projects, see "Airplanes of Paper" and "Origami".

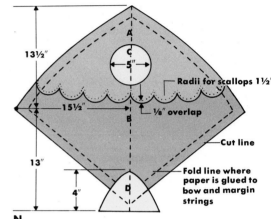

N

Figure N: The fighter kite wing surface is made of shapes cut from Madras tissue. To get the overall size and shape of the wing surface, trace the assembled frame on a large piece of brown paper, allowing a margin for folding and gluing. Draw in the smaller shapes, then cut the pieces apart to serve as patterns. Trace them on the tissue. If the tracing is not symmetrical, fold the tissue in half before cutting. Glue the pieces together, let dry, then glue the tissue edges over bow and margin strings.

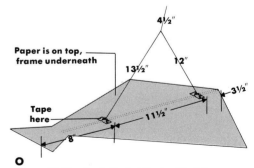

O

Figure O: To attach the bridle, lay the kite tissue-side up. Measure for the bridle holes and reinforce the kite with tape laid across the spine as shown. To make the holes, pierce both tape and tissue. Tie string for the bridle, making the legs 12 inches and 13½ inches long. Hold the bridle by its loop and adjust the balance by adding tape to the bow. The kite should hang evenly when you hold the loop.

# KNITTING TO FIT
# A Matter of Inches

Inches do count. You can know the basic knit and purl stitches, but if a knitted garment is to fit properly you must also know your inches — the inches in your measurements. You can try on ready-to-wear to check the fit before you buy; with your own knitting, you need to be sure of the fit before you start. It can be very frustrating to put a lot of time and love into a project, only to find when it's finished that the size is all wrong. Once you learn to knit to fit, and it's really quite simple, you'll never have that problem again. What you will have is great freedom to create your own designs, to copy clothes seen in expensive shops or magazines, and to make any written directions seem like they were written just for you.

### Know Your Measurements

You need to take two sets of measurements: your actual body measurements and the measurements of a similar-style sweater or skirt that fits the way you like. Everything you make will have an allowance for ease which is added to your body measurements; if you measure something that fits you well there will be no guesswork involved, the ease will have been taken into consideration. The amount of ease depends on the style and the way you like your clothes to fit. The hooded parka sweater, shown on page 1011, has an easy, loose fit so that it can be worn layered over another sweater for added warmth, while the kangaroo-pocket sweater shown on pages 1000 and 1007 is softly bloused above the waist for a fashion look. Turn to page 1003 for Craftnotes on taking measurements for a dress or sweater, pants and a skirt.

### Know Your Gauge

It may seem like a nuisance to knit a 4-inch square swatch that won't be part of the finished project, but this gauge swatch is the most important piece of knitting you will do. Besides, you can put all your gauge swatches together for a patchwork throw someday.

Once you choose the yarn and the stitch, experiment with different size needles until you find the ones that give the effect you want. Some yarn labels suggest needle sizes; generally the yarn and the needles are in direct proportion—the thicker the yarn, the larger the needles. You may vary from this rule of thumb for a special effect, or you can combine several yarns of varying thicknesses for a tweedy or multicolor look. Just be sure to use the exact yarns and stitch for the gauge swatch that will be used for the finished project.

Knit your gauge swatch 4 inches square—any smaller and the gauge may prove inaccurate. Any discrepancy of even ¼ inch will show up in a swatch 4 inches square. Press the swatch lightly and pin to a flat surface. With a tape measure or ruler and straight pins, find both the number of stitches and the number of rows per inch (photographs 1 and 2). In most cases, there will be more rows per inch than stitches per inch. Measure carefully—a fraction of an inch or half a stitch may seem insignificant, but it can make a big difference over the width of a sweater.

If you are following written directions, rather than creating your own, the gauge swatch will indicate whether or not you will achieve the same results as the designer. If your swatch does not measure up to the given gauge, change needle sizes until you find the correct one. Do not try to adjust the tension of your knitting to suit the gauge; this will be difficult to maintain for more than a short time. If you have more stitches per inch than given in the gauge, use larger needles; fewer stitches, use smaller needles. When the stitch gauge is correct, the row gauge usually follows. If not, you can always add or subtract a few rows to make up the difference. Write the gauge on the back of the yarn label and pin this to the gauge swatch for future reference.

Kangaroo-pocket sweater and below-the-knee skirt are knit in the round to eliminate seams and make the knitting easier. Directions and a close-up of the sweater are on page 1007.

*Kathryn Mendel Sorkin creates wearable works of art with yarn and knitting needles. Although influenced by traditional folk crafts, she adds to them her own very modern and colorful sense of design. Kathy is a member of the New York State Craftsmen, does free-lance designs, and has taught adult courses in Norwegian knitting near her home in West Orange, New Jersey.*

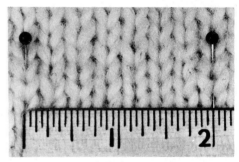

1: Stitch gauge is the number of stitches per inch. Measure even half a stitch—it will make a big difference multiplied across a row. If your gauge differs from that given, change needle size; don't try to alter your knitting tension.

2: Row gauge is the number of rows per inch. If the stitch gauge is accurate, the row gauge generally follows. If not, rows can be added or subtracted to comply with the directions.

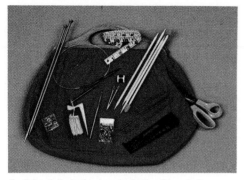

3: A basic knitting bag includes (Top, left to right): Straight and circular needles; tape measure; double-pointed needles, shown here with point protectors; scissors. (Center): row counter; yarn needles. (Bottom, left to right): plastic ring markers; yarn bobbins; crochet hook; straight pins; stitch holders; stitch and needle gauge.

## Abbreviations

| | | | |
|---|---|---|---|
| beg | beginning | rep | repeat |
| dec | decrease | rnd(s) | round(s) |
| g st | garter stitch | sl | slip |
| inc | increase | st st | stockinette |
| in(s) | inch(es) | | stitch |
| K | knit | st(s) | stitch(es) |
| P | purl | tog | together |
| pat | pattern | yo | yarn over |
| rem | remaining | | |

## Comparison of Ounces and Grams

28 grams = approximately 1 ounce
40 grams = approximately 1½ ounces
50 grams = approximately 1¾ ounces
100 grams = approximately 3½ ounces

## Bibliography

Creative Knitting by Mary Walker Phillips; Van Nostrand Reinhold.

Golden Hands Complete Book of Knitting and Crochet; Random House.

A Treasury of Knitting Patterns, Second Treasury of Knitting Patterns, and Charted Knitting Patterns by Barbara Walker; Scribners.

Knitting Without Tears by Elizabeth Zimmermann; Scribners.

Mary Thomas's Book of Knitting Patterns and Mary Thomas's Knitting Book; Dover.

Step-by-Step Knitting by Mary Walker Phillips; Golden Press.

The Textile Arts by Verla Birell; Schocken.

## (Number Of Inches) × (Stitches Per Inch) = Knitting That Fits

It's simple multiplication—you want a sweater to measure 38 inches around the hips and the gauge you've worked out is 5 stitches to the inch, so you cast on 190 stitches. Some patterns call for smaller needles to be used on ribbing or border stitches for a snug fit; the gauge then applies only to the body of the sweater worked on larger needles. Double check written directions to see if the gauge will give you the measurements you want. The pattern may allow more or less ease than you like and it is best to find that out before you start to knit, so adjustments can be made. Be sure to read through all the directions and note in writing any changes in number of stitches or inches before you start—you may forget later.

## Plan Ahead

It's a good idea to plan your sweater or other project ahead of time, using graph paper, to avoid last minute mistakes and ripped stitches. Use one square to represent one stitch and one line of squares for a row of stitches. Your drawing will not be worked to scale or life-size—it will simply be a guide to indicate changes of pattern, increases or decreases or other shaping, and changes of color. With such a guide, you may not even need written directions; you will be able to work directly from the plan. The cap on page 1006, and skirt on page 1008 are planned this way.

A favorite sewing pattern that is designed for sweater knits can also be used as a life-size guide for shaping your knitting. If you work on circular needles, eliminate the seam allowances altogether; if you use straight needles and plan to have seams, narrow the allowances to ¼ inch.

## Tools and Gadgets

As with any craft, the right tools can make the task easier and gadgets can make it more fun. The basic tools for knitting are the needles, either straight for back-and-forth knitting or circular or double-pointed for tubular pieces without seams, such as socks, mittens and skirts. The needles are usually aluminum or plastic with a few odd sizes available in wood. Sizes range from very small, No. 00, to very large, No. 15, with extra large sizes up to No. 50 sometimes used for special yarns. Straight needles come in lengths from 7 to 14 inches; use the longer ones for pieces with more stitches. For pieces with too many stitches for straight needles, use circular needles. Use them, too, when you want to eliminate seams and have the greatest elasticity. Double-pointed needles take some getting used to but they are useful for small seamless areas for which there are no circular needles short enough. Your basic knitting bag should also include a no-stretch tape measure or ruler; stitch holders which look like large safety pins; yarn or tapestry needles for sewing; straight pins and scissors. Other handy items are a row counter, a stitch and needle gauge to check the gauge and the sizes of double-pointed and circular needles which have no size markings (straight needles are marked on the flat end piece), point protectors, yarn bobbins if you plan to work argyle-type color patterns, and plastic ring markers and short lengths of yarn to mark rows and stitches (photograph 3).

## About the Yarn

Yarn will be the first thing you will consider when you plan a knitting project. In fact, it may be the color and texture of the yarn that inspires it. The amount of yarn a particular project will take will be determined by the thickness and the number of yards or ounces in a ball or skein of the yarn you choose. Types of yarn include, but are not limited to: baby and fingering yarns, which are very fine and soft; sport weight yarns, about half the thickness of knitting worsted; knitting worsted, the most popular and widely-available yarn, medium weight and 4-ply; rug yarns; bulky yarns; and novelties such as mohair, chenille and metallics. Ply is the term used for the number of spun single strands that are twisted together to create the finished yarn. The weight or thickness of the yarn is determined by the thickness of each ply, not by the number of plies, because a single strand can be spun to any thickness. For example, the bulky Lopi yarn that I used for the hooded parka sweater is single-ply but quite thick compared to the 2-ply Natuurwol used for the cap on page 1006. Most yarns, however, are 2-ply, 3-ply, or 4-ply and may be natural or synthetic fibers or a blend of both.

The more you knit, the better your instincts will become about the amount of yarn needed for a particular project. If you are designing your own, check written patterns for a similar style and use the amount of yarn indicated there as a guide. Remember that yardages vary greatly and all yarns are not interchangeable. You can use a yarn other than the one suggested by a pattern, but only if it will give you the same gauge.

It is better to buy too much, rather than too little. If you run out of yarn, you may not be able to match the color dye lot. The difference between dye lots may not be noticeable on the skein, but it can be very obvious on a finished sweater. Also, most stores and yarn shops will accept unopened balls or skeins of yarn for return or exchange. Or you can keep extra yarn for use in other needlecraft projects or to exchange with friends. Yarn is one of the most versatile materials around—it need never go to waste.

# CRAFTNOTES: TAKING MEASUREMENTS

Accurate measurements are essential for knitting that really fits. Always measure your knitting and compare the strategic measurements shown at the right. If you are knitting in the round, take the total measurement; if you are knitting flat pieces to be joined later, take the total measurement and divide for front and back or left and right sides, then add no more than ½ inch for seams. In either case, be sure to add an allowance for wearing ease to actual body measurements or measure a favorite pair of pants, sweater, dress or skirt.

When designing your own or changing the written directions for knitting with a color or stitch pattern, always consider the pattern repeat. If the number of stitches needed to make the change do not equal the number of stitches in the repeat, adjust to the nearest number of complete pattern repeats, unless the repeat is very large or intricate. You can always take a larger or smaller seam allowance or compensate when blocking. Knit fabric is very flexible, but it is easier to make a piece larger by blocking than to try to make it smaller. If the pattern repeat is too large or intricate, it is simplest to choose another pattern with a repeat that is adaptable to your size.

## For a skirt
A. Waist
B. Hip at fullest part
C. Length from waist to hip at side
D. Length from hip to hem at side
E. Desired width of hem
Skirts vary in design, but the basic A-line shape is flattering to most figures. Because the front and back are identical, it is easy to knit and can be done without seams on circular needles. An elastic casing waistband is most compatible with the elasticity of the knit.

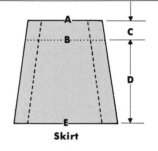

**Skirt**

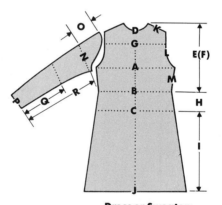

**Dress or Sweater**

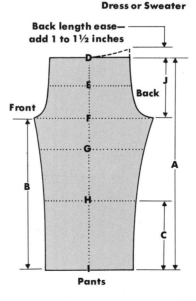

Back length ease— add 1 to 1½ inches

Front

Back

**Pants**

## For a sweater or dress
A. Bust
B. Waist
C. Hip at fullest part
D. Neck
E. Length from neck to waist at front
F. Length from neck to waist at back
G. Width across back at shoulders
H. Length from waist to hip
I. Length from hip to desired hem
J. Desired width of hem
K. Shoulder length
L. Armhole depth
M. Length from armhole to waist
N. Upper arm at widest part
O. Depth of sleeve cap
P. Wrist
Q. Length from wrist to elbow (inside arm)
R. Length from wrist to underarm

## For pants
A. Total side length from waist to hem
B. Inside leg length (inseam)
C. Length from knee to hem
D. Waist (add 1¼ inches total ease)
E. Upper hip (add 1¼ inches total ease)
F. Hip at widest part (add about 4½ inches total ease)
G. Upper leg, 3 inches below the crotch
H. Width around leg just above the knee
I. Desired width of hem
J. Crotch length. (Sit down for this and have a friend measure from your waist to the seat of the chair.)

Because of the elasticity of a knit, you can make a well-fitting pair of pants with an elastic waist and no side opening. Be sure to reverse shaping so that you have a left and a right leg. Pants can easily be worked without seams on circular needles. Each leg is worked separately and then joined just above the crotch where a small seam will be needed. The body is then worked completely around without seams.

# CRAFTNOTES:

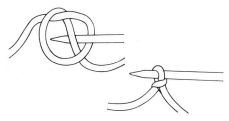

### Casting on with one needle

1. Make a slip knot around the needle, at a distance from the yarn end equal to about an inch for every stitch to be cast on.

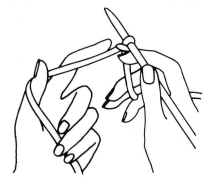

2. Hold the needle with the slip knot in your right hand and loop the short length of yarn around your left thumb.

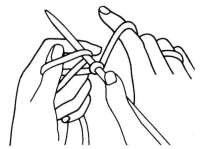

3. Insert the point of the needle under the loop on your thumb, and bring the yarn from ball over fingers of your right hand.

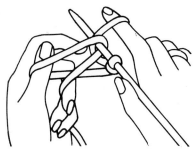

4. Wind yarn from ball under and over the needle and draw it through the loop, leaving the stitch on the needle.

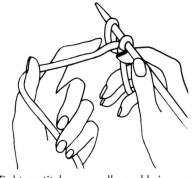

5. Tighten stitch on needle and bring yarn end around thumb, ready for next stitch. Repeat steps 3 through 5 until the desired number of stitches are cast on. Switch needle to left hand in preparation for knitting.

### Knit stitch

1. Hold needle with stitches in your left hand and the other needle in your right hand. Insert the right needle through the stitch on the left needle from **front to back**. Pass the yarn around the point of the right needle to form a loop.

2. Draw this loop through the stitch on the left needle, bringing it onto right needle.

3. Slip the stitch completely off the left needle. Repeat these steps until you have drawn loops through all the stitches on the left needle and onto the right one. You have knit one row. To work next row, change the needle holding stitches to your left hand and free needle to your right hand.

### Purl stitch

1. Hold needle with stitches in your left hand and the other needle in your right hand. Insert the right needle through the stitch on the left needle from **back to front**. Pass the yarn around the point of the right needle to form a loop.

2. Draw this loop through the stitch on the left needle, bringing it onto right needle.

3. Slip the stitch completely off the left needle. Repeat these steps until you have drawn loops through all the stitches on the left needle and onto the right one. You have purled one row. Change needles and work next row.

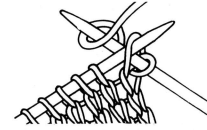

### Increasing

The simplest way to make an extra stitch is to knit or purl the stitch in the usual manner, but do not slip it off the left needle. Instead, insert the right needle into the **back** of the stitch and knit or purl into the stitch a second time. Slip both stitches onto the right needle. You have made two stitches from one.

# STITCHES

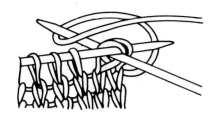

### Decreasing

To decrease one stitch (K 2 tog or P 2 tog) insert the right needle through two stitches on the left needle, instead of the usual one, and knit or purl together.

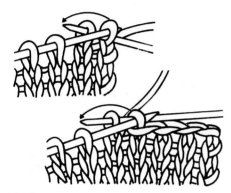

### Binding off

Work two stitches in pattern loosely. With left needle, lift first stitch over second stitch and off the right needle. This is one stitch bound off. Work next stitch and repeat process. To bind off six stitches at the beginning of a row, you will work seven stitches but the last stitch will remain on the right needle as the first stitch of the remainder of the row. To bind off a complete row, continue until all stitches but one are bound off. Break yarn and draw end through stitch, forming a loose knot.

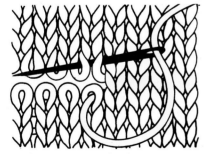

### Weaving

To weave two edges of stockinette stitch together, work on the right side with a yarn needle and a length of matching yarn about three or four times as long as the rows to be woven. Follow the illustration to form new knit stitches between the rows for an invisible finish.

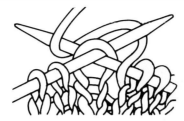

### Yarn over-knit

To make a yarn over (yo) when knitting, bring yarn **under** right needle to front of work, **then over** needle to back, ready to knit next stitch.

### Yarn over-purl

To make a yarn over (yo) when purling, bring yarn **over** right needle to back of work, **then under** needle to front, ready to purl next stitch.

### To slip a stitch

Insert right needle into stitch as if to purl the stitch (unless directions read "as if to knit") and slip stitch onto right needle without working, being careful not to twist it.

### To tie on a new strand of yarn

Join a new ball of yarn or a new color at the beginning of a row on straight needles by making a slip knot with the new strand around the working strand. Move knot up to edge of work and continue with new ball. On circular needles, leave 4-inch tails on the old and the new yarn and weave them into the back of the knitting in opposite directions.

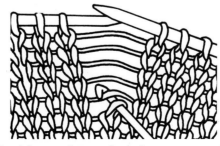

### To pick up a dropped stitch

From the knit side of work, insert a crochet hook through loop of dropped stitch from front to back, hook facing upward. Pull horizontal thread above stitch through loop on hook and onto needle.

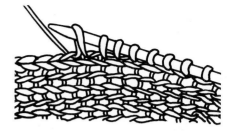

### To pick up stitches along an edge

To add a border along the neckline of a sweater, you will need to pick up, rather than cast on, the new stitches. Hold right side facing you, with edge where stitches will be added at top. Insert needle between first and second stitches and wrap new yarn around needle. Draw yarn through loop and keep on right needle for first stitch. Work this way all around.

### Markers

When directions tell you to "mark beg of rnd," slip a plastic ring marker on needle and always slip it from one needle to the other as you work. If directions read "mark row for turning ridge" or "mark stitch," tie a short length of contrasting yarn around end of row or stitch. Remove all markers when work is finished.

### Work even

Work in the same stitch or color pattern without increasing or decreasing.

### Working with two or more colors

When changing colors within a row, whether working on right or wrong side, pick up the new strand from **underneath** the dropped strand to prevent a hole in the work. Carry the unused color loosely across back of work. If unused color is carried for more than five stitches, twist it **loosely** around other color. Yarn bobbins will keep yarn untangled when working with small amounts such as in argyle patterns.

### Stockinette stitch

Knit 1 row, purl 1 row. On circular or double-pointed needles, knit every round.

### Garter stitch

Knit every row. On circular or double-pointed needles, knit 1 round, purl 1 round.

A tassel cap can be made to fit any size head, adult or child. You can create stripes of color by changing colors each time you change pattern.

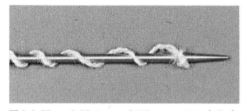

This is Unger's Natuurwol 100 percent wool, 2-ply yarn and a No. 5 straight knitting needle, actual size. (Use any yarn and needle that will give you the right gauge.)

## Needlecrafts
# Tassel cap

Cap is knit in alternating bands of garter stitch and stockinette stitch. For a striped cap, change colors as you change patterns. Key to abbreviations is on page 1002.

*Size:* Instructions are for average adult head size, 21 to 22 inches. To make cap larger or smaller, cast on the number of stitches which, based on the gauge, will give the proper size. Adjust all other references to number of stitches accordingly. *Note:* Because cap should fit comfortably snug, make it *smaller* than actual head measurement to allow for the natural elasticity of the knit.

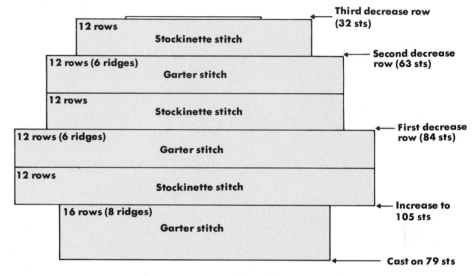

Figure A: Read from the bottom up. Tassel cap is knit in alternating bands of garter stitch and stockinette stitch. Keep cast-on stitches loose enough to stretch comfortably over the head.

*Materials:* Unger's Natuurwol 100 percent wool, 2-ply yarn: 2 balls of No. 5002 Natural White. One pair No. 5 straight knitting needles. Yarn needle. Cardboard rectangle, about 3 inches wide. *Gauge:* 5½ sts = 1 in; 11 sts = 2 ins; 7 rows = 1 in; in stockinette st. Knit stitches are shorter and wider than purl stitches. Garter stitch, which is all knit stitches, has greater elasticity and requires fewer stitches than stockinette stitch. When you combine the two, al- ways keep the garter stitch where you need the most horizontal stretch—at the beginning of a cap, the bottom edge of a sweater. *Cap (Figure A):* Cast on 79 sts, keeping this cast-on edge loose enough to stretch to the actual head measurement. Work in g st (K every row) for 16 rows (8 ridges). *Next row:* K across, inc 26 sts evenly across row (inc 1 st in every 3rd st, K last st) for a total of 105 sts. Work in st st (K 1 row, P 1 row) for 12 rows. Work in g st for 12

4: To make the tassel, wind yarn to the desired thickness around cardboard or another rectangle. (Kathy uses son Charlie's bicycle license plate).

5: Cut through one side of the loops with sharp shears. Don't worry about the tassel falling apart; it is so thick it will stay together until tied.

6: Tie cut loops through the middle and secure with a tight knot. Trim the ends and fluff into a round shape. Use tie ends to sew tassel to cap.

Figure A labels:
- Third decrease row (32 sts)
- 12 rows — Stockinette stitch
- Second decrease row (63 sts)
- 12 rows (6 ridges) — Garter stitch
- 12 rows — Stockinette stitch
- First decrease row (84 sts)
- 12 rows (6 ridges) — Garter stitch
- 12 rows — Stockinette stitch
- Increase to 105 sts
- 16 rows (8 ridges) — Garter stitch
- Cast on 79 sts

rows (6 ridges). *1st dec row:* (K 3, K 2 tog), rep across row. Work in st st for 11 more rows. Work in g st for 12 rows (6 ridges). *2nd dec row:* (K 2, K 2 tog), rep across row. Work in st st for 11 more rows. *3rd dec row:* (K 2 tog), rep across row. *Finishing:* Break yarn, leaving an end about 14 inches long. With yarn needle, draw this yarn end through stitches on knitting needle and gather together. Fasten, and weave back seam from top to bottom with the same end. *Tassel:* Wind yarn around cardboard to desired thickness. Cut through one side of loops; tie other side together for center of tassel (photographs 4, 5 and 6). Trim any uneven ends and fluff into shape. Sew to top of cap.

Collar and cuffs of the kangaroo-pocket sweater are done in a striking figure-eight design of brown and red on camel. Sweater and matching skirt are shown full-length on page 1000.

**Needlecrafts**

# Sweater and skirt

This skirt, and most of the sweater, are knit in the round on circular needles. This means few seams (none on the skirt) and easy knitting. For key to abbreviations, see Craftnotes on page 1002.

*Size:* Instructions are for size Medium (Misses' size 10-12; 33-34 inch bust, 35-36 inch hips). To make larger or smaller, cast on the number of stitches which, based on the gauge, will give the proper size. Adjust all other references to number of stitches accordingly.

*Materials:* Coats & Clark's Red Heart Wintuk 100 percent Orlon acrylic, 2-ply sport yarn: 9 skeins No. 360 Wood Brown, 1 skein No. 905 Red, 1 skein No. 327 Camel. No. 3 and No. 5 circular knitting needles. One pair No. 5 straight knitting needles. Stitch holder. Markers. Yarn needle. One yard ¾-inch elastic for skirt waistband.

*Gauge:* 6 sts = 1 in; 7 rows = 1 in; on No. 5 needles.

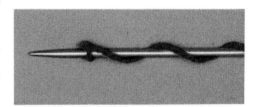

This is Coats & Clark's Red Heart Wintuk 100 percent Orlon acrylic, 2-ply sport yarn and a No. 5 straight knitting needle, actual size. (Use yarn and needle that will give you the right gauge.)

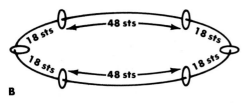

**B**

Figure B: At top of the skirt, put ring markers on your needle where the two side front, two side back and two side seams would be in a six-gore skirt. Increases are made at sides of markers.

7: Sewing the hem directly from needles gives a smoother hemline. If needles get in the way, pull them out a few inches at a time and lightly steam loops. Sew with yarn and yarn needle.

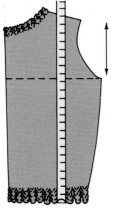

8: Sew the waistband facing to the skirt on the inside with yarn and yarn needle, encasing a circle of elastic inside the waistband as you sew. The elastic will be smaller than the skirt waistband.

**D**

Figure D: To check measurements against the directions, spread the knitting flat to the required width before measuring the length at the center of the piece. Do not measure around the curve of an armhole, but measure the depth on a straight line.

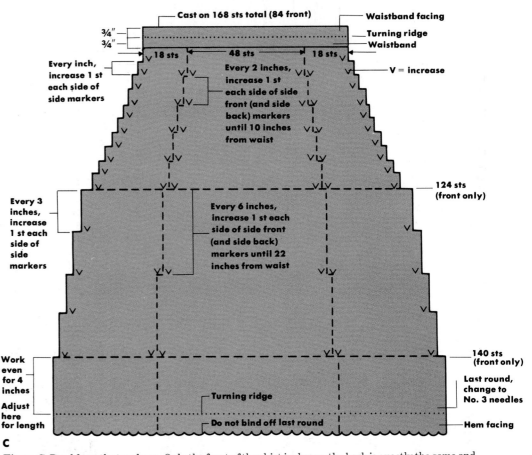

**C**

Figure C: Read from the top down. Only the front of the skirt is shown; the back is exactly the same and is worked in the round with the front, without side seams. This drawing, as any you will make, is not worked to scale. It shows the shape of the skirt and indicates the placement of increases.

## The Skirt

The skirt is knit from the waist down (Figure C), rather than by the usual hemline-up method. The advantages are fewer stitches to cast on and easier hem adjustment. (To lengthen a finished skirt which was knit from the bottom up, carefully pick out the last row of stitches and, working out from the edge, knit the number of rows desired. This works for stockinette stitch and garter stitch, but not for rib or pattern stitches.) Because this skirt is knit on circular needles, there are no bulky seams to sew or diminish elasticity and the only stitch needed for stockinette stitch is the knit stitch. *Waistband facing:* With Wood Brown and No. 5 needles, cast on 168 sts. Join, being careful not to twist sts, and mark for beg of rnd. K for ¾ in. *Next round:* (yo, K 2 tog), rep to end of rnd for turning ridge. *Waistband:* Work even for ¾ in. *Body of skirt:* Next rnd, put markers on needles at what would be the two side front, two side back and two side seams of a six-gore skirt. (Marker already on needles can be used for one side seam.)

There will be 48 sts between center markers and 18 sts between side and center markers (Figure B). *Increases:* Inc 1 st each side of markers every in at sides (4 sts every in) and every 2 ins at side front and side back markers (8 sts every 2 ins) until skirt measures 10 ins from waistband. Total number of sts: 248. Inc 1 st each side of markers every 3 ins at sides (4 sts every 3 ins) and every 6 ins at side fronts and side backs (8 sts every 6 ins) until skirt measures 22 ins from waistband. Total number of sts: 280. Work even for 4 ins (adjust here for hem). Change to No. 3 needles on last row of right side to keep hem from rippling. *Turning ridge:* K all sts through back of loops on next rnd. *Hem facing:* Continue to K for 1½ ins. Do not bind off. *Finishing:* With length of yarn and yarn needle, sew hem directly from knitting needles (photograph 7). Cut ¾-inch elastic to fit snugly around waist, with an extra inch for overlap. Lap ends and stitch securely. Sew waistband with yarn and yarn needle encasing elastic inside (photograph 8).

## The Sweater

*Waistband:* With Wood Brown and No. 3 circular needles, cast on 174 sts. Join, being careful not to twist sts. Work in K 1, P 1 ribbing for 3 ins. *Next rnd:* Change to No. 5 circular needles and inc 26 sts evenly over next rnd (inc 1 st in every 7th st to last 6 sts, K 4, inc 1 st in each of last 2 sts) for a total of 200 sts. Put markers on needle after the 100th st and at end of rnd. *Body of sweater:* Work in st st (K every rnd) for 1 in. *Kangaroo pocket back:* On next rnd, start pocket back and work as shown in Figure E. *Pocket front* is worked separately (Figure F). Pattern—Right side: K 6, sl 1, K 48, sl 1, K 6. Wrong side: P all sts. *Remainder of sweater:* After pocket is joined to body of sweater, work even until work measures 13 ins from beg. *Armhole shaping:* On next rnd, bind off 12 sts for each underarm (6 sts on both sides of side markers). Work front and back separately from now on. *Back:* Dec 1 st each side every other row 4 times (80 sts rem). Work even until back measures 7¼ ins or desired length from underarm to shoulder. *Shoulder shaping:* Bind off 5 sts at beg of next 6 rows (30 sts). Bind off 4 sts at beg of next 2 rows (8 sts). Sl rem 42 sts onto holder for back of neck. *Front:* Work as for Back until Front measures 4¼ ins from underarm. *Neck shaping:* On next row, sl center 26 sts onto holder for neck. Working on one side of neck only, bind off 2 sts at neck edge every other row 3 times. Dec 1 st at neck edge every other row 2 times. Work even on rem 19 sts until piece measures 7¼ ins from underarm or desired length. Bind off 5 sts at armhole edge 3 times. Bind off rem 4 sts. Work the other side of

the neckline, reversing shaping. *Cuff facing:* With Camel and No. 5 circular needles, cast on 49 sts. Join, being careful not to twist sts, and mark for beg of rnd. Work even for 23 rnds. Mark next rnd for turn of hem. *Cuff:* Work in color pat, following chart (Figure G). *Body of sleeve:* Change to Wood Brown and inc 15 sts evenly on next rnd for a total of 64 sts. Continue to work in st st, inc 1 st each side of beg marker every in until there are 84 sts on the needle. Work even until sleeve is 16½ ins from hem marker, or desired length to underarm. *Shape cap:* Bind off 6 sts each side of marker on next rnd. Dec 1 st each side every other rnd until cap of sleeve is 4¼ ins or desired depth. Bind off 3 sts at beg of next 4 rows. Bind off rem sts. *Neckband:* Weave shoulder seams. With Wood Brown and No. 3 circular needles, pick up approximately 130 sts around neck edge. Work in K 1, P 1 ribbing for 2 ins. Bind off loosely in ribbing. Fold neckband in half and slip stitch bound-off sts to wrong side. *Collar:* With Camel and No. 5 circular needles, cast on 104 sts. Join, being careful not to twist sts, and mark for beg of rnd. Work in st st for 32 rnds (underside of collar). Mark next rnd for turning rnd. Work top of collar in color pat, following chart (Figure G) for 23 rnds. Work 7 more rnds in Camel. Bind off. *Collar finishing:* See photographs 9 and 10. Sew long edges of collar to inside of neckband and fold collar to outside over band. *Sweater finishing:* Turn under pocket facings and slip stitch in place. Sew pocket front to body. Sew in sleeves. Turn under cuff facings and slip stitch in place.

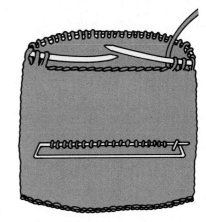

**E**

Figure E: The kangaroo pocket starts 1 inch above the ribbing. Slip 50 stitches at center front onto holder for pocket front. Cast on 50 stitches behind holder, join to body and work around for 5 inches. On next round, bind off center 50 stitches and work around to first bound-off stitch.

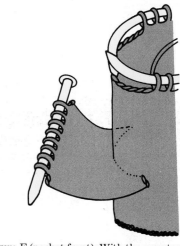

**F**

Figure F (pocket front): With the sweater facing you and using No. 5 straight needles, pick up stitches from holder, casting on 6 stitches at each side. Work in pattern (see text) for 5 inches; bind off 6 stitches on each side; put remaining 50 stitches on needles with body and work around.

9: The collar is knit in the round. To make it flat, machine stitch 2 rows each side of the beginning marker to prevent raveling. Then slash, being careful not to cut the machine stitches.

10: Fold the collar in half lengthwise, right sides outside. Turn short ends of the collar to the inside, hiding machine stitches, and blind stitch the edges together with matching yarn and yarn needle.

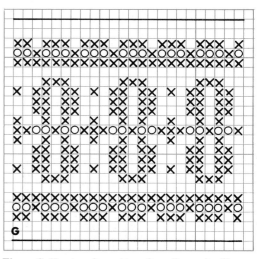

**G**

Figure G: Key to color pattern for collar and cuffs is: **X** = Brown; **O** = Red; **□** = Camel.

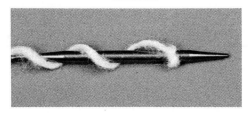

This is Reynold's Lopi 100 percent Icelandic sheep wool, 1-ply yarn and a No. 10 circular needle, actual size. (Use any yarn and needle that will give you the right gauge.)

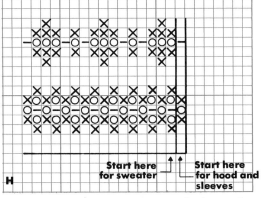

**Start here for sweater**

**Start here for hood and sleeves**

**H**

Figure H: Key to the color pattern for the sweater is: X = Blue; O= White; — = Red; □= Orange.

## Needlecrafts
# Hooded parka sweater

This pullover parka is great for skiers—because of its big, easy shape it can be worn over another sweater for added warmth. See page 1002 for key to abbreviations.

*Size:* Instructions are for size Medium (Misses' 10-12, 33-34, inch bust, 35-36 inch hips). To make larger or smaller, cast on the number of stitches which, based on the gauge, will give the proper size. Adjust all other references to number of stitches accordingly. *Note:* Sweater is designed to fit very loosely, with about 4 inches ease around body. *Materials:* Reynolds' Lopi 100 percent Icelandic sheep wool, 1-ply yarn; 2 skeins No. 71 Red, 2 skeins No. 51 White, 2 skeins No. 74 Blue, 5 skeins No. 67 Orange. ¼-yard Collins & Aikman's Shag fake fur. No. 8 and No. 10 circular knitting needles. No. 10 straight knitting needles. Stitch holders. Yarn needle. Markers. *Gauge:* 3½ sts = 1 in; 7 sts = 2 ins; 4 rows = 1 in; on No. 10 needles. *Pattern Repeat:* 6 sts; 14 rows. *Border:* With Red and No. 8 circular needles, cast on 128 sts. Join, being careful not to twist sts, and mark for beg of rnd. Work in g st (K 1 rnd, P 1 rnd on circular needles) for 2 ins. *Body:* Change to Orange and No. 10 circular needles. Work in st st (K every rnd), inc 10 sts evenly on 1st rnd (inc 1 st in every 12th st to last 8 sts, K rem sts) for a total of 138 sts. Work even in color pat, following chart (Figure H), until sweater measures 16½ ins from start, or desired length to underarm. *Divide for armholes* and work front and back separately from now on (69 sts each). *Back:* Work even in color pat until sweater measures 24 ins from start (7½ ins more). Work next row in Red. Do not bind off, but sl sts onto a holder. *Front:* Work as for Back until sweater measures 20 ins from start (3½ ins more). *Neck shaping:* Sl center 23 sts onto holder for neck on next row. Working on one side only, bind off 2 sts at neck edge every other row twice. Dec 1 st at neck edge once. Work even until sweater measures 24 ins from start. Work next row in Red. Do not bind off, but sl rem 18 sts onto holder for shoulder. Work other side of neck, reversing shaping. *Sleeves:* With Orange and No. 10 circular needles, cast on 46 sts. Join, being careful not to twist sts, and mark for

beg of rnd. Work even in st st for 7½ ins. Work remainder of sleeve in color pat, following chart (Figure H). After 7th rnd, inc 1 st each side of beg marker. Keeping in pat, continue to inc 1 st each side of marker every 1½ ins 3 times more. There are 54 sts on needle. Continuing in pat, work even until sleeve measures 19 ins from start or desired length to underarm. Work next 3 rnds in Red. Bind off. *For sleeves without fur trim:* With Red and No. 10 circular needles, cast on 46 sts and work in g st for 6½ ins. Change to Orange and work 4 rnds before starting color pat. *Shoulders:* With Red and yarn needle, weave shoulder sts of Front and Back tog, keeping center 33 sts of Back on holder for neck. *Neckband:* With Red, sew in sleeves. With red and No. 8 circular needles, pick up 92 sts around neck. Work in g st (K 1 rnd, P 1 rnd) for 2 rnds. On 3rd rnd, dec 5 sts evenly spaced. Continue to work in g st for a total of 1 in. Bind off on a P rnd (photograph 11). *Hood:* With Orange and No. 10 straight needles, cast on 59 sts. Work in color pat, following chart (Figure H), until hood measures 16 ins from start. Do not bind off. With Orange, weave sts tog. (To weave, hold needles side by side and weave sts off needles *or* sl sts off needles and steam lightly to hold their shape, then weave.) *Finishing:* Cut fake fur strip 6 inches wide to fit around front edge of hood. With right sides facing, stitch fur to hood by hand or machine. Turn fur to wrong side, sandwiching edge of hood inside, and slip stitch by hand (photograph 12). Sew hood to inside of neckband (photograph 13). Cut two fur strips about 7 inches wide to fit around cuffs of sleeves. Sew short ends together to form two circles of fur. With right side of fur facing wrong side of sleeve, stitch edges together by hand or machine. Turn fur cuff to outside and slip stitch to sleeve.

For related entries, see "Afghan Stitch," "Crochet," "Granny Squares," "Lace," "Traditional Knitting Patterns."

You don't have to look any farther than this page to find a sweater that's sure to keep you warm on the ski slopes. The hooded parka sweater is made of Icelandic wool yarn and trimmed with fake fur.

## CRAFTNOTES: FINISHING

### Seams

1. To **weave** seams, hold the edges together, right sides up. Using matching yarn and a yarn needle, bring the needle up through the first stitch on the left edge and down through the center of the first stitch on the right edge. Pass under two rows and draw the yarn through to the right side. Insert the needle into the center stitch on the corresponding row of the left edge and continue working from side to side, matching rows or patterns. Keep the seam flat and elastic; do not pull the yarn too tight or it will pucker.

2. To **back-stitch** seams, match rows or patterns and pin them with the right sides together. Make a row of back stitches about one stitch in from edge.

### Blocking and steaming

Put the knitting right side down on a padded surface and pin into shape around the edges. (To help you block to your exact measurements, there is Shape-A-Knit by Stacy, a non-woven fabric blocking aid with ruled guide lines. You can pin your knitting to the reusable fabric and spread it out wherever it is convenient. Look for it in the notions sections of department or chain stores.) Use rustproof pins, a steam iron, and a damp press cloth. Pass the iron slowly over the knitting, holding the weight of the iron in your hand. Do not let the iron touch the knitting, but hold it as close as possible to the surface. Do not block ribbing. Also, 100 percent acrylic yarn will stretch permanently if steam-blocked. Instead, pin it to the blocking measurements, cover with a damp cloth and allow it to dry naturally.

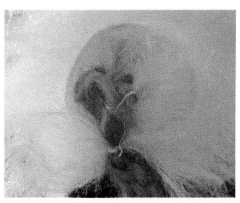

11: Neckband of the sweater is knit in garter stitch with red yarn. The inside of the sweater shows you how the back of multiple-color knitting should look.

12. Sandwich the edge of the hood inside the fur strip. With right sides facing, machine-stitch one edge of fur to the hood, turn fur to the wrong side, and stitch by hand.

13: Sew the fur-trimmed hood to the inside of the sweater neckband. This hood is optional. The sweater is complete without it; no special finishing is needed.

# Bobbins or Needles

*Brigita Fuhrmann is a lace-maker who uses traditional techniques to express her contemporary ideas. She studied textiles in her native country, Czechoslovakia, and in the U.S., including a year at the Rhode Island School of Design. Brigita directs seminars on lace making and her designs have been exhibited in craft shows and featured in several books. She and her family live in Reading, Mass. Brigita is a member of the Boston Weavers' Guild.*

Lace making, with its intricate structures balanced by a freedom of form, is one of the most expressive of all the textile crafts, and certainly one of the most traditional. However, there is growing interest in contemporary lace making that uses modern materials and takes unconventional shapes. So if you think only of bridal gowns and Elizabethan ruffs when you think of lace, consider this: Lace is also a wall hanging, a yarn sash or a modern art necklace, all of which you can learn to make. In a broad sense, the term *lace* embraces any openwork achieved by a textile technique. Such textile techniques as weaving, crochet and knitting can produce openwork as well as solid fabrics. But other techniques from their very beginnings have been used to create *only* openwork, with pattern achieved by threads that are an integral part of the structure. Two of these are needle lace and bobbin lace; therefore, they have been singled out as true laces.

The laces made by these two techniques might on first sight be mistaken for each other. Yet in spite of this design interchangeability, needle lace and bobbin lace differ considerably in their execution. Bobbin lace is a multiple-thread textile worked by twisting and crossing (not knotting) many strands of yarn or thread. It is related to macrame and sprang; the finished lace is soft and pliant. Needle lace is a single-thread textile worked by looping, twisting and knotting one continuous thread around itself with the help of a needle. This technique originated with, and is closely related to, embroidery and is also related to tatting and netting. Needle laces are somewhat stiff and crisp. Making bobbin lace is more like weaving; making needle lace is more like sewing.

This is a detail from a seventeenth-century Dutch painting by Nicolas Maes, "Woman Making Lace."

### Bobbin Lace

Bobbin lace is not limited to any fixed number of threads or any regular shape, so it is free to advance in any direction while it is being made. The multiple threads are wound on hand-held bobbins and the work is attached to a pillow with pins. Bobbin lace is sometimes called pillow lace because of this work surface.

A village church done in needle lace, using a technique similar to embroidery, makes a charming window hanging. Instructions and a pattern are on pages 1021 and 1023.

1: Bobbin lace is sometimes called pillow lace because the work is done on pillows. Sizes and stands vary, but the basic shapes are the bolster and the flat cookie (right center).

2: Pillows for lace making must be stuffed firmly with sawdust, hay or straw. A bolster can be improvised by wrapping several layers of a terry towel around a metal can.

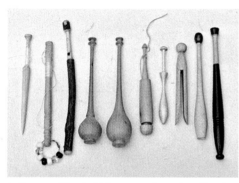

3: Lace making bobbins range from roundhead clothespins and whittled twigs to imported wood bobbins with covers over the shanks and antique bobbins with beaded spangles that dangle from the handles.

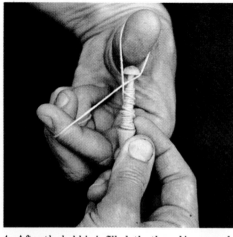

4: After the bobbin is filled, the thread is secured with a simple hitch near the head. Turn the bobbin in the direction opposite that of the winding to release the thread while at the same time maintaining the hitch knot.

## Pillows and Pins

Pillows most widely used are the bolster (the French mini-bolster being one variation) and the flat cookie pillow. The pillows can be held between your knees, set on a table or easel, or cradled in a floor stand or small wooden box (photograph 1). A flat pillow should be inclined at a 45-degree angle to make use of the tension that the bobbins give the threads.

A bolster pillow of any size can be made by sewing a fabric cylinder with flat endpieces and stuffing it solid with sawdust, hay or straw. As an alternative, you can wrap an oatmeal box, coffee can or shortening can with a length of terry cloth, woolen blanket, quilted fabric or other material that is easily penetrated by pins and holds them well (photograph 2). Be sure the covering is thick enough so the pins will not touch the hard core. A bolster pillow is the best kind to use for making lace tapes or continuous yardage. As the work progresses, the pillow is rotated to expose new work area.

To make a flat cookie pillow, simply cover a round piece of ¼-inch plywood with fabric and stuff with sawdust, hay or straw to achieve a rounded-top shape. Cut the fabric cover larger than the plywood to allow stuffing, and stuff it firmly enough so a pin stuck in the pillow will not be pulled out by the tension of the threads. The flat pillow is useful in making flat, shaped pieces such as collars and cuffs because it can be turned and the lace worked on from any side.

The pins should be long and made of brass or stainless steel so they do not stain the lace with rust marks. They should be strong enough to support the weight of bobbins. For fine lace, you can use brass dressmaker pins; for lace made of yarn or cord, use hat pins, glass-head florist pins or T-head pins. You will need to be careful with any headed pin so you avoid catching the lace on the head. Put each pin into the pillow at a right angle or angled slightly away from the work to give the pin strength and to keep it out of the way of the progressing lace.

## The Bobbins

The lace bobbins are spools shaped to be held comfortably in the hands and to be wound with lengths of yarn or thread. The basic parts are the handle, the shank where the yarn is wound, and the head which prevents the wound yarn from slipping off. Bobbins can be purchased at shops specializing in lace making supplies (see page 1015 for the names and addresses of two such shops). Or you can make your own from lightweight materials such as whittled twigs, old-fashioned roundhead clothespins, dowels or wooden furniture turnings (photograph 3). My husband has turned several wooden bobbins for me on his lathe. But the bobbins I use most came from Europe and have covers over the shanks to keep the wound thread clean. The musical clatter of the bobbins is a pleasant accompaniment as I work. If you make bobbins from dowels, choose dowels about ⅜-inch in diameter and cut them into 6- or 7-inch lengths. Cut a groove completely around one tip of each, about ½-inch from the end, to create a head for the bobbin.

To wind the yarn on a bobbin, start at the bottom of the shank, and with the bobbin held upright, wind counterclockwise around the shank. After the bobbin is filled, secure the yarn with a simple hitch as shown in photograph 4. As you work, twist the bobbin away from the direction of the winding to release the yarn a little at a time from the bobbin while maintaining the hitch knot. You can either wind each bobbin separately and tie two together with an overhand knot to form a pair, or cut a length of yarn sufficient to fill two bobbins and wind either end on a separate bobbin. If you run out of yarn on a bobbin while working, attach new yarn to old with a reef (square) knot. Because any knot will be on the top face of the lace, this will become your wrong side. However, except for the knots, the two faces will be exactly alike.

### Parchment Patterns
The stitches of bobbin lace are first drafted on graph paper and this draft is then transferred to a parchment or card stock the weight of an index card in a color contrasting with the yarn or thread. To make the transfer, hold the draft over the parchment and use a needle to prick through the design points which indicate where the pins will go. Outlines of the shape, texture indications, stitch types and the direction of the work can be indicated on the parchment (as well as on the draft) with non-smear ink. The pricked parchment, called the card, is then placed on the pillow and the lace is worked directly on top of it (photograph 5).

### Threads, Yarns and Cords
Traditional lace is made with only fine linen or cotton thread, but contemporary lace doesn't stop there. All types of yarn, macrame cords and twines, metallic threads and fibers—whatever suits your purpose—can be used. Yarns and other soft materials tend to emphasize overall shape and color, while threads and harder cords play up the stitches and the techniques. Linen and cotton threads are graded in numbers, the higher numbers indicating the finer threads.

### Suppliers
You can order lace making supplies and books from these shops (catalogs are available): Some Place, 2990 Adeline Street, Berkeley, Calif. 94703 or Robin & Russ Handweavers, 533 North Adams Street, McMinnville, Ore. 97128.

### Basic Movements
The stitches of intricate looking bobbin lace are all variations of two basic movements, the cross and the twist. Hang two pairs of bobbins over two pins stuck in your pillow close to each other on a horizontal line (one pair hangs from each pin). Hold and manipulate one pair of bobbins in each hand. With few exceptions, all movements are made simultaneously with two bobbins. The pairs of bobbins are numbered 1, 2, 3 and so on from left to right. Each time a pair changes its position, the instructions will refer to it by the number of its *new* position in relation to the other pairs, rather than by its original number.

Cross the right bobbin of the first pair over the left bobbin of the second pair (photograph 6). The two inner bobbins will exchange hands. This is a cross.

Twist the right bobbin of the first pair over the left bobbin of the same pair and twist the bobbins of the second pair in the same manner (photograph 7). The two twists should be done simultaneously using both hands. This is a twist.

The cross is made left over right; the twist is made right over left. This may sound confusing now, but since these two movements are repeated in all the different stitches and grounds, they will soon become second nature.

The combination of the cross and the twist is referred to as a half stitch. If you repeat the cross-twist again, the pairs will change positions completely, and you will have made a whole stitch. Repeating the cross-twist over and over employing the two pairs of bobbins will make a plait or braid.

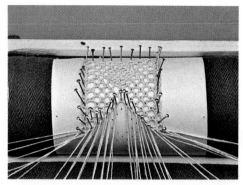

5: Bobbin lace is worked over a sheet of parchment that is pricked with a pattern of pinholes at the design points. As the lace is worked, pins are inserted in these holes to hold the threads in the proper formation.

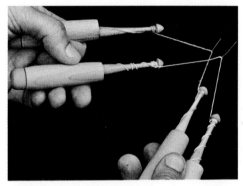

6: The cross is one of two basic movements in bobbin lace. With one pair of bobbins in each hand, cross the right bobbin of the first pair (yellow) over the left bobbin of the second pair (white). A cross is always made left over right.

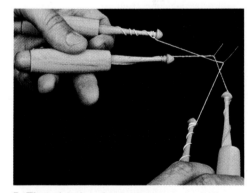

7: The twist, the other basic movement, is always made right over left. (Bobbin pairs are numbered from the left, according to their new positions.) Twist the right bobbin of each pair over the left bobbin of that same pair.

## Sampler of Grounds

A lace ground is the mesh or netting that forms the background or fills in between design elements. It is usually a uniform, repetitive pattern of a stitch using multiple bobbin pairs. Make a sampler of the grounds used in the following bobbin lace projects in order to become accustomed to the movements and to have a handy reference piece.

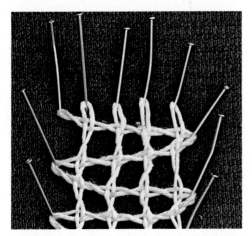

8: A sample of the whole stitch ground, and its draft zigzag line shows direction of leader pair.

▲
## Whole Stitch Ground

The 5 dots in a horizontal row across the top of this draft indicate a row of 5 pins to be inserted into the pillow over which 5 pairs of bobbins will be hung. The zigzag line is drawn to follow the direction of the leader pair (the first pair of bobbins at the extreme left side). The vertical columns of dots indicate the edge pins which will hold the leader pair in place at its turning points. Transfer all the dots to the pricking card as shown. The pairs of bobbins are numbered from left to right as 1 to 5. *1st row:* Cross-twist, cross-twist 1 and 2. Cross-twist, cross-twist 2 and 3. Cross-twist, cross-twist 3 and 4. Cross-twist, cross-twist 4 and 5. The leader pair of bobbins which was on the left side should now be on the extreme right side after weaving through the

other four pairs. Twist this leader pair twice and put a pin in the pricked hole under the twisted pair. *2nd row:* Starting at the right side, cross-twist, cross-twist 4 and 5; cross-twist, cross-twist 3 and 4; cross-twist, cross-twist 2 and 3; cross-twist, cross-twist 1 and 2. The leader pair should be back at the left side. Again, twist this pair twice and pin. Repeat these two rows for the whole stitch ground. Notice that the cross is always made toward the right and the twist is always made toward the left, regardless of the direction of the leader pair. These two basic movements never vary in their direction.

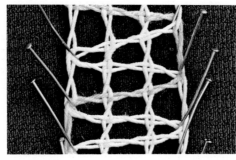

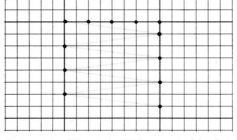

9: A sample of the whole stitch ground with a foot edge, and its draft.

▲
## Whole Stitch Ground with Foot Edge

The same pricking used for the whole stitch ground is used to create a whole stitch ground with a straight, strong edge called a foot. The foot edge is indicated on the draft by short bars connecting the vertical dots. *1st row:* Work the first row of the whole stitch ground ending with cross-twist, cross-twist 4 and 5. Put the pin under both pairs. *2nd row,* starting from the right: Cross-twist, cross-twist 3 and 4; cross-twist, cross-twist 2 and 3; cross-twist, cross-twist 1 and 2; put the pin under both pairs 1 and 2. *3rd row:* Cross-twist, cross-twist 2 and 3, and continue as 1st row. Repeat the 2nd and 3rd rows.

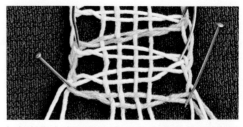

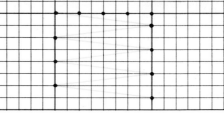

10: A sample of the linen stitch ground with a foot edge, and its draft.

▲
## Linen Stitch Ground with Foot Edge

The same 5 pairs of bobbins and the same pricking are used for the linen stitch ground with foot edge as for the whole stitch with foot edge. *1st row:* Cross-twist, cross-twist 1 and 2; cross-twist, cross 2 and 3; cross-twist, cross 3 and 4; twist 4; cross-twist, cross-twist 4 and 5; put pin under 4 and 5. *2nd row:* Cross-twist, cross 3 and 4; cross-twist, cross 2 and 3; twist 2; cross-twist, cross-twist 1 and 2; put pin under 1 and 2. Repeat these two rows. Notice that leaving out the last twist of the whole stitch in the center of each row changes the character of the stitch considerably, making it resemble woven linen; hence the name linen stitch.

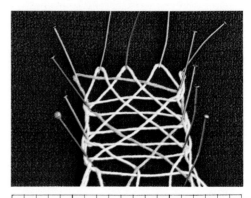

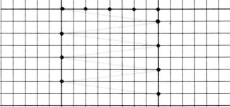

11: A sample of the half stitch ground, and its draft. Draft is same as for whole stitch ground.

### Half Stitch Ground (photograph 11)

This ground has the same draft and pricking as the whole stitch ground, yet it looks completely different in its structure. As the name implies, it is a half of the whole stitch. Again, use 5 pairs of bobbins. *1st row:* Cross-twist 1 and 2; cross-twist 2 and 3; cross-twist 3 and 4; cross-twist 4 and 5; twist-twist 5. Put pin under 5. *2nd row:* Cross-twist 4 and 5; cross-twist 3 and 4; cross-twist 2 and 3; cross-twist 1 and 2; twist-twist 1; put pin under 1. Repeat these two rows.

### Torchon Ground ▶

The whole stitch, half stitch and linen stitch use one or two bobbins for the leaders and basically their structure is on a right angle; the draft for the torchon ground is on a diagonal and all the pairs are equally employed with no one pair called the leader. This draft resembles a smocking pattern.

Draw rows of 4 and 3 dots in an alternating pattern as shown at right. For each alternating row, the stitches are staggered so that each new stitch is formed by splitting adjacent pairs of the two stitches above. Transfer all the dots throughout the design onto the pricking

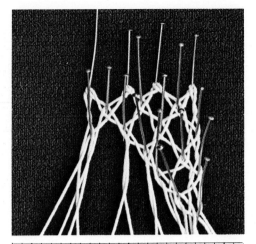

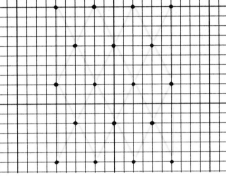

12: A sample of the torchon ground and its draft. Notice that there is no leader pair.

card. Put pins in the top 4 pinholes and hang 2 pairs of bobbins on each pin (8 pairs altogether). *1st row:* Cross-twist 2 and 3; put pin into the left hole of the row below, separating 2 and 3; cross-twist 2 and 3, enclosing the pin in the middle of the stitch; cross-twist 4 and 5; put pin into the center hole of the row below, separating 4 and 5; cross-twist 4 and 5, enclosing the pin in the middle of the stitch; cross-twist 6 and 7; put pin in the right hole of the row below, separating 6 and 7; cross-twist 6 and 7, enclosing pin in the middle of the stitch. In this row, pairs 1 and 8 are not worked. In the next row, they have to be twisted twice before being employed. *2nd row:* Twist-twist 1; cross-twist 1 and 2; pin to separate; cross-twist 1 and 2, enclosing pin; cross-twist 3 and 4; pin to separate; cross-twist 3 and 4, enclosing pin; cross-twist 5 and 6; pin to separate; cross-twist 5 and 6, enclosing pin; twist-twist 8; cross-twist 7 and 8; pin to separate; cross-twist 7 and 8, enclosing pin. Repeat these two rows. In this way, the torchon ground is worked horizontally. You can also work it diagonally (see instructions for bobbin lace sash below).

---

**Weaving, Braiding, Knotting**
# Bobbin lace sash    ¢ ◕ 🜊 🜋

This wide yarn sash is a combination of torchon ground and half-stitch diamonds. It can also be made in a linen thread (photograph, page 1018) and because they are the same thickness, the same draft and pricking can be used for either.

*Materials:* Cylindrical bolster pillow. Knitting worsted yarn, one 4-ounce skein, or linen thread No. 30/12. 18 pairs of large bobbins (such as round head clothespins) on which a length of yarn at least double the desired length of the sash can be wound. Pricker or needle. Parchment pattern. Pins.
*Size:* Red sash as shown is 61 inches long, 4 inches wide, and has 24 pattern repeats.
*Draft and pricking:* The draft (Figure B, page 1018) shows the design points where the pins will be inserted and the half-stitch diamonds are indicated by the zigzag lines. On the pricking, the pinholes forming the outlines of the diamonds will seem to be part of the torchon ground; you may find it easier to follow if you transfer the zigzag lines of the leader onto the pricking with

non-smear ink. Prick 2 cards, each with 2 or 3 repeats of the design, and leapfrog them to get a continuous pattern.
*Sash:* Wind 36 bobbins separately and tie 9 bunches of 4 bobbins together with overhand knots, leaving 3 or 4 inches of ends free to form the fringe. Attach pricked card to pillow. Pin through each overhand knot into the 9 pinholes on the top horizontal row of the card. (There will be 2 pairs on each pin.) The best way to work this design is to complete the torchon ground on the diagonal along the top half of the diamond, work the whole diamond in half stitch, then work the torchon ground along the bottom half of the first diamond and continue to the top half of the next diamond. Refer to your sampler and the directions for torchon ground and half stitch above.

A wide bobbin lace sash worked in bright red wool yarn shows how contemporary lace can be.

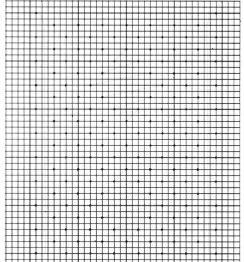

**A**

Figure A: This small draft reduces the width of the sash pattern from 4 to 1½ inches. Smaller bobbins and much finer thread, linen No. 30/3, are recommended. The length is variable; left short, the lace can be a bookmark; long, it can be an insert for a dress or for household linen.

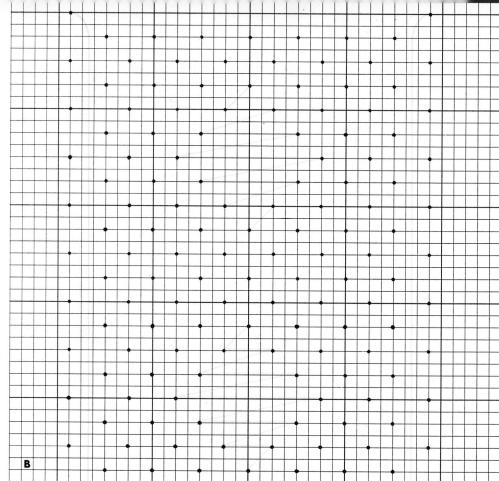

**B**

Figure B: This is an actual size draft (4 inches wide) of a section of the bobbin lace sash to be worked in wool yarn or linen thread. Reuse this draft until the sash is the desired length.

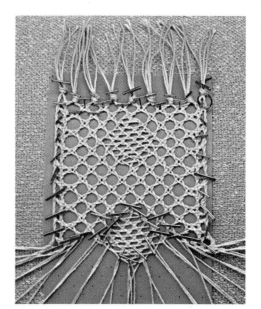

The bobbin lace sash can also be done with linen thread for another non-traditional look.

C = Cross; T = Twist

*Start* (left side of ground): C-T, C-T 2 and 3; T-T 1; C-T, C-T 1 and 2; pin under 1 and 2; C-T, C-T 2 and 3; C-T 4 and 5; pin, separating 4 and 5; C-T 4 and 5, enclosing pin; C-T 3 and 4; pin; C-T 3 and 4; C-T, C-T 2 and 3; T-T 1; C-T, C-T 1 and 2; pin under 1 and 2; C-T, C-T 2 and 3. Continue on the diagonal, each time employing one further pair and ending on the left side, with the foot edge. Observe that pair No. 2 goes straight down; this is the extra pair that strengthens the edge and is indicated by the vertical straight line on the draft.

*Right side of ground:* Work same as left side, starting with C-T, C-T 16 and 17; T-T 18; C-T, C-T 17 and 18; pin under 17 and 18; C-T, C-T 16 and 17; C-T 14 and 15; pin, separating 14 and 15; C-T 14 and 15, enclosing pin; C-T 15 and 16; pin; C-T 15 and 16; C-T, C-T 16 and 17; T-T 18; C-T, C-T 17 and 18; pin under 17 and 18; C-T, C-T 16 and 17. (Pair No. 17 goes straight down to strengthen the edge.)

*The half-stitch diamond* is worked from the topmost point: C-T 9 and 10; pin; C-T 9 and 10; C-T 8 and 9; pin under 8 and 9; C-T 9 and 10; C-T 10 and 11; pin under 10 and 11; C-T 9 and 10; C-T 8 and 9; C-T 7 and 8; pin under 7 and 8; C-T 8 and 9; C-T 9 and 10; C-T 10 and 11; C-T 11 and 12; pin under 11 and 12; C-T 10 and 11; C-T 9 and 10; C-T 8 and 9; C-T 7 and 8; C-T, C-T 6 and 7; pin under 6 and 7; C-T 7 and 8; C-T, C-T 8 and 9; C-T 9 and 10; C-T 10 and 11; C-T 11 and 12; C-T, C-T 12 and 13; pin under 12 and 13; C-T 11 and 12; C-T 10 and 11; C-T 9 and 10; C-T 8 and 9; C-T 7 and 8; pin under 7 and 8; C-T 8 and 9; C-T 9 and 10; C-T 10 and 11; C-T 11 and 12; pin under 11 and 12; C-T 10 and 11; C-T 9 and 10; C-T 8 and 9; pin under 8 and 9; C-T 9 and 10; pin; C-T 9 and 10. Continue working the torchon ground to the outline of the next diamond. When two repeats are finished, remove the pins near the top and roll the finished work onto itself. Do this as you go along the length of the sash. Finish the last repeat on a horizontal line, with one row of torchon ground stitches below the bottom point of the last diamond. Unwind the remaining yarn from the bobbins and tie 9 bunches of 4 strands each with overhand knots for fringe. Trim ends.

**Weaving, Braiding, Knotting**
# Bobbin lace collar and cuffs ¢ ● ♦ ⚙

This collar-and-cuffs set was designed to fit a particular dress, but the curved-tape design is adaptable to other sizes and shapes. If the patterns given on page 1020 won't fit your dress, use pieces from a sewing pattern or design your own.

A bobbin lace collar and cuffs adorn a dress worn by Nancy Bellantone, Brigita's neighbor. This dress is an original design by Nancy's mother, but you can adapt the lace pattern to fit any style of neckline and sleeves.

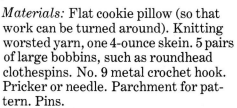

A close-up view of one half of the collar details the curves of the lace tape and the sewings that join it together. The straight edge is sewn to the inside of the dress neckline.

*Materials:* Flat cookie pillow (so that work can be turned around). Knitting worsted yarn, one 4-ounce skein. 5 pairs of large bobbins, such as roundhead clothespins. No. 9 metal crochet hook. Pricker or needle. Parchment for pattern. Pins.

*Size:* Each half of the collar is about 10 inches long on the inner edge. Each cuff is about 9 inches long. Can be adapted to fit any neckline and sleeve.

*Stitches:* Whole stitch and linen stitch. This lace is worked in a narrow tape and involves turning and attaching sections

of the tape together.

*Variation:* This design can also be used as an edging for a round doily (detail photograph this page and Figure C). The tape is much narrower and is worked with No. 50 cotton sewing thread. Directions are exactly the same as those for the cuff.

*Draft and pricking:* Graph paper cannot be used for this draft since this lace does not follow a straight line. Actually, designing the curving of the tape is very easy. If you choose to follow shapes other than those given in Figure D,

This delicate thread edging for a round doily shows how versatile lace can be; the scalloped lace is the same as the pattern for the yarn collar and cuffs, but on a smaller scale (Figure C).

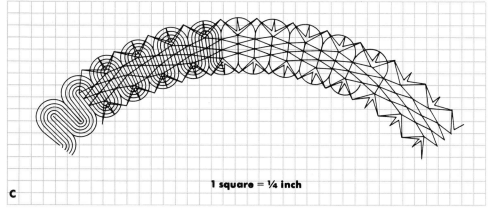

**1 square = ¼ inch**

C

Figure C: A draft for a scalloped doily edging is same pattern as is used in the collar and cuffs. One-quarter of the complete circle is shown. For how to enlarge this pattern, see page 57, Volume One.

page 1020, try to keep the tape a uniform width throughout for best results. You may find it helpful to transfer the design outlines and directional lines from the draft onto the pricking card with non-smear ink.

*Cuff:* Attach the pricked card to the pillow. In the center of the straight edge, put 5 pins an equal distance apart on one zigzag line which slants as in Figure D. Turn the pillow so that the scalloped edge is on the right and the straight edge is on the left. This will cause the line of pins to slope down to the right. Hang one pair of bobbins on each pin.

*C = Cross; T = Twist*

*1st row (starting at the left):* C-T, C-T 1 and 2; C-T, C 2 and 3; C-T, C 3 and 4; C-T, C 4 and 5; T-T 5; pin under 5.
*2nd row:* C-T, C 4 and 5; C-T, C 3 and 4; C-T, C2 and 3; T2; C-T, C-T 1 and 2; pin under 1 and 2.
*3rd row:* C-T, C 2 and 3; C-T, C-T 3 and 4; C-T, C 4 and 5; T-T 5; pin under 5.
*Repeat 2nd and 3rd rows to the corner.* As the work rounds the corner, the width of the tape increases and it turns right. When you reach the pinhole at point A, work *1st corner row* (left to right): C-T, C 2 and 3; C-T, C 3 and 4; C-T, C-T 4 and 5; no pin. *2nd corner row* (right to left): C-T, C 3 and 4; C-T, C 2 and 3; T 2; C-T, C-T 1 and 2; T-T 1; pin

Figure D: Below are the patterns for the bobbin-lace collar and cuffs that are pictured on page 1019. For how to enlarge the pattern, see Craftnotes, page 57, Volume One.

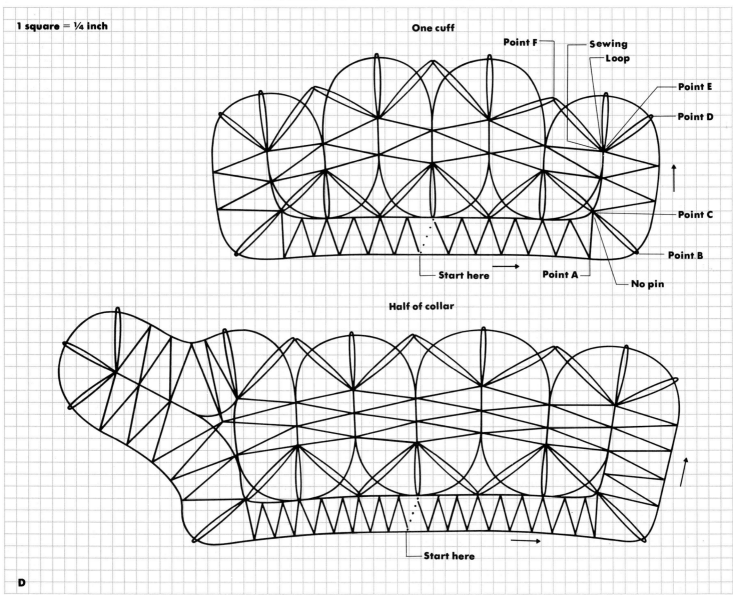

1 square = ¼ inch

One cuff

Point F — Sewing
Loop

Point E

Point D

Point C

Point B

Start here → Point A

No pin

Half of collar

Start here

under 1. The pin should be inserted in the pinhole at point B. *3rd corner row* (left to right): C-T, C-T 1 and 2; C-T, C 2 and 3; C-T, C 3 and 4; T 4; C-T, C-T 4 and 5; T-T 5; pin under 5. This pin should be inserted in the pinhole at point C. By avoiding this pinhole in the 1st row, the tape turned the corner and is now proceeding toward the scalloped edge with the rest of the cuff on the right.
*1st side row* (right to left): C-T, C-T 4 and 5; C-T, C 3 and 4; C-T, C 2 and 3; T 2; C-T, C-T 1 and 2; T-T 1; pin under 1.
*2nd side row* (left to right): C-T, C-T 1 and 2; C-T, C 2 and 3; C-T, C 3 and 4; T 4; C-T, C-T 4 and 5; T-T 5.
*Repeat these 2 side rows once more.*
Repeat 1st row again, reaching point D.
*Next row:* (left to right): Continuing in linen stitch, finish by looping pair 1 around a pin inserted in the pinhole at point E.
*Next row* (right to left): Continue in linen stitch, ending with foot edge.
*Next row* (left to right): Continue in same stitch, looping end pair around the pin at point E.
*Next row* (right to left): Continue in linen stitch, ending at point F.
*Next row* (left to right): Continue to

point E; remove pin holding the loops at point E. With crochet hook, enter the released loop from the top, catch one of the strands of pair 5 and pull it through, forming a large loop. Push the other bobbin of pair 5 through this loop, handle first (photograph 13). Remove the hook and tighten the loop. This is called a sewing and it connects the tapes together. Continue to work in linen stitch and at each turn in the design, twice form the foot edge without inserting a pin and sew the loops which share a pin as before. Where there are 3 loops sharing the same pin, two loops go around the pin and the third connects them with a sewing. When the work comes back to the beginning, sew the pairs into the loops which are at the starting points, then tie each pair in a reef (square) knot and cut as short as ⅛ inch. (This is also the way to join the edging on the round doily as shown in Figure C and photograph, page 1019.)
*Other cuff:* Make a mirror-image copy of the pattern and work as the first cuff.
*Collar:* The directions for the cuff also pertain to the collar, differing only in size and number of scallops. This can easily be read from the draft.

13: The technique for joining two sections of lace together as the lace is being worked is called a sewing. This is done with the help of a crochet hook and a lace bobbin.

## Needlecrafts
# Needle lace window hanging ¢ ▨ ⚥ ⚐

The needle lace technique, which is very similar to embroidery, is simple and easy to learn. In fact, you may already be familiar with some of the stitches if you do any type of embroidery. Needle lace is portable and in the eighteenth century, European men used to take their needle lace work with them when they attended parties at the royal court.

The only tools needed are a small sharp needle and a larger blunt-point needle. The lace is worked on a sheet of construction paper (for stiffness) which is basted onto fabric (to keep the paper from tearing). In the past, black paper was used as a sharp contrast to the traditional white linen thread. Now, any color paper that contrasts with your choice of yarn or thread is suitable. A piece of old sheet is fine for the fabric backing.

### Basic Stitches
There are innumerable stitches of needle lace, all variations of the buttonhole stitch and the filet knot.

First, a thread must be couched to the paper background to outline the desired shape. The thickness of this thread depends on how thick you want the outline. For the sample stitches, a thread thicker than the work thread is used. This shape is then filled in with a chosen stitch. The two faces will look almost exactly alike, but the top face will be the right side.

For the sampler of stitches on page 1022, I have chosen square shapes because they are the simplest. In a square, the number of stitches in each row should be the same. When filling irregular shapes, the number of stitches per row will vary, decreasing as the shape narrows, increasing as it widens. Following in the Craftnotes are the needle lace stitches that are used in this and the next project.

# CRAFTNOTES: NEEDLE LACE STITCHES

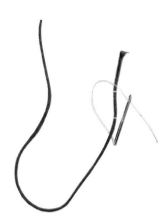

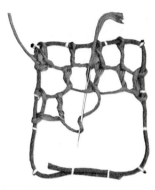

### Couching
Outline the lace shape on the fabric-backed paper with pinholes about ¼ inch apart. With a sharp needle and sewing thread, sew the outline thread to the paper, bringing the needle up and taking it back through the same hole. Continue around until the ends of the outline thread overlap.

### Twisted buttonhole stitch
This is another variation of the buttonhole stitch. The loop is formed to the right of the needle, then twisted once around the needle. This results in twisted bars between the rows and a squared-off appearance in the stitches.

### Filet knot
Form a complete loop to the right of the needle, then slip the needle down under the top thread and through the loop. Insert a pin into the loop to control the size and draw the knot tight. After each row, carry the thread back to the left side and work from left to right, slipping the needle under both the loop of the stitch above and the thread that was carried across.

Close buttonhole stitch

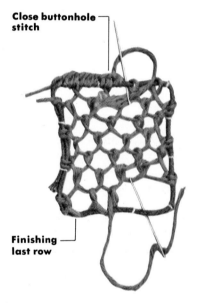

Finishing last row

### Buttonhole stitch
Tie the working thread to the outline thread at the upper left corner. With a blunt needle, bring the thread down under the top outline thread, forming a loop under and to the right of the needle. Keep the loops fairly loose and alternate the direction of each succeeding row.

### Darning
This is a simple over-and-under weaving of the working thread between the opposite sides of the outline thread. If there are other threads parallel to the outline thread, weave in an over-one, under-one pattern.

### Finishing (bottom)
On the last row of any stitch, loop the thread around the bottom outline thread after each stitch.

### Close buttonhole stitch (top)
Cover the outline thread with a row of buttonhole stitches very close together after the filling stitches are completed.

### Double buttonhole stitch
This is a variation of the buttonhole stitch above. Instead of a single stitch formed on the horizontal thread, two stitches are worked close together. The loops should be less rounded than those of the buttonhole stitch. Notice, too, how the rows of stitches are staggered.

### Spider motif
Attach the outline thread in a circle, then stretch the working thread across the center of the circle several times. Carry the working thread to the center and weave over and under the radius threads in ever-bigger circles.

**The Village Church in Lace**

Enlarge the pattern (Figure E) and transfer onto construction paper. Outline the shapes with the outline thread, then fill the spaces with the indicated stitches. (The key to the stitches is at upper right; see also the color photograph on page 1013.) Hide all the ends of thread in the final outline of close buttonhole stitch. Do not outline the darned sections with close buttonhole stitch. For the hanging as shown, use one 2-ounce spool of white linen thread, No. 10/2. If you wish to make the hanging smaller or larger, use a thickness of thread that is in proportion. After removing the lace from the paper, mount it between two squares of clear glass or acrylic plastic and suspend it with nylon monofilament or fishing line.

**Key to stitches**
D = Darning
1 = Buttonhole stitch
2 = Double buttonhole stitch
3 = Twisted buttonhole stitch
4 = Filet knot

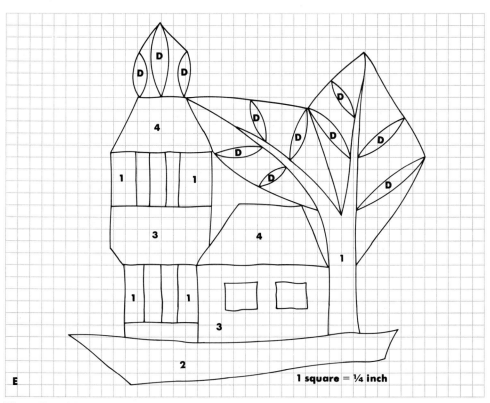

1 square = ¼ inch

Figure E: This is the pattern for the village church hanging shown in the color photograph on page 1013. The stitch key is at the upper right; directions for enlarging the pattern are on page 57, Volume One.

**Needlecrafts**
# Modern art necklace ¢●♦☕

This necklace is a combination of needle lace and bobbin lace (Figure F, page 1024). The center circle of the pendant is needle lace and should be worked first. As shown in the photograph at right, none of the shapes (other than the edge of the circle) are outlined in close buttonhole stitch but you can outline them if you wish. Use three 2-ounce spools of No. 10/2 linen thread, one each in red, orange and yellow; follow the photograph for placement of colors. The key to the stitches is on page 1024.

The rest of the necklace is bobbin lace tape, which is worked according to the directions for the collar and cuffs (page 1019). Pin the needle lace circle into the empty space on the draft for the bobbin lace, and work the bobbin lace tape around it. As you work, join the bobbin lace to the needle lace with sewings.

Start the bobbin lace at the back opening and work around to the opposite end where the ends of the thread will form a button loop. Work close buttonhole stitch over this loop and sew a small button on the other end. When the tape is finished, the two parts will be completely connected.

For related crafts and projects, see "Crewel Embroidery," "Crochet," "Embroidery," "Knitting to Fit," "Macrame," "Sprang Weaving," and "Weaving."

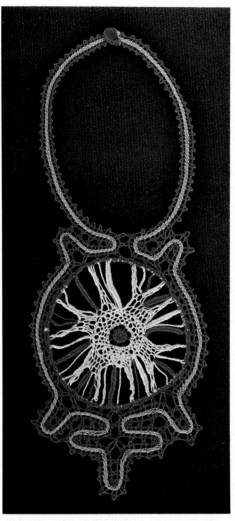

The modern art necklace is a combination of two lace techniques: the inner circle of the pendant is needle lace and the curved outer tape is a continuous length of bobbin lace.

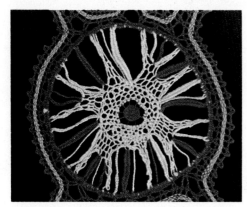

The needle lace circle above is the center of the pendant in the combination lace necklace.

## Key to stitches

S = Spider
1 = Buttonhole stitch
2 = Twisted buttonhole stitch

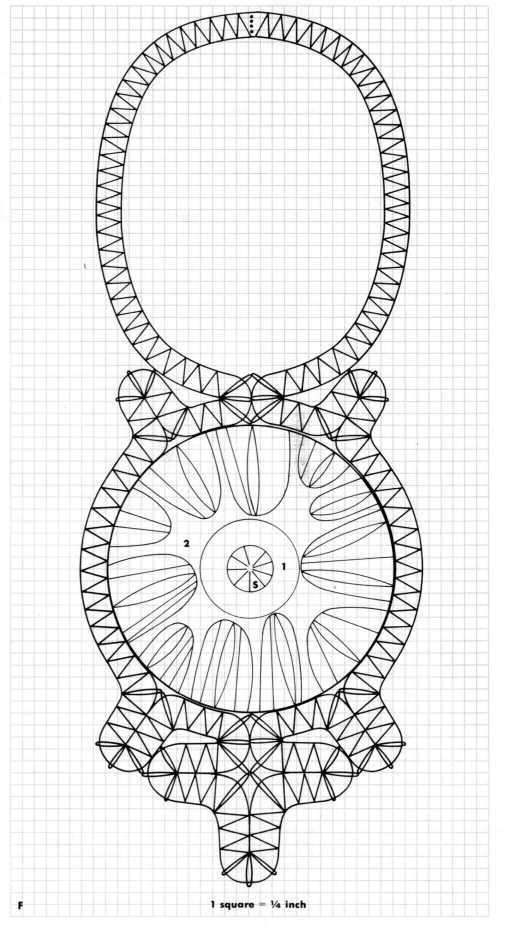

Figure F: At right is the pattern for the combination lace necklace. See the stitch key above and instructions for enlarging patterns on page 57, Volume One.

F

1 square = ¼ inch